Courts applying the law
Tribunaux appliquant la loi

Cultures juridiques et politiques

Stéphanie Rohlfing-Dijoux & Otmar Seul

VOL. 21

Remus Titiriga (ed.)

Courts applying the law
Tribunaux appliquant la loi

Perspectives from Europe and Asia
Perspectives d'Europe et d'Asie

PETER LANG
Bruxelles · Berlin · Chennai · Lausanne · New York · Oxford

Bibliographic information published by the Deutsche Nationalbibliothek. The German National Library lists this publication in the German National Bibliography; detailed bibliographic data is available on the Internet at http://dnb.d-nb.de.

A catalogue record for this book is available from the British Library.
Library of Congress Cataloging-in-Publication Data

Names: Titiriga, Remus, editor.
Title: Courts applying the law : perspectives from Europe and Asia / edited by Remus Titiriga.
Description: New York : Peter Lang, 2025. | Series: Cultures juridiques et politiques, 2235-1078 ; volume 21 | Includes bibliographical references.
Identifiers: LCCN 2025015835 (print) | LCCN 2025015836 (ebook) | ISBN 9783034355551 (paperback) | ISBN 9783034355575 (ebook) | ISBN 9783034355582 (epub)
Subjects: LCSH: Courts--Europe. | Courts--Asia. | Justice, Administration of--Europe. | Justice, Administration of--Asia. | Practice of law--Europe. | Practice of law--Asia.
Classification: LCC K2100 .C68 2025 (print) | LCC K2100 (ebook) | DDC 347/.01--dc23/eng/20250403
LC record available at https://lccn.loc.gov/2025015835
LC ebook record available at https://lccn.loc.gov/2025015836

Funding information: The editor wishes to acknowledge the support received from the LEXFEIM research center of Le Havre Normandie University, making this publication possible, as well as several members of LEXFEIM, who are authors of a chapter in the book.
L'éditeur tient à remercier le soutien reçu du centre de recherche LEXFEIM de Le Havre Normandie Université, qui a rendu possible cette publication, ainsi que plusieurs membres de LEXFEIM, auteurs d'un chapitre de l'ouvrage

Confection de la couverture : Peter Lang Group AG

ISSN 2235-1078
ISBN 978-3-0343-5555-1 (Print)
ISBN 978-3-0343-5557-5 (E-PDF)
ISBN 978-3-0343-5558-2 (E-PUB)
DOI 10.3726/b22955
D/2025/5678/25

Publié par/Published by Peter Lang Éditions Scientifiques Internationales - P.I.E., Bruxelles, Belgique

info@peterlang.com http://www.peterlang.com/

This publication has been peer reviewed.

Contents

Foreword

The present book, which focuses on courts applying law to cases, results from a vibrant dialogue and support. Our journey began in the fall of 2022 with a proposal of Professor Pierre Chabal, a respected scholar and mentor, to publish an old paper of mine on *Interessenjurisprudenz*. The paper was completed twelve years ago and remains unpublished. Professor Chabal offered the insightful suggestion that I publish my article in an edited volume, incorporating other scholars' contributions. His unwavering moral and intellectual support has been the cornerstone of this project and has brought it to fruition.

The project's official start was hosted in Le Havre in Professor Chabal's laboratory in mid-January 2023. At this point, the book's frame and eventual contributors were decided, ensuring a comprehensive exploration of the subject from many viewpoints. My task was to elaborate on the academic frame, a comprehensive and systematic approach to the subject matter, and a guide to the collaborators' development. This frame was designed to ensure a cohesive and in-depth topic exploration, incorporating diverse perspectives and insights. In parallel, I completely rewrote my initial paper and added one more article (both in English, present in this volume, and discussing the *Interessenjurisprudenz*).

I submitted a questionnaire sheet to contributors, inviting them to write anything they deemed interesting about the interpretations that played out in their national courts. I continued online dialogues with the endeavor's participants, who steadily provided their papers. From that moment on, I was responsible for editing all papers to create a coherent whole. Throughout the process, Professor Chabal's advice and direct contribution have been indispensable. I extend my deepest thanks and appreciation to him. I also want to thank the other contributors who have enriched this volume with their unique insights and perspectives. As the editor, I take responsibility for any potential drawbacks of the volume. Finally, as chance would have it, the journey on which this book rests came to its conclusion recently in Le Havre, where I participated in an international seminar on "economic activities and fundamental rights."

Le Havre, France
November 7, 2024

Remus Titiriga

Introduction: Contextualizing the Contributions in the Volume[1]

Remus Titiriga
University of the West, Romania

This book examines courts' practice of adopting case law. Contributions have a European-Asian reach and relate primarily to judicial practice in Europe (France, Germany, or the UK) and Asia (Kazakhstan, Russia). As for the approach, the book's focus, themes and contributions can be divided into three parts that also shape the volume's structure. The first group of papers about courts deals with interpretation (methods or mechanisms) in civil and criminal law matters. The second set dwells on the specific application of law by national courts as a result of an extension of the control of constitutionality. The third set deals with courts crossing the borders between legal orders, more precisely, national courts applying specific conventions of international public law. This triple division of the contributions will be equally followed in this Introduction.

Methods and mechanisms of interpretation by the courts in civil and penal matters

Germany's landscape of legal interpretation

In the first contribution in this volume, "Profile of the *Interessenjurisprudenz* as a Normative Interpretation Proposed to the German Courts," Remus Titiriga analyzes a historical legal methodology called *Interessenjurisprudenz* (Jurisprudence of Interests) proposed by the Tübingen School of legal theory and its founder, Philipp Heck, as a counterpart to normative theories like *Begriffsjurisprudenz* (Conceptual Doctrine) or School of Free Law. A key theme in this first paper is the tension or gap between normative interpretative theories proposed by legal doctrines and the practical application of such interpretative theories by courts. In Germany, law

1 This introduction also serves as a conclusion. We recommend reading it before the contributions in the volume and revisiting it afterward.

professors created a normative methodology outlining the methods that courts should adopt. These normative theories of interpretation were later integrated in German courts.

This tension is still evident in the second contribution, "Illustrating how *Interessenjurisprudenz* Applies in Real German Cases" by Remus Titiriga, which provides a deeper understanding of the practical use of legal doctrine in German courts beginning around 1930. Heck's proposals were highly controversial initially, but they were increasingly used and widely accepted in the 1920s and early 1930s and became commonplace among civil law practitioners. To understand where *Interessenjurisprudenz* stands within the German methodological landscape, a deeper examination of the history of legal theories of interpretation in Germany is required.

Germany's historical developments of concepts and methods for legal interpretation

In the German methodological literature, one must differentiate[2] between "methods" and "systems" (or schools) of interpretation.[3] The methods came into being through Friedrich Karl von Savigny, the leader of the Historical School, who summarized the state of German legal methodology in his "System of Today's Roman Law" of 1840.[4] He highlighted four "elements" or methods of interpretation: grammatical, logical, historical, and systematic.[5] Later, a new dichotomy emerged: the subjective versus objective methods of interpretation.

2 I. Mircea Manolescu, *Teoria si practica dreptului* (Bucuresti: Fundatia Regele Mihai I, 1946), 258–59.

3 There is a difference between rules of interpretation and arguments of interpretation. The latter is intended to convince another person, while their use for the discovery of legal truth gives them the quality of rules of interpretation. See Manolescu, op. cit., 259.

4 Friedrich Karl von Savigny, *System des heutigen römischen Rechts*, vol. 1 (Berlin: Berlin Veit 1840), 215.

5 Grammatical interpretation considers the language applied by the legislature. Logical interpretation explains the rational relationship between the individual parts of the law. Historical interpretation compares the legal regulation with the older legal situation that it modified. Systematic interpretation considers the relationship of the law to the entire legal system.

This dichotomy between subjective and objective theories of legal interpretation remains a crucial aspect of German legal theory and emerged by the late ninteenth century. The "subjective theory" focuses on determining "the (original) will of the legislator" or "the intention of Parliament," while the "objective theory" aims to determine the "objective" or "true meaning of the statute" itself.[6] The subjective theory of interpretation has certain variations. One variant is known as the original interpretation.[7] The other is the "historical-purposive" interpretation of Philipp Heck, the key figure of the *Interessenjurisprudenz*.

Heck shifted from considering lawmakers' real and psychological intent to their normative or regulative intent. The correct path in interpreting the law is historical research into commandments and the purpose of norms. These norms resulted in the legislator's evaluation and weighting of social interests. In other words, *Interessenjurisprudenz* was using grammatical interpretation, systematical interpretation and historical interpretation (Savigny's canon) to determine the normative purpose of the historical legislator, not his psychological will. Hence, *Interessenjurisprudenz* belongs to a particular variant of the subjective theories of interpretation.

On the other hand, an objective theory of interpretation, which is not covered by any contributions in the volume, emerged towards the end of the nineteenth century in Germany. It was formulated almost simultaneously by three of the most important legal scholars of the time: Karl Binding (1841–1920), Adolf Wach (1843–1926), and Josef Kohler (1849–1919).[8] This

---

6 A debate has recently been revived in the United States between "originalists" and "intentionalists," on the one side, and "textualists" and those favoring a "dynamic approach," on the other. See Stefan Vogenauer, "Statutory interpretation," in *Elgar Encyclopedia of Comparative Law*, edited by J. M. Smits (Cheltenham, UK: Edward Elgar Publishing, 2006), 686.

7 As one of the theory's prominent early advocates, Bernhard Windscheid argues that the interpreter "must…think his way as fully as possible into the soul of the legislator" by examining all available sources. See Karl Larenz, *Methodenlehre der Rechtswissenschaft* (Berlin: Springer, 1991), 28ff.

8 Karl Lorenz Binding, *Handbuch des Strafrechts*, vol. 1 (Lipsia: Duncker & Humblot, 1885), 450; Adolph Wach, *Handbuch des deutschen Civilprozessrechts*, vol. 1 (Lipsia: Duncker & Humblot, 1885), 254ff; Josef Kohler, "Über die interpretation von gesetzen," *Zeitschrift für das Privat- und öffentliche Recht der Gegenwart (Grünhuts Zeitschrift)* 13 (1886): 1–61; Cited by Larenz, *Methodenlehre der Rechtswissenschaft*, 32.

objective theory of interpretation considers how a statute's interpretation must be separated from its historical origin. The legal meaning is not what the legislature thinks but what is intrinsic to the objective law.[9] The terms of a legal rule should be separated from their historical surroundings, and therefore, according to this theory, the historical interpretation method should be abandoned altogether and placed into the current environment to be interpreted as if they were adopted today.

At the core of objective interpretation is a new method known as objective teolology, which focuses on "the goal pursued" by the statute. This new method comprises two steps. First, there is a search for actual social conditions that the statute should meet. Afterward, according to today's ideas, there is a search for a more suitable solution. The solution "that is the best response to that purpose" must be chosen from several literal interpretations.[10] Since these conditions are subject to change over time, the interpretation of a legal sentence must also follow the change. Interpretation must, therefore, always be related to the present.

A second dichotomy: Interpretation versus lawmaking (rechtfortbuildung)

From the end of the nineteenth century onward, German writings on statutory interpretation emphasize a clear distinction between interpretation itself and the "further development of the law" *(Rechtsfortbildung)* by the interpreter,[11] especially judges.[12] The dividing line depends on whether the "borderline of the literal meaning" (*Wortsinngrenze*) has been crossed.[13] Recent

---

9 See Kohler, cited by Larenz, *Methodenlehre der Rechtswissenschaft*, 33.

10 Larenz, *Methodenlehre der Rechtswissenschaft*, 33.

11 Stefan Vogenauer, "Statutory Interpretation," in *Elgar Encyclopedia of Comparative Law*, ed. J. M. Smits (Cheltenham, UK: Edward Elgar Publishing, 2006), 685ff.

12 This distinction did not exist for the late Savigny. See Baldus Ronny, "Legal binding, interpretation and analogy: Basics and significance of the 19th century," in *European Methodology*, ed. Karl Riesenhuber (Berlin: De Gruyter, 2021), 56.

13 According to a widespread opinion, although the distinctive criteria are still controversial, one must differentiate between the interpretation of the law and the development of law when the hypothetical decision lies beyond the potential meaning of the word. One must simultaneously not contradict the law, the limit of which is the possible meaning of the word by grammatical interpretation. In the second case, the law remains silent about the problem.

German tradition sharply separates interpretation from analogy, placing interpretation on one side of the literal meaning boundary.[14]

There are intricate categorizations of the various types of *Rechtsfortbildung* and the "gaps" and "implicit gaps" required to engage in this activity. Once such a gap is identified, the limits on further developing the law to differentiate between "legitimate" and "illegitimate" judicial lawmaking arise. The prevailing German legal view today is that the instrument for such legitimate lawmaking is the analogy and the connected arguments (*a fortiori*, *a contrario*). By considering them, the judge does not create law but merely operates within legal loopholes.

Taken together, these studies on *Interessenjurisprudenz* illustrate that Von Heck embraced the tool of analogy or the use of related arguments for filling gaps and loopholes in the law. However, he did not consider an analogy of commandments or factual parts linking legal norms. Rather he considered an analogy of similar interests, which demands a complex understanding of the law's hidden evaluations.

France's landscape of law interpretation

The third paper, "Remarques à propos de l'interprétation des textes de droit civil et penal par le juge français" by Didier Guével and Luc-Michel Nivôse, deals with Civil and Criminal matters as interpreted by the French civil or criminal courts or by the French Constitutional Council.

The study begins with a detailed introduction to the fundamental concepts of legal interpretation. The first part of the document is devoted to a detailed examination of the various traditional methods of interpretation employed by judges in the French legal system. The analysis is organized around two main axes. The first is an in-depth study of principles specific to civil and commercial law, where interpretation can prove more adaptable. The second is a survey of principles specific to criminal law, characterized by their rigor and strict interpretation.

In the first part dealing with civil law, the authors cover various traditional French methods of interpretation belonging to the School of Exegesis and mention the Free Scientific Research School of François Geny. The second part explores the complex dynamics of relationships between legislative and

---

14 Stefan Vogenauer, op. cit, 685.

judicial powers. It highlights the subtle interactions between parliament, the source of law and the judges who represent its privileged interpreters. This section thoroughly analyzes how case law and legislation mutually influence each other in a constant dialogue, thus shaping the evolution of law. It also examines how judicial decisions can sometimes lead to legislative modifications, creating a virtuous circle of continuous improvement in law.

What follows is a closer look at aspects of the French interpretative frame and landscape that contextualizes certain French interpretative methods and theories within the methodological frame and landscape we developed for the German context above. We will cover the School of Exegesis, the Free Scientific Research of Francois Geny, and the Teleological or "objective" method. In France, scholarly writers utilize diverse categorizations like these to illustrate various approaches to statutory interpretation.[15]

The School of Exegesis

The School of Exegesis emerged in the nineteenth century after adopting the Civil Code. Its principal authors were Duranton, Demolombe, Aubry, and Rau. The Civil Code was considered the law *par excellence* and the sole source of rights. The entire body of law was deemed contained within the Codes, and interpretation was centered on the text. For this initial School of Exegesis, the law is complete – everything is in the law, and everything must be deducible from the law. The heyday of this initial exegetical school included a pivotal transfer from German methodological doctrine – namely, the textbook on French Civil Law by Zachariä von Lingenthal, translated by Aubry and Rau with its first edition published in 1838.

The textbook became the defining stylistic textbook of that era. In it, Zachariä adopted the German interpretive categories common at that time,

[15] Jean Carbonnier, for example, portrays three primary methods of statutory interpretation: the exegetical technique, the approach of social intent and the free scientific investigation method. According to a logic similar to the one exposed above for Germany, Rene David differentiates between grammatical, historical such as legislative history, logical and teleological interpretations. Alfred Rieg distinguishes between the legislature's aim, which is particularly suitable for recent laws, and examining the social purpose of the law, particularly for old laws. See Claire M. Germain, "Approaches to Statutory Interpretation and Legislative History in France," *Duke Journal of Comparative and International Law* 13, no. 3 (2003): 201ff.

which preceded that of Savigny: grammatical and logical interpretation.[16] Zachariä then formally defined analogy, but not according to the criterion of a textual limit, as was the case later in Germany. He also did not define analogy as a means of creating law, which was a distinction characteristic to German legal culture between interpretation and the development of law (*Rechtfortbildung*). This is absent in French law as a result of the borrowing of pre-Savignian methodologies in the French legal space.[17]

In other words, "logical reasoning" was added to the interpretative canons of the exegesis to resolve difficulties in applying the code. If the language was silent on a problem, one could employ the norm of a comparable case using one of the following methods: analogy, reasoning *a contrario* to the rule in the text, reasoning by induction from rules given in other instances or *analogia juris*, and reasoning deductively, which derives from the legislator's expressed principle and extension it to different situations.

Even later, the Exegesis School introduced some other modifications. It acknowledged the need for a flexible approach based on "legislative history" and accepted the use of specific external sources, such as legal history and preparatory works, to aid in interpreting ambiguous or unclear provisions of the law. By now, the exegetical method emphasizes the observance of the drafters' intent. Therefore, if the law is unambiguous, a jurist must apply it without interpretation. If ambiguous, a jurist will examine preparatory works to discern legislative purpose and the meaning of obscure provisions in the clear conception of the assembly. In this way, we obtain an interpretative doctrine of exegesis that belongs, according to the interpretative framework developed in relation to Germany, to the subjective interpretation. More than that, the German and French interpretative perspectives go back to ideas of the modern legal era. To put it simply, the German perspective goes back to the early nineteenth century with Savigny, and the French go back centuries before that with Thomasius, the famous Natural Law scholar.[18]

---

16 With Thomasius, a distinction was made between "grammatical" interpretation (from the words of the law) and "logical" interpretation (from other circumstances). See Baldus, op. cit., 39.

17 ibid. 66ff.

18 Baldus Ronny, "Legal binding, interpretation and analogy: Basics and significance of the 19th century," in *European Methodology*, ed. Karl Riesenhuber (Berlin: De Gruyter, 2021), 39.

New approaches to overcoming exegesis: The free scientific research of François Geny

By the end of the nineteenth century, scholarly authors observed that tribunals were less likely to strictly interpret legislation than to craft an equitable interpretation of the legal instruments. Some code provisions had become antiquated, and the Industrial Revolution and economic, political and other societal changes had occurred. In his seminal work, first published in 1900, Geny urged the frank recognition of gaps in the statutory framework and argued for what he called free scientific research.[19]

François Gény did not wholly reject the previous interpretive method that relies on ascertaining the legislator's historical intent. He acknowledged that respecting and seeking to understand the legislator's original purpose is not inherently illegitimate.[20] However, Gény contends that confining the interpreter to this pursuit of historical intent is an absurd constraint, particularly when grappling with legal issues that have arisen long after the enactment of the Civil Code. At a particular juncture, the interpreter must confront the reality that the law contains gaps and lacunae that render it incapable of resolving the specific conflict brought before the judge. Here the judge must become a legislator and examine social needs, the ideals of the moment, comparative law, and history, which will show institutional evolution. This stage is free scientific research beyond interpretation. This movement was parallel to similar approaches in Germany, such as the *Freirechtsschule*. However, French tribunals did not adopt this doctrine, which parallels how German jurisdictions rejected the *Freirechtsschule* approach. In fact, while taking liberties with legal instruments, French tribunals did not openly free themselves from the law in the ways advocated by Geny.

---

19 François Geny, *Méthode d'interprétation et sources en droit privé positif* (Paris: L.G.D.J., 1919).

20 In this way, Geny is more deeply involved than certain parallel branches of *Freirechtsschule* in Germany, which at that time rejected all methods of interpretation except strict textualism.

The teleological or objective method[21]

Considering the statute's social objective, a new teleological method has emerged. This evolutionary doctrine is a type of teleological interpretation also called flexible textualism. A jurist using this method looks only at the legal text, acknowledging that inquiry into legislative will may be futile given societal changes post-enactment. This doctrine considers social needs constantly evolving, allowing a jurist broad discretion to adapt the text to meet contemporary community interests based on discerning contemporary legislative sentiment. This purposeful doctrine, advocated by Louis Josserand, identifies the legislation's intended social object or goal. In this way, we obtain an interpretative doctrine that belongs (according to the interpretative frame developed in relation to Germany) to the "objective interpretation theory."

A post-Soviet specificity: The instrument of regulatory decisions of interpretation by the Supreme Court of Kazakhstan

The fourth contribution, "The normative resolutions of interpretation by the Supreme Court of Kazakhstan" by Zhuldyz Sairambayeva, focuses on general norms adopted by the Supreme Court in specific matters, and in this case, interpretation. The study addresses mostly judges and the broader legal administration. One can connect these norms intellectually with a specific instrument from the history of French law. In France, to interpret the statute, Article 4 of the Civil Code states that a judge who refuses to render a judgment under the pretext of the law's silence, obscurity, or insufficiency may be prosecuted for denying justice. However, a judge's power is limited to decisions concerning specific cases.

Article 5 of the Civil Code prohibits judges from issuing general, lawmaking provisions on matters submitted to them, called an "arrêt de règlement." This historical peculiarity stems from the revolutionaries' hostility toward judges in the Parliaments who issued general rulings before the French Revolution and opposed the King's attempts at reform.[22] The normative interpretation resolutions by the Supreme Court of Kazakhstan are precisely

21 The teleological (objective) method is not covered in the third contribution of the volume, but it is important for the history of legal methods in France and deserves a brief presentation.

22 Germain, "Approaches to Statutory Interpretation and Legislative History in France," 196.

"arrêts de règlement" regarding the understanding of legal texts. This arrangement is a remnant from Soviet times but serves a different function in Kazakhstan, a country transitioning to democracy. In the modern legal system of the Republic of Kazakhstan, the Supreme Court has jurisdiction to adopt normative interpretation resolutions to address various legal issues, including analyzing laws, filling legislative gaps, and regulating legal relations. These normative interpretations, therefore, serve as foundational elements for the operations of judicial bodies. They are directed toward clarity in legal interpretation, fostering uniformity in judicial practice and preventing the occurrence of judicial errors.

The paper analyses how such regulatory decisions were employed in unifying the decisions of the ordinary (civil/criminal) courts. In unifying the interpretation, such decisions act as obligatory directives of interpretation addressed to the inferior courts. They represent a mechanism of interpretation that employs the methods of interpretation covered supra, and this is the reason for the article to be atached in this section of the Introduction and the first part of the volume.

Transitions in the constitutional control by the courts

The expansion of protection of fundamental rights in French constitutional law

The fifth contribution, *Nouveau regard sur les réserves (d'interprétation) transitoires du Conseil constitutionnel* by Maxime Charité, deals with strategies used by the Constitutional Council of France to avoid retroactivity in its rulings. This reservation of interpretation consists of supporting a decision to repeal a contested legislative provision with deferred effect and with an interpretation consistent with the Constitution, where the repeal takes place between the date of the decision and the date the repeal takes effect. A brief review of the history of constitutional review in France is required to contextualize the article's content.

The evolution of constitutional control in France has been from a system of absolute parliamentary supremacy to a sophisticated mechanism of constitutional oversight. Before 1958, France operated without any real system of constitutional review. The Third and Fourth Republics (1875–1958) maintained parliament's absolute sovereignty, reflecting a deep-seated resistance to any form of judicial oversight of legislative acts. That changed dramatically with the establishment of the Fifth Republic in 1958, which created the Constitutional Council. The referral methods were restricted by action within one month before the promulgation of the law and only by the President of the Republic, the Prime Minister, the President of the National Assembly, and the President of the Senate. Though initially conceived with limited powers, primarily focused on ensuring proper election conduct and reviewing laws before their promulgation, this institution would gradually evolve into a more robust guardian of constitutional rights. A pivotal moment came in 1971 with the Freedom of Association decision when the Constitutional Council significantly expanded its scope of review. By incorporating both the 1789 Declaration of Rights of Man and the Preamble of the 1946 Constitution into what became known as the "bloc de constitutionnalité," the Council created a broader framework of constitutional norms against which laws could be evaluated.

The 1974 reform strengthened constitutional control by allowing 60 deputies or 60 senators to refer laws to the Constitutional Council before promulgating. This change dramatically increased the Council's activity and importance, as opposition parties gained the ability to challenge legislation passed by the majority, introducing a new dynamic in the legislative process. The most significant recent development came with the 2008 constitutional reform, which introduced the Question Prioritaire de Constitutionnalité (QPC). For the first time, this new mechanism allowed citizens to challenge (á posteriori) the constitutionality of laws already in force through a referral system via ordinary courts to the Constitutional Council. This reform marked a fundamental shift from purely preventive review to include the possibility of examining existing laws, bringing France closer to other modern democracies' constitutional protection systems (like Germany or Italy) while maintaining its distinctive characteristics.

The July 23, 2008 reform introduced the priority question of constitutionality, allowing control by exception. The new article 61-1 of the Constitution provides that "When during proceedings in progress before a court, it is maintained that a legislative provision infringes the rights and freedoms that the constitution guarantees, the Constitutional Council may be seized of this question upon referral from the Council of State or the Court of Cassation, which rules within a specified period." If the Constitutional Council considers the provision unconstitutional, it is set aside for the current dispute and repealed as soon as the decision of the Constitutional Council is published unless the latter decides otherwise by setting a deadline or a date for repeal.

Under Article 62, the provision is repealed upon the Constitutional Council's declaration of unconstitutionality. The Council may also set a later date for repeal. This setting of a later date allows the French Parliament to quickly vote on a new law to fill the potential legal void that the repeal will have generated. The article of Maxime Charité inserts its pointed analysis here. In a way, France is following the steps of the constitutional control already implemented in Italy and Germany. Transitional interpretative reservations represent a vital tool in modern constitutional adjudication. This mechanism illustrates the broader evolution of French constitutional law from rigid formalism toward pragmatic constitutionalism. It reflects a sophisticated understanding that constitutional change often requires careful management of transitions to be effective and legitimate.

The expansion of protection of the fundamental rights in UK constitutional law by the Human Rights Act of 1998

In the sixth article, "De la rule of law au Human Rights Act: évolution des droits et libertés au Royaume-Uni," Louis-Philippe Gratton examines the evolution of judges' apprehension of rights and freedoms by focusing on the differences observed before and after the adoption of the Human Rights Act of 1998. The Constitution of the United Kingdom is an uncodified fundamental law comprising various statutes, judicial precedents, conventions, treaties and other sources. Beginning in the Middle Ages, the Constitution developed gradually in response to multiple crises. By the twentieth century, the British monarchy had become a constitutional and ceremonial monarchy, and parliament developed into a representative body exercising parliamentary sovereignty.

Regarding the constitution, we speak of diffuse constitutional control when several or all the courts of a legal system are competent to control the constitutionality of a norm or, in other words, when no specific constitutional jurisdiction is necessary. In this case, ordinary judges examine the question of constitutionality. The UK is, hence, aligning with the American model of constitutional justice, which also uses diffuse control. The UK is also a dualistic country. Hence, international public law instruments need to be incorporated into internal law. The Act incorporated into British law the provisions of the

European Convention on Human Rights (ECHR), which provide individuals with a remedy in the event of a violation of their fundamental rights.

The Human Rights Act 1998 is a pivotal Act of the Parliament of the United Kingdom. It received royal assent on November 9, 1998, and came into force on October 2, 2000. Its primary objective was to incorporate into UK law the rights enshrined in the European Convention on Human Rights, thereby providing a domestic remedy for breach of a Convention right without the need to go to the European Court of Human Rights (ECHR) in Strasbourg. This legislation has profoundly transformed the UK legal landscape and has led to significant changes in judges' approach when tackling cases relating to rights and freedoms. Before the promulgation of the law, they relied on various methods of interpretation influenced by common law (jurisprudence or case law), the principles of statutory interpretation (statutory interpretation), and specific references to international instruments. The Human Rights Act, providing a statutory framework for the protection and implementation of rights and freedoms, has modified the approach by the UK judges to favor a proportionality test.

In particular, the act makes it unlawful for any public body to act incompatibility with the Convention unless the wording of any other primary legislation provides no other choice. It also requires the judiciary, including tribunals, to take account of any decisions, judgments or opinions of the European Court of Human Rights and to interpret legislation, as far as possible, in a way compatible with Convention rights. However, it is impossible to interpret an Act of Parliament to make it compatible with the Convention. In that case, the judges cannot override the Act of Parliament. All they can do is issue a declaration of incompatibility. This declaration does not affect the validity of the Act of Parliament. In that way, the Human Rights Act seeks to maintain the principle of parliamentary sovereignty under the Constitution of the United Kingdom. However, judges may strike down secondary legislation. Under the Act, individuals retain the right to sue in the Strasbourg court.

Transitions and expansion of constitutional control in Kazakhstan

The seventh article, "Emergence of Constitutional controle in Kazakhstan" by Yesbol Omirzhanov, covers the evolution of constitutional control in the Republic of Kazakhstan after the country became independent. The analysis follows the first, second, and initial practices of the third Constitutional

Court of Kazakhstan chronologically, illustrating through cases another case of expansion of constitutional control. The evolution of constitutional control in Kazakhstan presents a fascinating journey from Soviet-era legal traditions to a modern constitutional system, particularly marked by the country's independence in 1991. During the Soviet period, Kazakhstan, like other Soviet republics, operated without formal constitutional review, with the Supreme Soviet wielding supreme legislative power and courts having minimal authority to question legislation.

The early independence period (1991–1995) saw Kazakhstan's first attempt to establish independent constitutional control through the creation of a Constitutional Court in 1992. However, this institution operated under significant political constraints and with limited jurisdiction. A major transformation occurred with adopting the 1995 Constitution, which abolished the Constitutional Court and established the Constitutional Council, modeled after the French system, which functioned until 2022. Inspired by the French system, this transformation from a court to a Council model represented a significant shift in Kazakhstan's approach to constitutional control. The Council's different structure and competencies, along with its landmark decisions, particularly demonstrated the evolution of constitutional oversight during this extended period of Kazakhstan's development.

The most recent chapter began in January 2023 with the establishment of the current Constitutional Court, marking a return to a court model but with significantly expanded competencies. This latest iteration reflects Kazakhstan's contemporary approach to constitutional justice, incorporating lessons learned from previous experiences while adapting to modern constitutional challenges. The Court's enhanced structure and broader jurisdiction, exemplified through its recent case law, suggests a maturation of constitutional control in Kazakhstan. However, the system still needs to improve, including the limited citizen access, the strong executive influence and questions about independence and enforcement mechanisms.

Courts crossing borders between legal orders: National courts applying conventional international law

The eighth paper, "Les juges nationaux face à la Convention relative au contrat de transport international de Marchandises par Route (CMR)" by Sandie

Calme is focusing on national courts applying the specific CMR treaty. This treaty was adopted in Geneva, Switzerland, in 1956. The CMR Convention provides a uniform legal framework for the international transportation of goods by road, and it establishes rights and obligations for the parties involved in the transport of goods, as well as a standard contract and a system for the settlement of disputes. The CMR Convention aims to facilitate international trade and to ensure the safe and efficient transportation of goods by road.

The ninth paper, "Double Taxation Treaties before the Courts of Kazakhstan and Russia" by Sagyngaliy Aidarbayev and Ilya Lifshits, delves into the interpretation of Double Taxation Treaties (DDTs) by national courts, a topic of direct relevance due to their applicability to international instruments. The existing OECD Model Tax Convention and its Commentaries, as well as specific nonbinding instruments containing special directives for interpreting DTTs dispositions, further enhance the significance of the author's analysis. There are some useful remarks on the use of commentaries to the Model Law in Russia and absence thereof in Kazakhstan. The authors thoroughly consider the pivotal role of DTTs within the legal systems of Kazakhstan and Russia, underscoring the importance of this research.

PART I

Methods and mechanisms of interpretation by the courts in civil and penal matters

Profile of the *Interessenjurisprudenz* as a Normative Interpretation Proposed to the German courts

Remus Titiriga
University of the West, Romania

Interessenjurisprudenz (The Jurisprudence of Interests) is a German methodological school that was developed at the beginning of the twentieth century. It emerged at the University of Tübingen around Philip Heck,[1] a professor of civil law. It was enriched by the contributions of other Tübingen professors such as Heinrich Stoll and Max Rümelin, who were also specialists in private law. *Interessenjurisprudenz* proposed a normative interpretative doctrine, asserting what a judge should do, based on the legal balance of interests. It guided the judge to protect the interests favored by the legislator. Its essential achievement was the return to social and political realities and the legal-political purposes of legal norms.

Moreover, *Interessenjurisprudenz* has developed a comprehensive interpretation theory for court practice, unprecedented in its coherence and, in many ways, still state of the art today.[2] It became dominant in Germany in the twentieth century, and the judges embraced this approach in a simplified version from the 1930s onward. Despite its paramount importance in the evolution of methodological thinking and juridical practice, the *Interessenjurisprudenz* remains to be discovered outside of Germany. The first part of this paper is devoted to an examination of the context of its emergence in the historical, methodological debate in Germany. The second part offers an overview of its interpretative doctrine according to Heck,[3] the leader of the school.

---

1 Philipp Heck (1858–1943) became a law professor at the University of Tübingen in 1902. In Tübingen, he remained until his emeritus in 1928. His writings cover German legal history, admiralty, commercial law, the law of obligations and the law of property.

2 That is the recent assertion of authors like Bernd Rüthers, Christian Fischer, and Axel Birk, *Grundrisse des Rechts* (Berlin: Verlag C.H. Beck, 2010), 360.

3 Among Heck's outstanding contributions to legal methods, used as primary sources for this article, we can cite Philipp Heck, *Gesetzesauslegung und Interessenjurisprudenz* (Tübingen: Mohr, 1914); *Begriffsbildung und Interessenjurisprudenz* (Tübingen: Mohr,

The *Interessenjurisprudenz* in the German Methodological Debate

Begriffsjurisprudenz

The nineteenth century in Germany was dominated by the positivism of the historical school, which focused on interpreting Roman legal sources (*Corpus juris civilis*). From the middle of the nineteenth century onward, this historical school attempted, notably in the work of G.F. Puchta, to build a deductive or pyramidal logical system of legal concepts.[4] This systematic vision transformed Savigny's organic connection between legal institutions into a logical connection between concepts, seen as a cognitive source of new norms. It explicitly adds science, or doctrine, as a third source to the two traditional sources of law, namely statute and custom.

Begriffsjurisprudenz, or the Doctrine of Concepts, was given its name by Jhering and is a resumption and accentuation of Puchta's systematic construction. Jhering understands[5] the systematic theme as a decomposition of institutions and legal rules into their "logical elements," followed by a recomposition to produce further legal rules. In this way, one can obtain a "multiplication of law on its basis" or a "growth from within' because "concepts are productive...couple and generate new concepts" through a process, exclusively inductive, identical to that of exact natural sciences.[6]

1932). The second contribution, *Begriffsbildung und Interessenjurisprudenz*, was translated into English and published as P. Heck, "The Formation of Concepts and the Jurisprudence of Interests', in *The Jurisprudence of Interests: Selected Writings*, ed. and tr. Magdalena Schoch (Cambridge: Harvard University Press, 1948) and will be referenced as such. The movement's best summary is in Philipp Heck, *Interessenjurisprudenz* (Tübingen: Mohr, 1933).

4 In this manifestation of a "science of pandects," the system presented itself as a set of concepts extracted by formal analysis of the content of the law to obtain interdependent concepts in a deductive manner and going vertically – towards the top of a "conceptual pyramid" – to the concept of subjective right, which expresses the autonomy of will of the subject. See Karl Larenz, *Storia del metodo nella scienza giuridica* (Milan: Giuffre Editore, 1966), 22.

5 That is the logic exposed in *The Spirit of Roman Law* from 1852–1858.

6 Larenz, *Storia*, 28.

Jhering distinguished two levels of the doctrine.[7] On the first level, *Begriffsjurisprudenz* extracted legal concepts from legal sources using abstract interpretation. On this level, the so-called low doctrine focuses on the interpretation and clarification of existing law, the clarification of ambiguities and contradictions, and the arrangement (condensation) of legal material using classification concepts. On the second level, the high doctrine was the legal science domain. It did not address the results of the general classification of concepts as mere condensations but as legal entities with a structure similar to natural bodies. For each concept (obtained by condensation), one should accurately determine its inner structure. For example, each right had to be examined to determine its object, content and purpose.[8] The ultimate result must be, according to Ihering, a "formula" or a definition. In this way, the concept was "interpreted" or constructed. Afterwards, that definition must be strictly respected and used as a basis for new rules and deciding new cases. According to Ihering, this unlimited use of "constructions" is precisely its principal value. Therefore, these concepts and their "system" will be seen as an endless source of new legal materials.

Begriffsjurisprudenz has constrained the judge to apply the law by logically inserting (subsuming) the facts of a case under legal concepts. The judge was prohibited from making any independent evaluation since his activity was cognitive and modeled on mathematics. He was only supposed to comprehend the rules through the concepts. The judge may eventually obtain a missing rule from the concept that was the ground for the other existing rules. This procedure was promoted to the dignity of a general method and was applied not only for normative concepts, found in legal texts, but also

---

7 Heck, "The Formation of Concepts," 38–40.

8 We can illustrate what Jhering considered structural problems: "In a co-ownership, is it the ownership, the right, or the value of the property that is divided? Is the *obligatio correalis* of Roman law a plurality of obligations with identical content, or is it an obligation with several subjects?" See Heck, 38.

for classification concepts produced by legal science.[9] Thus, legal gaps were solved using classification concepts as a basis for new rules.[10]

The school of free law

Between the end of the nineteenth century and the beginning of the twentieth century, the *Begriffsjurisprudenz* declined in Germany. From now on, law is seen increasingly as the product of political decisions, as the means of confirming social relationships based on choices. In other words, the law stops being seen as an autonomous system and becomes an integral part of social reality, a subsystem of the social system. That leads to a rejection of the system of concepts. Among those acting in this direction were the members of the *Freirecht Schule* (School of Free Law).

The ideas of the *Freirecht Schule* became visible and peaked towards the end of the nineteenth century and the beginning of the twentieth century. Several elements favored its advent.[11] First was the arrival of the codification of the Civil Code (BGB), which revealed many things that could have been improved in the legal order. Not all problems were anticipated, and there was no way to fill or work around the gaps in the Code's provisions. One thus discovers the creative activity of the judge, who resorted to the general notions of the Code such as good faith and morals, to rule out the special provisions. In principle, however, the particular rules prevail over the general rules. In this context, the freedoms of the judges of the English Superior Courts and the Supreme Court of the United States were admired.

---

9 Thus, the protection determination for the author's works (intellectual property) was based on constructing a general classification concept for property rights in general (starting from a normative concept of common property rights). Then, it was obtained by a purely intellectual construction the protection regime for authors' rights (as immaterial property).

10 This procedure was later called the "method of inversion" by *Interessenjurisprudenz*. See infra for an example of inversion used to determine the legal regime of a patent right.

11 The German school will be more active than the French school (represented, in fact, only by François Geny) because the German law and customs of the time of the Pandects were incomplete.

All these reasons led to the position taken by Ehrich, who in 1903 affirmed the "free discovery of law" and "free legal science."[12] Likewise, in 1906, Kantorowicz's work *The Fight for the Science of Law*[13] considered that in the presence of a gap, the judge must be able to find a solution freely. In other words, he must create the rule himself. This idea of judicial discretion represents the most substantial challenge of the *Freirecht Schule* to *Begriffsjurisprudenz*. The main idea of Ehrlich and some of his successors is that the judge can decide the best way on a case if he is free to evaluate its characteristics without worrying about the rules of law.[14] The reasons for the decision can be drawn from the case because each case carries its law, *sua lex*, in itself.[15]

When this movement emerged, its protagonists passionately criticized court practice and classical legal theory (*Begriffsjurisprudentz*). This type of propaganda was undoubtedly effective because if the discussion had been conducted calmly between experts, it would have taken the movement longer to achieve its goals.

However, the chosen formula also had significant drawbacks.[16] The way the arguments were presented provoked heated opposition and prevented calm consideration of the proposed approach. That is exemplified by the equivocal term "Free Law,"[17] which was subsequently abandoned and replaced by the

---

12 Ehrlich invented the expression "free law" in his 1917 article on legal logic, "Die juristische Logik," reprinted in Ehrlich Eugen, *Fundamental Principles of the Sociology of Law* (Cambridge: Harvard University Press, 1936). He also examined the positive principles that govern the cases and promised a theory of the Free Search for Law (*Freie Rechtsfindung*).

13 Hermann Kantorowicz, *Der Kampf um die Rechtswissenschaft* (Heidelberg: C. Winter, 1906).

14 Therefore, this decision can be called a "lawless decision."

15 It is the reason for the rejection by this school of the idea of filling the gaps in the law based on solutions found in the law itself by resorting to arguments such as *analogia legis*, *analogia juris* and *argumentum per a contrario*.

16 Max Rumelin, "Legal Theory and Teaching," in *The Jurisprudence of Interests*, ed. and tr. Magdalena Schoch (Cambridge: Harvard University Press, 1948), 21.

17 The term "Free Law" has been used to express different ideas. Some jurists have asserted that a law's binding force depends on its effectiveness. Others, proceeding from the theory of objective interpretation, have held that the content of law must be limited to the "clear and unequivocal expression of the terms" of the law. Some have reached the conclusion (which has not been accepted by all supporters of "Free Law") that the judge has the right, in certain circumstances, to refuse obedience to the law or, as has been sometimes said, to change the law. See Rumelin, "Legal Theory and Teaching," 23.

more neutral term "sociological Jurisprudence." The latter helped clarify the controversy and pacify minds. Ultimately, the doctrine of Free Law did not succeed in having its vision of the role and practice of the judge adopted. This theory has been criticized because, in typical cases, applying general rules according to the law's intention gives more satisfactory results. It was also argued that there were limits to the insight and impartiality of the judge and, finally, that in many areas of life, the predictability of judicial decisions was more important than their substantive correctness.[18] Nevertheless, this doctrine revealed some flaws in the doctrine of *Begrifssjurisprudenz*, which from that moment onward, left the legal spotlight. The parallel and rival school of *Interessenjurisprudenz* then occupied the methodological space, thus being liberated by the Freirecht Schule.

Interessenjurisprudenz in the German methodological debate

Jhering departs from his initial *Begriffsjurisprudentz* vision by discovering that not only legal norms but also the dogmatic concepts determined by "construction" are transformed with time in the four volumes of *The Spirit of Roman Law*, specifically the 1864 edition.[19] Later, Jhering started considering that legal rules are based on practical reasons. The author will use the terms good, value, enjoyment, and interest and define subjective rights as legally protected interests.[20] The relationship between law and society through interests will be explored further in *Der Zweck im Recht,* where Jhering uses the concept of interest to explain individual and collective action and the law elaboration.[21] However, Jhering could not propose an alternative practical methodology for the judge. Only Interessenjurisprudenz will achieve that.

The fight against *Begriffsjurisprudenz* will be a constant concern of the *Interessenjurisprudenz.*[22] As for the application of law, the opposition is not directed against the formation of concepts, nor against the adoption of

[18] Rudolph von Jhering, *L'esprit du droit romain dans les diverses phases de son développement*, vol. 4 (Paris: Marescq, 1880), 325.

[19] See the third volume of *L'esprit du droit romain* devoted to subjective rights.

[20] Jhering, *L'esprit*, 327.

[21] Rudolph von Jhering, *L'évolution du Droit* (Paris: Marescq, 1901), 173–74.

[22] Heck, "The Formation of Concepts," 107.

judicial decisions based on the concepts used in legislation.[23] The opposition is concerned with deducing new legal rules from classification concepts by interpreting laws through "constructions." According to Heck, the error is in the "inversion," the idea that one can deduce norms from legal concepts.[24] The "inversion" results from confusion between the end (the norm) and the means (the concept). For Heck, the norm preexists the concept.

The concept is only how our consciousness comprehends the norm, allowing us to translate and express its content in a way likewise seen in the work of Pawlowki.[25] In Pawlowski's example, "A is the owner of a patent right. B announces that he wants to use the patent-protected process without A's consent; A then sues B for an injunction. The judge finds the following relevant "law disposition" below:

1. If there is a risk of disruption to someone's property, the owner can sue for an injunction against the person causing the disturbance.
2. If there is a threat of disruption to his mortgage (*pfandrecht*), the pledgee can sue the person disrupting to cease.
3. Anyone who has a right to a name can demand that others refrain from using their name and
4. The buyer cannot sue for injunctive relief if his claim to the purchased item is threatened by disruption.

The judge uses abstraction to form the general term "absolute right" from the terms "property", "mortgage" (*pfandrecht*), and "right to name" (the right

---

23 However, normative concepts remain helpful, unlike dogmatic (classification) concepts. Heck considers that normative concepts, which are elements detached from legal provisions, must be reinserted into the rule when the rule is applied. They are as authoritative to the judge as other disposition components. These application situations have nothing in common with the method (contested by Heck), which derives a new rule from classification concepts (construction through concepts). See Heck, "The Formation of Concepts," 107.

24 Inversion means that the contents of the terms abstracted from the existing legal sentences serve as the source for a new commandment. The common elements of these terms would be combined into more general terms and defined precisely. These "general terms" would then be used to fill the gap by deriving the decision of the new case from that definition. Heck, "The Jurisprudence of Interests," 37–38.

25 Hans-Martin Pawlowski, *Methodenlehre für Juristen: Theorie der Norm und des Gesetzes* (Heidelberg,: Müller, 1981), 53–54.

to purchase is not included since it is a "relative right") and thus arrives at the "general legal principle:" the owner of an absolute right, if there is a threat to his right, can sue for an injunction against the disruptor. The judge then determines that patent law is also an absolute right and can now award a lawsuit-injunction. That is because after the abstract replacement of property, mortgage (*pfandrecht*), and name right by the concept of "absolute right" from the legal sentences 1–3, "it can be deduced" that the sanction "injunction" stipulated therein can also be ordered for disruptions to patent rights."

Heck similarly rejects the idea of the legal system's logical closure and the negation of the judge‘s creative role by *Begriffsjurisprudenz*. The second front of *Interessenjurisprudenz* was directed against the School of Free Law.[26] To the extent that the followers of the Free Law School aimed to free jurisprudence from the yoke of conceptualism, they were objective allies of the *Interessenjurisprudenz*. While the former school benefited from the dynamism of the latter, since these two movements were often confused, *Interessenjurisprudenz* also suffered from the violent reaction that arose against the doctrine of Free Law.[27]

However, the two methodological schools are different. The *Interessenjurisprudenz* is far from a freely developed law as understood by the *Freierecht Schule* and criticizes its insufficient respect for the constitutional framework.[28] Also, *Freierecht Schule* advocates a rigorously objective interpretation method based on the law‘s text. Hence, the inadequacy of the norm (the text) and the case requiring a solution is relatively frequent.[29] To fill such gaps, the authors of the *Freierecht Schule* assign the judge a mission of *Freie Rechtsfindung*, in which the magistrate must identify the rule capable of resolving the case within the society. For the *Interessenjurisprudenz*, this last

---

26 Heck, "The Formation of Concepts," 108.

27 That is the first reason that Heck emphasizes his opposition to this theory. Indeed, the Interessenjurisprudenz has often been treated as a variant of the theory of Free Law. Heck cites the case of Ross, who informs his readers that after the first successes of Free Law theory, many of its adherents left it. The only reference mentioned is an article by Heck from 1912. That is a double error for Heck since the chronological order of events would be precisely the opposite, the Interessenjurisprudenz being the oldest school and the School of Free Law a later manifestation. See Heck, "The Formation of Concepts," 108.

28 Heck, "The Jurisprudence of Interests," 32.

29 Heck, "The Formation of Concepts," 108.

step is inadmissible since it infringes on the legislator's supremacy over the judiciary. The judge is bound to uphold the rules of law and the separation of powers within the constitutional order. When ruling, a judge should not act freely but must adhere to interpretations and the legal community's prevailing social and ethical views. The judge's views should play only a subsidiary role.

The doctrine of *Interessenjurisprudenz* about the application of the law

General aspects

There are specific elements for the definition and the application of law as proposed by the *Interessenjurisprudenz*. The logic of a legislator is that of emotional thinking,[30] the law is an act of evaluation by the legislator, and the law is a product of interests.[31] The legislator's action corresponds to evaluation or "weighing of interests," falling under what Heck has called the "genetic theory of interests."[32] As for the application of the law, the judge's activity is also not submitted to the logic of cognitive thinking but to that of emotional thinking, where the ideal is not the truth but an evaluation of life and the interests.[33] However, since the judge is subject to the law, he must refer to the legislator's ideals and value judgments and the original weighing of interests in solving a case. As a general rule, the judge only transposes the legislative judgments. In the ordinary situation, there is no conflict between applying the law and the legislator's initial weighing of interests.

---

30 "The function of establishing rules involves questions about what ought to be. These normative problems are problems of emotional thinking." Heck, "The Formation of Concepts," 192.

31 Heck, "The Jurisprudence of Interests," 40.

32 Its counterpart is the "productive theory of interests," which analyzes legal phenomena downstream from legislative creation through the grid of interests. Heck, "The Formation of Concepts," 125.

33 "The logic of the judge's activity does not belong to the logic of cognitive thinking, but to that of emotional thinking. Its ideal is not the truth, but the life or value interest value of the results of thought." Heck, *Gesetzeauslegung und Interessenjurisprudenz* (Tübingen: Mohr, 1914), 11.

Heck also foresees the need for a judge's complementary weighing of interests, which could or should be carried out in exceptional cases.[34] In such cases, the judge acts as a subsidiary, like a legislator. This second evaluative moment in the activity of the judge makes Interessenjurisprudenz qualify the judge as an intelligent assistant to the legislator.[35]

Law elaboration: The genetic doctrine of interests

This part of *Interessenjurisprudenz*'s theory falls under the so-called "genetic theory of interests." The *Interessenjurisprudenz* wants the "satisfaction of the needs of life, desires and existing tendencies in the legal community, material or ideal."[36] Heck named "interests" such "desires and tendencies." The infinity of interests pursued by individuals constitutes the starting point. Left to itself, the multitude of conflicting interests is socially costly because satisfying one particular interest means sacrificing another. It is often impossible to attack the conflict's source. Hence, it is desirable to reduce social instability by setting orders of preference. That is the legislator's task. The interest the legislator chooses to protect implies that he agrees to sacrifice another interest, which may be worthy of protection.

Although this is a matter of will and discretionary, it is not entirely random. It results from the relationships of present social forces, social stability and so-called superior interest, which includes the practicability of the solution to material justice.[37]

---

34 "If we attempt to characterize judicial decision...we cannot describe it as a mere cognitive function. The judge has to do more than apply ready-made rules of law and frame rules himself. Creating laws is one of his functions. To be sure, his established rules have a different force than legislative rules. They are not binding on other judges. In particular, the judge is less free than the legislator. He is bound by those evaluations of interests laid down by legislation; his evaluation may intervene only in a subsidiary capacity." Heck, "The Jurisprudence of Interests," 42.

35 "What our law and life need is a judge who assists the legislator as a thinking assistant, who not only observes the words and commandments but penetrates the legislator's intentions and realises the value judgments of the law even for unregulated situations on the basis of his own examination of interests." Heck, "The Formation of Concepts," 178.

36 Larenz, *Storia*, 65.

37 See Wilfred Kallfass, *Die Tübinger Schule der Interessenjurisprudenz* (Frankfurt am Maim: V. Klostermann, 1972), 14.

Typologies of interests

The term "interest" refers to the significance and desirability of life values for human beings. It encompasses a concept beyond material desires by including latent inclinations present below the surface of consciousness. Such underlying interests can be awakened by a stimulus and manifest as actual demands or claims. However, interests differ from such demands, as people do not constantly have active demands but enduring dispositions that may spark demands when triggered.[38] Interests apply to tangible and intangible goods like ethics, nationality, religion and ideals. One can also identify individual interests (private or personal) and collective interests (community or public interests).

Private interests are essential in private law, while public interests play a decisive role outside private law. However, public interests also exist in private law, even if they are less significant since a minimum of public interests must always be present. When even such a minimum is missing, there are no legal rules, and the conflict of interests is outside the legal sphere.[39] The diversity of interests that legislators must consider mirrors the complexity of life. For analytical purposes, Heck distinguishes between "interests of actual life" that the law aims to promote in order to achieve material justice[40] and "interests of legal technique", concerned with the applicability or easiness of application of legal rules.[41]

---

38 Heck, "The Formation of Concepts," 130.

39 Compared with private interests, public interests are strongly emphasized in mandatory (imperative) rules, while they are less critical for rules of a permissive character (dispositive rules). Their relative significance is minor where the community is merely interested in maintaining peace or order, i.e., it demands that conflicts of private interests be solved but is indifferent about how they shall be solved. Heck, "The Formation of Concepts," 132.

40 The substantive "interests of actual life" that laws seek to promote can be called the "ultimately effective interests." Their realization accomplishes "material justice" by crafting laws that adequately accommodate the realities of people's lived experiences. Sometimes, the fundamental interest is establishing a regulating norm; other times, the rule's content must closely fit societal expectations. Heck, "The Formation of Concepts," 133.

41 In contrast to this first group of interests, the "interests of legal technique" relate to the form and implementation of the law itself. It includes the "interest of practicability"—the law must be capable of being effectively applied, not just state aspirational goals. Rules must translate into workable, real-world solutions. It also includes the

Conflict theory: The weight of interests by the legislator

The legislator takes a comprehensive perspective when looking at the various interests and concerns of individuals or the legal community. He evaluates and differentiates these myriad interests from one another, and the resulting law can be seen as a product of these competing interests that struggle for recognition within the legal order. The law's outcome, purpose and content show that a particular interest is deemed more important and should receive legal protection through the norm.[42] Protecting this particular interest can only be achieved by setting aside other interests, and with hindsight, satisfying that interest is the purpose of the legal rule.

Legal elaboration primarily occurs through balancing the substantive interests of the parties involved. However, suppose one wants to shape the law according to ideas about the social order. In that case, the objective legal values necessary for the community (public interests) must also be considered in the weighting process.[43] According to Heck, three types of conflict may be distinguished:

- "Private" conflicts where the legislator faces a collision of private interests, which he has to adjust. Here, legislator interests come into play merely as normative reasons and standards. It is the case in "dispositive" or "permissive" rules of private law, [*ius dispositivum*, i.e., rules which govern cases only when the parties have not agreed otherwise], as distinguished from "mandatory" rules, [*ius cogens*]. The law of contracts, for example, is essentially a "dispositive" law.
- Internal conflicts of the legislator occur when the legislator has to choose between opposing legislative ideals. Such a conflict frequently occurs between the ideals (interests) of substantive appropriateness

"interest of presentation"—the law aiming to be easily applied in practice. That encompasses clarity, consistency, accessibility and other facets affecting ease of use and comprehension. These technical legal interests shape the form and structure of legislation, codes, and other legal instruments. They represent additional aspects the legislator must consider alongside the underlying substantive interests at stake. Heck, "The Formation of Concepts," 133

42 Heck, "The Formation of Concepts," 137–38.

43 These three types of conflict are frequently intermingled. Heck, "The Formation of Concepts," 132.

and practicability. The result of the legislator's choice is an imperative (or mandatory) rule that the parties cannot modify or eliminate by agreement. Rules prescribing formalities and most family law rules illustrate this type of rule.

- There are also conflicts of compulsion, where public and private interests are opposed. The problem is whether and to what extent private interests should be sacrificed to public interests. The outcome may be mandatory rules in private or criminal law.

The legislator's decision on conflicting interests results from this weighting, a complex process that considers "value ideas" and produces an "evaluation judgment." Heck did not specify the exact criteria for such evaluations. He did not try to provide a material theory of values within a ranking of life's goods[44] since *Interessenjurisprudenz* is "not a general philosophy, nor does it belong to that department of philosophy which is termed legal philosophy."[45]

The judicial activity: The "productive doctrine of interests"

Interessenjurisprudenz is devoted primarily to the application of law and aims at finding principles that judges should follow in deciding cases.[46] We saw that *Interessenjurisprudenz* maintains that the intellectual processes triggered by the judge do not relate to formal logic but to emotional thinking. The judge faced with a dispute is deciding about a conflict of interests, the resolution of which involves a value judgment. Since the judge, under the constitutional regime, is subordinate to the legislator, its decision must refer, except in particular situations, to the scale of values and the evaluation emerging from the legal order as a whole.

Contrary to *Begriffsjurisprudenz*, the judge's work cannot be limited to subsumption, where at first glance, the state of the affair should be covered under the typical factual elements of the legal norm hypothesis. For *Interessenjurisprudenz*,

44 "...the Interessenjurisprudenz is not a theory of substantive values. We do not dream of dictating to the legal community which interests it must protect in preference to other." Heck, "The Formation of Concepts," 123.

45 Heck, "The Formation of Concepts," 31.

46 ibid.

the judge must carefully verify that, in addition to subsumption, the opposition of specific interests in the actual case corresponds to the constellation of interests apprehended by the legislator. Therefore, an evaluative moment is always present, even if subconsciously.[47] As we will see below, the judge's subordination to the legislator does not negate his creative activity in gap-filling.

The theory of interpretation of *Interessenjurisprudenz*

The theory of interpretation of *Interessenjurisprudenz* distinguishes two steps. The first step concerns the interpretation as research of interests. At this stage, the judge must identify the content of the norm regarding all the interests that causally determined its development. For this historical research of interests, essential are, as we will see below, the legislative materials with normative value and the use of linguistic methods in elucidating the meaning of words and the preparatory works of the law.

In the second stage, on further development of the law, while the judge compares the product of his first research to the case at hand, he might observe that the norm needs to be completed or corrected. At this stage, the judge faces issues such as gaps and the judicial creation of law.

The interpretation proper: A historical research of interests

Determining the law evaluation of interests requires, according to Heck, historical research that must ultimately bring to light the normative will or purpose of the legislator and not his psychological will.[48] The motives behind the setting of the norm, which have prevailed in the legislative process, are

[47] Heck, "The Formation of Concepts," 185.

[48] Heck rejects the objective interpretation, which considers the law on itself as separated by its author, the legislator. However, he also differentiates Interessenjurisprudenz's interpretation from the Subjective interpretation. He rejects the "psychological will" of the legislature that emerges from the preparatory works of the proponents of the subjective-historical method: "..[our] historical interpretation should not be purely subjective. It determines the human ideas that emerged during the legislative process. However, it goes beyond these ideas to the interests that are causal for the law...If one wanted to summarize the entire activity...as an interpretation, one would have to describe this activity as a historical-teleological interpretation." Heck, *Gesetzauslegung*, 8.

decisive for determining the purpose of the regulation.[49] Within the interpretative process, the interpreter will juxtapose various images formed by different means to represent the norm correctly.

The first of these images will result from the text of the law, interpreted using the usual means whether grammatical or philological.[50] Heck insists on the relativity of this approach. The text provision is just a statement,[51] not the norm itself. While the *linguistic tools* have heuristic value, according to Heck, they cannot decisively dictate how laws should be interpreted[52] and rather provide just an initial source of knowledge. When interpreting individual terms, a legal practitioner must consider the entire set of ideas the term might represent rather than limiting their analysis to the literal meaning of the word alone (principle of free research).[53]

Furthermore, understanding does not occur through words in isolation.[54] The judge must research the context around individual words and concepts used in the law when the statute was adopted.[55] That involves understanding each term of the norm's legal facts and legal consequences at that moment in time. The second image concerns the circumstances and reasons that led to the enactment of the norm. Based on preparatory and committee works, this research focuses on the interests expressed in the legislative process. Since legal norms are based on the balancing of interests, as shown in genetic interests theory, the judge must go beyond the terms and, with their help, reach interests considered by not only the law, but also the law's

---

49 For this purpose, all indications that have significantly influenced the establishment of the norm should be used. That includes the entire sociopolitical context, that is, the interest-related nature of the regulatory matter and its historical-social roots ("interest research" and "occasion legis") as well as the materials of the legislative process (government draft, commission deliberations, counter-drafts, official reasons). Bernd Rüthers, Christian Fisher, *Grundrisse des Recht*, 494.

50 Heck, *Gesetzauslegung*, 120.

51 ibid., 121.

52 ibid., 120.

53 ibid., 92, 156.

54 ibid., 157.

55 In order to interpret the historical idea and achieve an insight into the train of thought that accompanied the creation of the words of the law, the published and unpublished legal materials (all the records of the internal development process of law) are informative in addition to the wording of the law. Heck, *Gesetzauslegung*, 106ff.

value judgments and value ideas.[56] The judge must clarify the interests the legislator had in mind, how and why it recognized them and how the law affects the interests. As Heck explains, this is the "practical peak of interest jurisprudence."[57]

Initially, interest research aims to determine the purpose of the law, which promotes the "predominant interest." Such predominant interest can be recognized from the law when viewed retrospectively. However, to fully understand the content of a legal norm as a result of a balancing of interests, the judge must also clarify the opposing interests.[58] The third step consists of searching for the legislative process's unspoken elements, which influenced the decision without being stated in the preparatory works.[59]

At the end of this process, the judge has a global representation of the norm, and the final image allows the judge to apply the law while respecting the genuine will of the legislator. That means the judge must refrain from any value judgment as long as the legislator's normative will corresponds to the state of the affair.

The domain of further development of law by the judge

The starting point for every case decision is a comparison between the conflict of interests in the case and the one decided by the law. Against this background, the historical interpretation of the law can lead to different results, which according to Heck, can be summarized into three large groups of cases[60] that include standard cases, more complicated cases and loophole (gap) cases.[61]

In the so-called standard cases, the judge should decide based on facts stemming from conflicting interests that the legislature has anticipated and

56 Heck, "The Formation of Concepts," 140.

57 Heck, *Gesetzauslegung*, 96.

58 Heck, "The Formation of Concepts," 137–38.

59 ".. It is also possible that the delimitation of the interests under consideration was influenced by value judgments that the people involved were not aware of but which nevertheless had an effect on the judgment or the formulation. Such "dispositions of consciousness must also be taken into account." Heck, *Gesetzauslegung*, 95.

60 The last two situations are the only ones covered by the further development of the law.

61 Heck, "The Formation of Concepts," 180ff.

regulated. The judge's role is then limited to logical deduction (subsumption), meaning that hypothetical facts of the norm match the facts of the case.[62] This allows the value judgment of the law to be transferred to the conflict of interests in need of a solution. According to *Interessenjurisprudenz* and Heck, the interests must always be examined without exception, even if, in such simple situations, this process is done subliminally.[63]

Heck identifies more complex cases as those where direct legal subsumption under an existing norm is impossible, including cases where there are gaps in the narrow sense, gaps *intra legem*, or delegation gaps. That happens where the statute refers the judge to his judgment, either by express delegation (judicial discretion) or by the use of indeterminate words that demand an appraisal of values,[64] such as the phrase "important ground" or "sufficient basis."[65]

The third group refers to cases in which, as a result of historical interest research, it emerges that there is a "gap" in law, or a gap in the narrow sense.[66] The judge performs here an evaluative formation of commandments, considering the interests that conflict with the decision, comparing them and

62 ibid., 180.

63 Stoll, one of the followers of the *Interessenjurisprudenz*, states that in simple situations, the decision can be obtained not by analyzing the conflict of interests but by logical subsumption due to its simplicity. Weighing interests would only be helpful for complex cases rather than routine ones. Heinrich Stoll, *The Role of Concepts and Construction in the Theory of the Jurisprudence of Interests*, in *The Jurisprudence of Interests: Selected Writings*, ed. and tr. Magdalena Schoch (Cambridge: Harvard University Press, 1948), 259ff. Heck agrees but emphasizes that an intuitive weighing of interests exists even in routine cases. The simple logical subsumption can be used where the result of the logical subsumption is consistent with the result of the analysis of the interests and where this result seems obvious. In such cases, the analysis of interests is present but is done intuitively in the judge's subconscious. It remains essential, however, because if the judge considers that the result is inconsistent with the interests at stake, he would hesitate to apply logical subsumption. Here, the analysis of interests has less of a role of conscious motivation but rather that of a control tool, an alarm device (*Alarmapparat*) that awakes the judge each time submission is inadequate, and the subsequent conscious and detailed analysis is needed. Cf. P. Heck, *The Formation of Concepts*, in Magdalena Scoch, op. cit., 185.

64 Heck, "The Formation of Concepts," 180.

65 ibid., 41.

66 Heck, *Gesetzauslegung*, 161.

weighing them up based on a value judgment.[67] For *Interessenjurisprudenz*, the law only sometimes provides clear answers since it is impossible for legislators to fully anticipate all situations due to the diversity and evolving nature of life. Hence, the laws must be revised and completed. This doctrine of the gap in the law is central to Heck, who developed a typology of gaps[68] based on their characteristics.[69]

Heck proposes two approaches for addressing the identified gaps in the law. On the one hand, the judge can use historical research to assess prevailing societal interests and recognize the ranking of the various interests in the legislation (remote effect of the law).[70] In case of real gaps, whether primary or secondary, Heck instructs the judges to supplement the missing requirement by examining whether the same or a similar conflict of interest has been resolved in law in one way or another. Such legal evaluation is groundbreaking for similar facts, and the judge can use it. If the same or a similar conflict of interests has been resolved in law, the value judgment should be transferred by analogy[71] in an analogy of interests and not the old analogy of concepts.[72]

On the other hand, the judge can rely on their own knowledge and life experience to determine interests worthy of protection (judicial evaluation).[73]

---

67 ibid., 225.

68 For detailed gap terminology, see Heck, *Gesetzauslegung*, 168ff.

69 For example, according to their genesis, Heck divides gaps into primary gaps inherent in the law at its creation and secondary gaps arising through the change of time. Heck, *Gesetzauslegung*, 168- 69, 172, 176.

70 Heck, *Gesetzauslegung*, 232ff.

71 "Whenever the statute does not foresee the facts of a particular case, the judge must first envisage the conflict of interests which underlies the dispute. Then, he must examine whether or not the same conflict of interests underlies other factual situations that have been expressly regulated by legislation. If the answer is affirmative, he must transfer the value decision in the statute to the facts of his case; that is to say, he must decide identical conflicts of interest similarly." Heck, "The Formation of Concepts," 41.

72 "About the delimitation of interests, the legal relationship of the official residence of a Reich civil servant shows greater agreement [analogy, our remark] with the legal relationship of a tenement than, for example, with a Reichstag resolution. Given the conflicts of interest that arise, the institution of the court settlement *is* often closer to out-of-court settlements than the institution of the bailiff...." Philipp Heck, *Grundriß des Schuldrechts* (Tübingen: Mohr, 1929), 479–80.

73 Heck, *Gesetzauslegung*, 227.

However, this latter approach only applies if there is a missing evaluation judgment (an evaluation gap)[74] in the law. The judge's evaluation may only be used if neither the law itself nor customs or the constitution can provide criteria for evaluation.[75]

Conclusion: The doctrine of interests winning the methodological contest and the practitioners

Interessenjurisprudenz, a leading "challenger" in the German methodological debates, finally overcame rival currents due to its intrinsic qualities and coherence. *Interessenjurisprudenz* became the interest of magistrates and the courts in the 1920s and 1930s. Heck himself mentions[76] two articles by Wachinger an Imperial Supreme Court's magistrate that testify to *Interessenjurisprudenz* expansion. In the first article of the *Deutschen Richterzeitung* (German Judges" Magazine)[77] Wachinger answers "What should it do?" in reference to the jurisprudence. He describes in detail the method of *Interessenjurisprudenz*, referring to the writings of Heck and Müller-Erzbach. He emphasizes the enormous demands this method places on the judge and the benefits it entails for satisfying the demands of life. Wachinger ends his description with these words: "Such a method of searching for the right is what we need." In another article in the *Juristischen Wochenschrift* (Legal Weekly),[78] the same Wachinger summarized the balance of interests. According to

74 ibid., 238.

75 ".. [the judge] may sometimes find himself in a position where he has to decide a conflict of interests according to his own evaluation...such an appraisal of interests on the part of the judge is required in all cases where it is demanded by the guiding ideas pervading the legal system as a whole, but where statutory evaluations are contradictory or entirely lacking. In such cases the judge must render that decision which he would propose if he were the legislator. This is the rule contained in the famous article 1 of the Swiss Civil Code. In its substance it is valid for the German judge as well as for the Swiss judge." Heck, "The Formation of Concepts," 41.

76 Philipp Heck, "Die Leugnung der Interessenjurisprudenz. Eine Erwiederung," in *Archiv für die civilistische Praxis* 137, no. 17 (1933): 55–56.

77 Burghart Wachinger, "Was not tut," *Deutsche Richterzeitung* 24 (1932): 225.

78 Burghart Wachinger, "Zur Frage der Erzwingbarkeit von Untersuchungen für die Blutgruppenbestimmung: Bedeutung und Grenzen der richterlichen Interessenabwägung," *Juristische Wochenschrift* 15, no. 10 (1932): 3041ff.

Heck, it is significant that a member of the Supreme Court embraced the *Interessenjurisprudenz*. It is also significant that this characterization of the weighting of interests is not carried out on the occasion of a civil matter but rather for treating a procedural problem. Practitioners have noticed early on the potential and difficulties of using *Interessenjurisprudenz* to solve cases. Our following paper will illustrate both these aspects with some applications of the *Interessenjurisprudenz* in actual cases.

Illustrating How *Interessenjurisprudenz* Applies in Real German Cases

Remus Titiriga
University of the West, Romania

This second article about *Interessenjurisprudenz* complements the theoretical developments of our first paper and illustrates how this methodological doctrine is applied to actual cases. The first part follows Heck's examination of a case about a clause *donatio mortis causa* within a contract in favor of a third party. Heck exposes it in an article from 1933, which updates some of his old research on the problem. He criticized a case decision by Reichsgericht in 1917, which used a conceptualistic approach that was a revised form of *Begriffsjurisprudenz*, and followed through on a constant practice. At the same time, in an inspiring and dense presentation, Heck offered his solution to the problem using the *Interessenjurisprudenz*.

The second part again analyzes a case where Heck critically examines Reichsgericht‘s famous decision about revaluating monetary obligations at the height of German hyperinflation in 1923. In the most relevant part, Heck exposes his solution based on a well-articulated application of Interessenjurisprudenz. The last part of the paper covers two linked cases about a German patent procedure in 1932. Norber Sohn, an attorney from Berlin at that time, reconstructed the methodological reasoning in the two cases as an essential but hidden use of *Interessenjurisprudenz*. ParentAmt also distanced itself from a conceptual, methodological approach, including *Begrifssjurisprudenz* in all of its manifestations. The two cases express German jurisdictions' adoption of a silentious and simplified version of *Interessenjurisprudenz* as the choice method in complex cases.

The case of third-party donation concurring with inheritance law

Interessenjurisprudenz attacked the inversion conceptual construction used by *Begriffsjurisprudentz* during the nineteenth century to find new solutions based on classification concepts.[1] This initial *Begriffsjurisprudenz* faded away and was replaced by a new *Begriffsjurisprudenz* based on concepts and terms within the law and its normative concepts. In this revised form, the solution to real problems was determined by German judges in a purely cognitive way from legal terms by theoretical, conceptual constructions.[2] What was missing in such situations was, according to Heck, the consideration of the practical life needs or an examination of interests and purposes that are causal to the norms.[3] Heck was critically examining a Reichsgericht (RG) decision involving a contract in favor of a third party based on this type of *Begriffsjurisprudenz* and was proposing a different solution using *Interessenjurisprudenz*.

The case and the Reichsgericht solution

The case of 1917

In a case dating to 1917,[4] a rentier with several nieces favored them in his testament or will with several legacies of equal amounts. However, by mistake, he forgot one of his nieces. Instead of modifying his will, the uncle deposited the corresponding sum in a bank, understanding that he would be free to dispose of the money during his lifetime and that, unless he disposed of it, that particular niece would receive the capital on his death. The uncle died, and it was discovered that the debts of the inheritance were more significant

---

1 Philipp Heck, "The Jurisprudence of Interests," in *The Jurisprudence of Interests: Selected Writings*," ed. and tr. Magdalena Schoch (Cambridge: Harvard University Press, 1948) 38–39.

2 Specific authors note that this sort of *Begriffsjurisprudenz*, an interpretation based on formal legal expressions, is still widespread today. Rolf Wank, *Juristische Methodenlehre* (Munich: Franz Vahlen, 2020), 2.

3 "The study of interests and the effect of interests is still neglected. The formation of concepts, even if they are only concepts of order, is still treated as a problem of knowledge and elevated to the subject of methodologically incorrectly conducted disputes." Philipp Heck, *Grundriß des Schuldrechts* (Tübingen: Mohr1929), 479–80.

4 The facts underlie a case decided by the Reichsgericht and published in volume 88 of the *Entscheidungen des Reichsgericht in Zivilsachen* (1917). Heck, "The Jurisprudence of Interests," 42.

than its assets. The problem or question was the following: Who should be entitled to the capital? Should it be that niece or the estate's creditors?

We have in this scenario a contract in favor of a third-party,[5] from which someone other than the contracting parties should acquire a right. Such a contract enables an indirect transfer of assets, a sort of an "indirect donation," while the promisee makes a sacrifice that advances the beneficiary's interests. The asset goes to the beneficiary through the "third-party clause" in the contract.[6] According to article 328 (1) BGB (German Civil Code), it can be agreed that the third party acquires the right "immediately."[7]

The contract of the two parties included the uncle, the promisee, and, the bank the promisor, and it was made in favor of a third party, namely the the forgotten niece who was the beneficiary. It was to become effective in case the contracting party, namely the promisee, dies. Before that, the uncle could freely dispose of the money in his account. According to a provision of Article 331 (1), if the benefit was to follow the death of the promisee (a *mortis causa* clause in a contract in favor of a third party),[8] the third party's right

[5] In principle, a contract under the Law of Obligations only binds the contracting parties. However, a corresponding agreement can be made into a contract in favor of third parties. This contract type is characterized by the debtor (promisor) having to provide the service owed to a third party (beneficiary), not to his creditor or contractual partner (promisee).

[6] It consists of three legal relationships: a) the cover relationship between the debtor (promisor) and the creditor (promisee). The underlying transaction can be of various types: a mutual contract, purchase, work contract, or insurance contract. In our precise case, it is a banking service contract for a savings account by the uncle. b) the value relationship between the creditor (promisee) and the third party (beneficiary). This value relationship is the causal relationship between the promisee and the beneficiary: the legal reason that causes the promisee to make an indirect donation. [It can also be an unrestricted donation, like in our case, our remark]. c) the execution relationship between the debtor (promisor) and the third party. It cannot be ruled out that the promisor also sees himself compelled to make his promise not only by his relationships with the promissee but also by his relationships with the beneficiary. In this situation, there is a joint donation. [That is not the case for our bank contract, our remark]. Heck, *Grundriss des Schuldrecht*, 144.

[7] Article 328 (1) BGB: "A performance to a third party may be agreed by contract with the effect that the third party acquires immediately [unmittelebar] the right to demand the performance."

[8] Article 331 (1) BGB states: "If performance (of a contract) in favor of a third party is to be rendered after the death of the promisee, in case of doubt, the third party acquires the right to performance upon the death of the promisee..."

should only be acquired upon the death of the promisee.[9] While the case can be subsumed under articles 228 (1) and 331 (1), there is no immediate answer in the BGB about the position of the third-party beneficiary concerning the estate's creditors. In conclusion, there is a gap in the law.[10]

The conceptual solution of the Reichsgericht

Reichsgericht solves the case by favoring the niece over the estate's creditors. The court's solution is based on an argument often used before and after,[11] the immediacy theory[12] developed in three steps. The first is the observation that the beneficiary's right in Article 328 can be acquired "immediately" from the contract. The second is that the beneficiary acquires it "immediately," which means his right was never part of the promisee's assets. Third is that this right was never subject to the restrictions that apply to the promisee's disposal of assets.

According to Heck, based on the second step, the word "immediately" is used in a sense that it might apply in general but not precisely here.[13] Simply speaking, there is some ambiguity since "immediately" can signify both the right acquired directly (a substantive meaning) or the non-requirement of accession or acceptance (a procedural meaning) by the third party. An examination of the legislative history of article 328 (1) leaves no room for doubt: in the relationship between the third party and the promisor, "immediately" means "without collaboration' or a need for acceptance by the third

9 This provision says two things. 1) Before this time (death of promisee), the interests of the person concerned enjoy no protection against the contracting parties. The nomination can be canceled without the beneficiary's consent, depending on the agreement in the contract, or, as a rule, unilaterally by the promisee. 2) Before the promisee's death, the third person's interests are treated only as an actual prospect, like the prospect of someone named (legatee) in a will. Therefore, his creditors cannot access it through seizure or bankruptcy. Heck, *Grundriss*, 146.

10 This primary gap was already present when the Civil Code (BGB) was elaborated.

11 RG uses the same argument in RGZ, vol. 51, 405 (1902); RGZ, vol. 71, p. 327 (1909); RGZ, vol. 80, 177 (1912); RGZ, vol. 88, 137 (1917); RGZ, vol. 106, 1 (1923). Heck, "The Jurisprudence of Interests," 45.

12 Heck, *Grundriß des Schuldrechts* (Tübingen: Mohr, 1929), 149.

13 ibid., 149.

party (the second procedural meaning).[14] The *Reichsgericht*, choosing the first meaning, has derived from a term covering a strictly limited mandate content, a new legal norm. According to Heck, besides that, the RG's more profound error is the attempt to derive a decision from a concept (with an argument of *Begriffsjurisprudenz* on its second iteration) instead of returning to the interests and value judgments of the law.

The solution of Heck using Interessenjurisprudenz

Heck's 1933 text devoted to these developments is very brief and almost cryptical.[15] Therefore, his other contributions could help reconstruct his reasoning steps. The author elaborated on some aspects in his opus, *Grundriss des Schuldrechts* of 1929.[16] But Heck made more significant developments in a paper from 1890,[17] before the adoption of the BGB (German Civil Code), and producing such an impression abroad that was immediately translated into French.[18] A brief reading confirms that this initial inquiry was conducted strictly using the Jurisprudence of Interests method while proposing, at that time, *de lege ferenda* solutions.

Rejecting the conceptual solution of the RG, Heck solves the case using *Interessenjurisprudenz*. According to the doctrine covered in our previous article, the judge should assess prevailing societal interests and the ranking of various legal interests to fill this legal gap. He should determine whether a similar factual hypothesis and an analogous conflict of interests to the case at hand have been determined in the law in one way or another (remote effect of the law). In that situation, the judge should apply the same evaluation to the case (analogy of weighted interests).

---

14 The argument can be cited: "..such a contract can be concluded with the effect that the third party directly, *without his accession or declaration of acceptance* [italics added], acquires the right to claim the performance." See "Memorandum 1239» in Beno Mugdan, *Die gesammten Materialien zu den Reichs-Justizgesetzen*, vol. 2, (Berlin: Verlag, 1897–98).

15 Heck, "The Jurisprudence of Interests," 42–46.

16 Heck, *Grundriß des Schuldrechts* (Tübingen: Mohr, 1929), 587.

17 Heck, "Die Lebensversicherung zugunsten Dritten, eine Schenkung auf den Todesfall," *Archiv fur Burgerliches Recht* 17, vol. 4 (1890).

18 Philipp Heck, *L'assurance sur la vie au profit d'un tiers et la donation a cause de mort, annoté par M. J. Lefort*, tr. M. J. Brissand (Paris: BNF, 1891).

The case at hand

The case relates to a contract between a promisee (the uncle) and a promisor (the bank) containing a revocable *mortis causa* clause in favor of a third party, the niece. Since it acts as an "indirect donation" (with a *mortis causa* element), the search for analogies, factual hypotheses, and balances of interests must naturally start with donations *inter vivos* and then adjust them to create donations *mortis causa*.

The pattern of interests and their legal evaluation in contractual obligations in general

The Law of Obligations governs the rights and duties of creditors and debtors. The creditor has a relative right to demand action or performance from the debtor, who has the corresponding duty (or obligation in the restricted sense)[19] to act or perform.[20] Obligations as relationships involve conflicting interests that the law must balance. The creditor's interest is to receive the promised action or performance, while the debtor's interest is to avoid an excessive sacrifice or burden. Satisfying the creditor is the purpose behind obligations and the predominant interest, which is legally protected, but the law must weigh the competing interests, too.

Donations inter vivos and the relevant interests

The departing point in Heck's reconstructed overview is the donation, a gift through which a donor enriches the recipient from his assets. According to today's reglementation, both parties agree through a contract that the gift is free of charge (§ 516 para. 1 BGB) as a legal transaction. A donation is a unilateral contract binding only on one side because only the donor (the debtor of the donation) has to provide a service. The interests (and their intensity) of the parties in a donation are different from other transactions

---

19 The law uses the term obligation in a broader and restricted sense. The former describes the legal relationship between debtors and creditors, such as a sales contract. The term obligation, in the narrower sense, on the other hand, refers to the individual claims that result from such a legal relationship, such as the buyer's claim against the seller for ownership of the purchased item.

20 The link between rights and interests lies in the affirmation of Ihering that subjective rights are legally protected interests. See our first paper for the discussion relative to Ihering.

since the donation is altruistic in a world of egoists.[21] A donation is made with no counterpart from the recipient (enrichment), and in return, the donor's assets are reduced (de-enrichment), and there is a fundamental risk that the donor's interests could be particularly endangered. Therefore, the law grants the receiver of the donation (the creditor of the donation) less protection than otherwise is usual in non-altruistic legal transactions. The legal balance between the interests of the debtor vs. the interest of the creditor is slightly truncated for specific factual hypotheses in favor of the debtor (the donor).[22] Hence, one can identify the evaluative judgment in the law as protecting the party making a sacrifice. This legal evaluation will reverberate as leitmotiv further on.

The interests in the donation mortis causa (promise of donation) in general

Heck examines the mechanisms allowing a shift from transactions that, according to their regular form, operate between living persons (donations *inter vivos*) to transactions having their effect in whole or in part after the death of the person making them (*mortis causa*). Such a shift would be the deferral of a donation. A complete deferral occurs when the gift is freely revocable, and a partial one occurs when the revocation is excluded, but the immediate enjoyment of the receiver is prevented.[23]

Regarding the greater sphere of other interests, including the donor's creditors, dispositions in the event of death through a donation *mortis causa* differ significantly from those in a donation *inter vivos*. The interests situation

---

21 Heck, *Grundriss*, 289.

22 For example, several situations give the donor the right to cancel the donation within the scope of revocation (Section 530ff. *Bürgerliches Gesetzbuch*) and the right of objection (emergency requirements Section 519 *Bürgerliches Gesetzbuch*).

23 In *Die Lebensversicherung*, Heck elaborates (in 1890, before the adoption of the *Bürgerliches Gesetzbuch*) about the legal situation during the donor's lifetime: "According to Justinian and common law, the effect of the *mortis causa* donation during the donor's lifetime depends only on his will. He can establish a revocable right or postpone creating a subjective right for the person concerned until his death."

- In the first case [of a revocable right, our remark], the receiver has only an actual prospect, which must be treated like the last will. Therefore, it is not subject to sale, seizure, or, in general, inheritance. This weakening of the effect compared to *inter-vivo* transactions is legally justified. If a revocable liberality is given to is characterized by the words that Roman law uses for the *mortis causa* donation (§ 95. II, 7, "mortis causa donatio est, cum magis se quis velit habere uam eum, cui donatur, magisque eum, cui donat, quam heredem suum"), "a donation in a case of death, is when a person wishes to have himself more than the one to whom he gives, and the one to whom he gives more than to his heir" [or creditors, our remark].[24]

The donor *mortis causa* does not want to deprive himself of anything and gives what death would take away from his hands. The absence of sacrifice by deceased donors shapes protections differently than typical *inter vivos* donations. On the one hand, the *mortis causa* donation's interest in maintaining the estate is weaker than that of the *inter vivo* donation.[25] On the other hand, the estate's creditors need more legal protection than in an *inter vivos* donation.[26] If a donor *mortis causa* could withdraw the estate from his creditors in favor of others without his sacrifice, the estate's creditors would be endangered or would be sacrificed. Their transactions should be protected more than in donations *inter vivos*. The evaluative leitmotif of the legislator

another, the donor can be expected to resort to revocation and destroy the gift. The inadmissibility of this transfer saves such a detour.

- In the second case [of a postponed right, our remark], a more comprehensive power of disposal of the receiver is intended (...). In both eventualities, the revocable right or the postponed right is subject to the free access of the donor's creditor, which he cannot exclude." Heck, *Die Lebensversicherung*, op. cit, Section 32, 70.

24 Heck, *Grundriss*, Section 95, 299.

25 "The interests are weaker. Those who only want to reduce their estate demonstrate a lesser motive for devotion than those who impose personal deprivation on their account [a lesser interest, our remark]. The receiver, who has only achieved a prospect of enjoyment after the death of another, can rely on this only in time. The realization of an uncertain increase in assets for the receiver does not have the same weight as for the receiver of an immediately effective donation; He will be less inclined and less empowered to choose it as the basis for his life plans and economic arrangements and will, therefore, more easily endure the thwarting of his hopes for the benefit of those interested in inheriting [or estate's creditors, our remark]. [He also has a lesser interest, our remark]." Heck, *Die Lebensversicherung*, Section 3, 24.

26 "The need for legal protection of those inheriting [or estate's creditors, our remark] is more significant than in *inter vivos* dispositions. The egoism of the disposing party in *inter vivos* dispositions protects those interested in inheriting [or estate's creditors, our remark] since anyone who wants to deprive themselves of their assets in this way can only do that at their own expense." Heck, *Die Lebensversicherung*, Section 3, 24.

trying to protect those who make a sacrifice, or those whose interests might be sacrificed, is relevant again.

Conclusions about the actual legal regime in the BGB for the deferred donations

The two ways of realizing the deferral of donations open up two different legal regimes implemented in the BGB. The first is the postponement of donation, linked to a term-a delay (the death of the donor) and opening a contractual regime implemented by the BGB as a promise of donation.[27] All other aspects regarding the estate creditors' interests vis-a-vis the receiver's interest apply identically and were implemented in the BGB accordingly. The other variant, of introducing the revocability in a donation by implementing it *mortis causa,* closes the access to the contractual sphere of obligations. This kind of transfer of an asset stops being a donation or promise of donation as a legal type. A potestative condition (the revocability of obligation by the donor's will) implies no desire to assume an obligation by contract. The revocability in this situation makes the transaction become a unilateral act and, hence, escapes the Law of Obligations. As a *mortis causa*, this revocable transfer of goods belongs to the Inheritance law in the BGB – the will with legacy, which is analyzed below.

The last will with legacy, the relevant interests and their evaluations

A last will is a unilateral declaration of intent by the testator regarding his assets that simultaneously requires formality, can be revoked at any time and only takes effect in the event of his death (inheritance). In German Inheritance Law, the legacy grants a specific financial benefit based on a will to the person intended by the legacy (the legatee). The object of a legacy can be the gift of any asset. Sometimes, the legatee does not even know about his position. The legatee does not acquire the item immediately upon the testator's death. He only obtains a claim against the heir or heirs burdened

27 See Article 2301 (BGB) Promises of gifts because of death: 1. "The provisions on dispositions mortis causa shall apply to a promise to make a donation which is made on the condition that the donee survives the donor...." 2. "If the donor executes the gift by making payment for the object granted, the provisions on gifts inter vivos shall apply."

with the legacy. Before the testator's death, the legatee had no subjective rights, while the testator's creditors still had subjective rights. After a testator's death, the conflict of interests between the estate's creditors and the legatees is legally resolved. Creditors must be protected. This is an imperative legal norm, not a dispositive one.[28] It is not something resulting from the alleged content of the will, and the testator has no possibility of placing his legatee in a preferential situation regarding his creditors.[29]

Examining the contract with mortis causa clause in favor of a third party, the relevant interests and their evaluations

The above detour was meant to help understand the case at hand: the contract between parties (the uncle and the bank) containing a revocable *mortis causa* clause in favor of a third party (the niece). We saw that the real significance of contracts for the benefit of third parties is that they enable the indirect transfer of assets (the indirect donation) from the promisee to the third party. Similar to the shift operated for regular direct donation is the "indirect donation" through forms, which is designed to be effective between the living and can be postponed until the death of the promisee through a particular clause. That clause is the right of withdrawal. That is, the appointment of a third-party beneficiary can be revoked at any time during the recipient's lifetime.

If this is a deviation from the right of the *mortis causa* donation (promise of donation),[30] it merely contains a further approximation (analogy) to the law of legacies.[31] The third-party (the niece) does not need to accept the (indirect) "donation" since she may not receive any knowledge of it during

28 Inheritance Law contains mostly imperative rules.

29 Heck, "The Jurisprudence of Interests," 43.

30 If the uncle had used a promise of donation while he lived, the receiver niece would already have a subjective right, even if a relative (personal) right under term (the uncle's death). A subjective right means a more substantial interest (high-intensity interest). This interest is more robust than in our contract in favor of third-party beneficiaries (the forgotten niece). Therefore, the interests in the two situations are unequal and cannot constitute a basis for a further analogy. They can be used only in support of an argument *a fortiori*. For further details, see Heck, "The Jurisprudence of Interests," 43.

31 Heck, *Grundriss*, Section 95, 299.

the promissee's lifetime (like a legatee in a will), influencing the formation of the conflict of interests. In that situation, she not only has no reason to rely on obtaining it but cannot even do so. As long as the uncle lives, the niece has not acquired a subjective right but only an expectation lacking protection against him (like a legatee in a will vs. the testator).

After the uncle's (promisee) death, one must consider that the promisee spent nothing during his lifetime for the third party. His sacrifice is missing, just as for a testator in a will. If the promisee could withdraw the estate from his creditors in favor of others (the third parties) without his sacrifice, the creditors would be endangered. That is, it would be sacrificed. The need to protect the promisee's estate's creditors is like in a will for the testator's creditors. The promisor's interest is irrelevant here. He will execute the third-party clause in favor of the beneficiary in the same way as the heirs burdened with the legacy shall do in a will.

Analogy of interests between the legacy will and our contract in favor of a third party

We identified the legal balance between the interests of legatees and the interests of the estate's creditors, a balance weighted by law in favor of the estate's creditors. We also identified the equality in the interests of the niece favored by the third-party contract and the legatee in a will both before and after the promisee's or testator's death. The position of the estate creditors is the same in the two situations, and the evaluative reason (preventing and protecting against unjust sacrifices) should apply the same in the balance with the estate creditors' interests.

The balance of the law for legatee versus the estate's creditors' interests applies by analogy, given the similarity of factual situations and the equality of interests, to the balance between the interests of the contract's third party and the interests of the estate's creditors. Contrary to the RG's decision, this balance should be weighted in favor of the estate's creditors. Hecks critique and proposed solution using *Interessenjurisprudenz* offered a compelling alternative to Reichsgericht's approach, demonstrating the importance of his holistic legal reasoning. This considers the practical implications and societal values at stake rather than adhering to a localized conceptual formalism.

A famous reevaluation judgment analyzed and reconstructed according to *Interessenjurisprudenz* by Heck

Before August 1914, the stability of the German mark's value was secured by its link to the value of gold, the rule of the gold standard. At the outbreak of the First World War, this gold convertibility was suspended in Germany by monetary laws, allowing unrestricted expansion of the note issue and making paper money legal tender.[32]

From then onward, every creditor had to be content with being paid the nominal amount of the debt in paper marks under the principle "[paper] Mark equals [gold] Mark." The rule also applied retroactively to the extent that claims established before 1914 monetary laws were also affected. With the end of the War in 1918, the mark had officially lost more than half of its value, or more precisely, purchasing power, both internally and externally. The actual cause of the increasing inflation from 1919, which turned into hyperinflation from mid-1922, was the massive expansion of the money supply by the State in the early years of the Weimar Republic due to the high reparation payments.[33]

As a result, debtors could free themselves by paying nominal amounts in marks no longer related to the original gold mark value. The falling value of money meant a corresponding devaluation of creditors' rights, including mortgage claims. A legal reaction to this was not to be expected since the

---

[32] A previous Law of June 1, 1909 (RGBl., p. 315) declared the Reichsbank notes legal tender. The monetary laws of 1914 extended that under the following specific laws: 1. the Law of August 4, 1914 (RGBl. p. 341), which transferred the same regulation to the Reich treasury notes until further notice and at the same time lifted the obligation to redeem until further notice; 2. the Law of August 4, 1914 (RGBl. p. 326) regarding changes to the coinage law, which applies to the exchange of silver coins put paper money on an equal footing with gold coins; and 3. these provisions had been supplemented by a Bundesrat decree (BRVO) dated September 26, 1914 (RGBl. p. 417), expressly abrogating the gold clause in contracts made prior to July 31, 1914, and authorizing payment in paper money. Cf. Ph. Heck, "Das Urteil des Reichsgerichts vom 28. November 1923 über die Aufwertung von Hypotheken und die Grenzen der Richtermacht" (The ruling of the Reich Court of November 28, 1923 on the revaluation of mortgages and the limits of judges' power), *Archiv für die civilistische Praxis*, 122. Bd., H. 2 (1924), p. 204.

[33] See John P. Dawson, "Effects of Inflation on Private Contracts: Germany, 1914–1924," *Michigan Law Review*, 33, no. 2, (1934): 172.

German state benefited from the situation as the debtor of the war bonds.[34] In this context, the "Marks equal Marks" principle was upheld and ratified by the German courts, which systematically denied creditors' claims to revaluate the mortgage obligations.

However, the public mood changed. Jurists and economists insistently asked the legislators to act and remedy the injustice the 1914 laws were causing. In December 1922, a bill to this effect had been presented to the German Parliament, and it seemed that the legislator intended to revalue obligations. However, this intention had already been expressed and postponed on previous occasions.[35] As hyperinflation was accentuated, the political-economical situation became tense, and the German Supreme Court (Reichsgericht-RG) decided to push the legislature. In the summer of 1923, the Council of Magistrates of the Court addressed the Minister of Justice, asking him to adopt some measures because the situation caused severe problems of conscience for the judges. Shortly after, it warned the Minister that a legislative intervention that disregards the creditors' right to revaluation would be contrary to the principle of good faith and could be disobeyed by the courts.[36]

This unprecedented manifestation of the magistrates was followed by a judicial reversal of the higher jurisdiction on November 28 1923 at the height of the hyperinflation.[37] That day, the RG authorized the creditor of a mortgage loan contracted before the war[38] to deny the debtor the cancellation of the debt when offered the nominal value of the loan in paper money.[39]

---

34 Dieter Grimm, *Neue Juristische Wochenschrift*, 50 (1997): 2724.

35 Heck, *Das Urteil*, 222–23.

36 ibid., 223.

37 In November 1923, a gold mark was traded with 522 billion paper marks; in December of the same year, the price had risen to 1 trillion paper marks. Dawson, "Effects of Inflation on Private Contracts," 174.

38 The plaintiff owned land in South West Africa (an old German colony) and had mortgaged it in favor of the creditor. When the mortgage claim of 13.000 marks fell due on April 1, 1920, the mortgage creditor refused to accept payment because the actual value of the principal and interest was a fraction of the sum he had anticipated when the mortgage loan had been made. The plaintiff (mortgage debtor) sued for a declaration that the mortgage had been redeemed by payment of the stipulated sum in paper marks at their nominal value. Basil S. Markesinis, Hannes Unberath, and Angus Johnston, *The German Law of Contract* (London: Hart, 2006), 801.

39 RGZ, vol. 107, 78.

The Court relied on Section §242 of the German Civil Code (BGB) and thus granted the judges the authority to set a new exchange rate (revaluation).[40] Heck analyzed this decision critically and proposed his solution based on *Interessenjurisprudenz*. According to him, the reasons for the judgment in an upbeat section give a legal basis for the revaluation. In contrast, the negative section states that the monetary laws do not stop the revaluation. The negative part was decisive, according to Heck, and he focused on this side of the Court's arguments to systematically reject it.

The historical interpretation and the rejection of the constancy meaning of the RG

The RG attributes to the monetary laws of August 1914 the view that banknotes and cash receipts were meant to be equal in value to metal money. The possibility of such a currency decline that "the conclusions resulting from the currency regulations are no longer compatible with the principles of good faith" was not considered. In conclusion, the "intended adherence to the currency regulations is impossible for RG in the present case." One would be here in the presence of a primary gap where the legislator has not regulated a situation because he has not foreseen it.[41] Heck, call this the constancy interpretation.[42] He recognizes that if the authors of monetary laws did not consider the possibility of devaluation and therefore did not want the inevitable damage to creditors in such a case, there would have been no obstacle for a revaluation according to §242[43] Since the law's wording does not support this restrictive view, a historical interpretation is needed here.

---

40 In the decision, the Court says: "When issuing the regulation, the legislature did not have any expectation of a significant devaluation of paper money, especially one of such a magnitude as has become increasingly reality after the unfortunate outcome of the world war and after the revolution thought." From this, the RG derived the authority to adjust the numerical amount of a debt to the changed monetary value, even without a corresponding clause in the contract. With no other options left, the Reich Court chose the Civil Code's Section 242 (good faith). Dawson, "Effects of Inflation on Private Contracts," 28ff.

41 Heck, *Das Urteil*, 209.

42 ibid., 211.

43 Article Section 242 (BGB), Performance in good faith, states: "The debtor is obliged to provide the service in a way that is required by good faith and in consideration of standard practice."

Assessing the ideas prevailing at the time (August and September 1914) regarding monetary laws and the notorious situation of interests in which the German Empire found itself leads to a different conclusion: monetary laws were intended to support the value of paper money (and exclude revaluation).

Heck calls this interest of the state in compulsory exchange rates of paper money monetary interest.[44] As a rule of historical experience, non-redeemable paper money was used in political turmoil and wars. Heck proves it furthermore by examining society's values and common ideas at the outbreak of the War,[45] and by considering that the legislator should have aligned with those ideas.[46]

Heck determines the opposite interest after establishing this purpose, which coincides with the dominant interest. Achieving the monetary interest was associated with hardship. A war, any war, means death and suffering, and Germany was prepared to endure unheard-of hardships. Given the life sacrifices required from those fighting the war, a minor sacrifice of the *financial interests of creditors* should be readily accepted. The state could only obtain the means of payment it needed through the compulsory exchange rate at the expense of the creditors.[47]

This balance suppressed creditors' interests in favor of *currency interests* and corresponded to the ideas at the origin and the causal interests. Consequently, contrary to RG, monetary laws did not intend to avoid damage to creditors and did not assume the constant value of money. Furthermore, RG bases its constancy interpretation on only two grounds Heck finds inconclusive.[48] The court considers the monetary laws based on the assumption of equivalence between paper money and banknotes as "entirely justified given the healthy state of the German national economy." Heck recognizes that the German national economy was healthy before the war. Nevertheless, the laws were intended for the future. Moreover, for the prognosis of the future, it was

44 Heck, *Das Urteil*, 210.
45 ibid., 210.
46 ibid., 210.
47 ibid., 211.
48 ibid., 211.

logically not the previous state that was decisive but the impact of the war and its outcome.[49]

Secondly, the RG relies on the official justification of the BRVO of September 26, 1914, regarding the repeal of the gold clause. The measure affirms that "the public unrestrictedly recognizes the full value of the notes and that the temporary suspension of the gold clause does not disadvantage the creditor in any way." According to Heck, the Court must consider the unexpressed and implicit reasons here. Given the historical context, certain things about the future could not have been made public in the motivation of such a legal instrument.[50] These historical interpretations prove that arguments for deviation from the precise wording of the law and an upgrade (revaluation) of monetary laws based on Section 242 BGB need to be corrected.

Rejecting the dispositive interpretation of monetary laws

The RG finally interprets the contract according to §157 BGB.[51] In the case of loan agreements, this interpretation leads to the result that if the devaluation were foreseen, the parties would have agreed that the creditor should receive a correspondingly higher amount. The court added that the monetary laws allowed such tacit agreements of the parties to be considered valid. If the first affirmation is correct, the second is invalid, according to Heck.[52] The compulsory rate of paper money is not a defeat of the ordinary party will but rather involves sacrificing the party will in favor of public interests. A party's will, determined according to Section 157, cannot have a more substantial effect than one expressly formulated in a monetary law (an imperative law).

---

49 ibid., 211.

50 "Even if there were grave fears about the future of our credit at this time (immediately after the Battle of the Marne-[first significant defeat of the German Army on the Western front with a perspective of a more protracted war, our remark]), their inclusion in an official memorandum was neither required nor permitted because the seriousness of the situation was notorious." Heck, *Das Urteil*, 213. Here is an example of the legislative process's unspoken elements mentioned in our other paper (section about A Historical Research of Interests) influencing the decision without being stated in the preparatory works.

51 Civil Code (BGB) Section 157: "Contracts must be interpreted as good faith and fairness required, considering common practice."

52 Heck, *Das Urteil*, 214.

The moment the interest of the state comes into play, private interests must give way because the law has given priority to the former.[53]

The temporal adjustment and the need for revaluation

In the second part of his analysis, Heck recognizes that the interests decisive for enacting the monetary laws no longer exist at the time of RG's decision. Hyperinflation has increasingly and hopelessly damaged the interests of creditors and finally destroyed them definitively. Next to it, the achievement of its purpose and national interest and the preservation of the German currency, which initially forced and thereby justified the unfair treatment of creditors, became impossible in the eyes of observers and participants. The sacrifice of the creditors not only increased enormously but also became pointless.[54] The sense of justice led to outrage, and the problem of revaluation became about the temporal adjustment of outdated laws[55] which, according to Heck, took three forms: automatic cancellation of the law, a judge‘s rule that deviates from an outdated law, and a new legislative act.

The automatic cancellation of the law is excluded[56]

The three commandments set out on August 4, 1914, contain the clause "until further notice" and are, therefore, limited in time. The limit is determined by Article 4, which authorizes the Federal Council to determine the moment in time when the law will expire. The automatic termination cannot be reconciled with this norm. The only position that could seem reasonable in August 1914 was the expectation that in the event of a significant change in the situation of interests, the suspension of laws would be determined by the Federal Council by Section 4 of the law. However, until then, the laws should continue to apply even if circumstances change.

---

53 Here, there is not just a conflict of two private interests (interests of the creditor versus interests of the debtor), but a conflict of public interest (monetary interest of the State) with a private interest (creditor interest) weighted by law in favor of the public interest.

54 Heck, *Das Urteil*, 216.

55 Here, we are facing a secondary gap in the law related to a change of circumstances. See our first article for other details.

56 Heck, *Das Urteil*, 218.

Cancellation by the judge's decision

A judge's rule can also temporally adjust outdated laws, meaning the judge no longer applies the law to the changed interest situation. According to Heck, the power of the judge to change the law in such a context is highly controversial.[57]

A first restriction is imposed by the need for continuity (legal security)

There is no objective standard for balancing the interests of the two groups, namely creditors and debtors. The difficulty lies not only in the fact that the individual cases are different. The judge could do justice to that. Instead, since there is no objective standard for the recognized situation of interests, only an arbitrary (subjective) decision case by case is possible. Therefore, the results would differ from judge to judge, affecting legal security.

The consideration of the autonomy of the legal community (the legislator)

This is the second crucial obstacle. The primacy of the law over the judge is a fundamental principle. The judge is the servant and helper of the law, but not its master. He may only deviate from a law if it is beyond doubt that the legislative factors would have changed the law for this case if they had been given the occasion.

The only solution acknowledged by Heck is a legal intervention

According to Heck, the judge cannot pre-empt a legislative decision. Therefore, he concludes that the judge should have postponed the right to revaluation until a final legal regulation had been adopted.[58] With its revolutionary decision, the *Reichsgericht* claimed the right to set a new exchange rate instead of the legislator, whose inactivity ultimately expropriated the creditor's money. At its core, a constitutional conflict between legislation and the judiciary arose from the judges' distress of conscience. They were no longer willing to share responsibility for the unjust consequences of galloping inflation by obeying

57 ibid., 219–21.
58 ibid., 221–22.

the law.[59] Faced with an unprecedented constitutional crisis requiring an extraordinary solution, the RG used its methods only to hide its actions as a legislator. The Reichsgericht's decision, while practically necessary, strained constitutional boundaries by usurping the legislator's role before finally catalyzing legislative action. In November 1923, the Reich government started dealing with the legal regulation of the problem.[60]

The hidden use of *Interessenjurisprudenz* in a German patent procedure

Norbert Sohn, a lawyer in Berlin, analyzed two decisions of the German Imperial Patent Office (*Reichspatentamt*) in an article from 1933[61] abandoning a long-standing practice, which has given rise to a lively academic debate. The article discusses three groups of essays reacting to the Patent Office's decision. The first group approves the decision's result and justification. The second group approves the result but considers it "unconstructible," meaning it cannot be obtained from conceptual arguments (*Begriffsjurisprudenz*), and rejects it for constructive reasons. The third group rejects both the result and the reasoning behind it. In the most critical part of his analysis, the author proceeds to solve the issue using Interesenjurisprudenz's method. His analysis showcases how the Imperial Patent Office decisions, though not explicitly invoking Interessenjurisprudenz, applied its core principles.

---

59 Bernd Rüthers, Christian Fischer, and Axel Birk, *Grundrisse des Rechts* (Berlin: Verlag C.H. Beck, 2010), 586.

60 Promulgated under the authority conferred by legislation passed in late 1923, the Third Emergency Tax Decree of February 1924 delineated, albeit hastily and ambiguously, the broad contours of a national economic policy that would find more comprehensive and detailed expression in the seminal Revalorization Act adopted in 1925, as well as the avalanche of ancillary laws and regulations that built upon that foundational statute in ensuing years. Dawson, "Effects of Inflation on Private Contracts," 213.

61 Norbert Sohn, "Interessenjurisprudenz und Patentamt. Ein Beitrag zum Methodenstreit" (Interests doctrine and patent office. A contribution to the dispute over methods), *Archiv für die civilistische Praxis*, 137, no. 3 (1933): 345–60.

The Appellate Division's decision

During patent proceedings before the Imperial Patent Office, anyone can object[62] to the intended grant of a patent after its publication (Section 23 Patent Gesetz-PG), under Section 24 (II) PG about "Opposition." Suppose the Application Division nevertheless decides to grant the patent. In that case, the opponent may appeal against this decision under Section 26 PG about "Appeal." In such a case, the legal problem is related to the opponent declaring during the appeal proceedings that he had initiated that he wished to "withdraw" the appeal. The Reichspatentamt had, in an established practice, regarded the proceedings as being settled with the withdrawal of the appeal.

However, the Appellate Division I of the Reichspatentamt, for the first time in a decision of May 18, 1932, took the opposite position, namely that it was entitled and obliged to continue *ex officio* the examination of the application for patentability despite the "withdrawal" of the appeal. After rejecting the analogous application of the ZPO (German Civil Procedure) to the case, as that would lead to an "unsatisfactory" result, the Appellate Division derives its conclusion from the "aim" and "purpose" of the patent procedure of "granting patents which fulfill the conditions of the law." The Appellate Divisions could not fulfill this purpose if the opponent's withdrawal of the appeal brought the proceedings to a substantive end.[63]

At this stage, Sohn approached the decision of the Appellate Division through the *Interessenjurisprudenz* approach by identifying under the manifest reasoning the relevant interests and their relative weight.[64] The purpose, specifically the "causal interest" that prompted the legislator to create the

62 Patent applications were made in writing to the Patent Office (*Patentamt*) in Berlin. Once the Patent Office granted a patent, there was a three-month window open for opposition filings. Any third party could oppose the validity of a newly granted patent by filing an opposition within this period after patent publication. An Opposition Division of the Patent Office would then examine the opposition. Based on these proceedings, it would decide whether to revoke the patent, uphold it as granted, or maintain it with amended claims. This decision on the patent, refusing application, or opposition could then be appealed to the Appeals Divisions and higher courts. If the Appeals Divisions upheld the examiner's refusal, the applicant could make a further appeal to the Reichspatent Court (acting as a particular patent court system for higher appeals and litigations).

63 Norbert Sohn, "İnteressenjurisprudenz," 347.

64 ibid., 351–55.

Patent Act in the first place was to stimulate technical progress by granting the inventor a monopoly right to the exclusive commercial exploitation of an invention for a certain period in return for its disclosure. Inventive activity is thus rewarded with a premium.

This monopoly right represents an impairment of the free commercial activity of the general public and can only be justified if the disclosure of the invention enriches the general public. Therefore, there is a conflict between the applicant's interest in obtaining protection for the disclosure of a technical innovation and the public's interest in granting the discloser a monopoly right only if the public can expect an enrichment by the disclosure. Even if, considering this conflict of interests, the legislator has established conditions for the entitlement of the exclusive right, it was necessary to determine whether these conditions were fulfilled in a given case. Hence, a patent office and a patent granting procedure had to be created. The causal interest in instituting the patent grant procedure was to determine whether the applicant was entitled to granting a monopoly right, referred to by Sohn as "interest in granting." When designing the details of the patent grant procedure, it was and is always necessary to ensure that the interest in granting is given sufficient consideration in all circumstances. Let us suppose that the decisive body has become aware of concerns about the monopoly claim. The patent grant procedure was created to examine such concerns and the "withdrawal" of the appeal, which is the declaration by the opponent that he is no longer interested in the examination should be irrelevant given the mandatory consideration of the interest in granting.

However, another interest, which is also recognized and valued by the legislator, is essential in the design of a patent-granting procedure. It is the common interest of the applicant and the public to ensure that the granting procedure does not extend indefinitely but ends as soon as possible ("finality interest" or interest in celerity). The general public and the applicant should know as soon as possible whether the protection exists.[65] This finality interest alone would terminate proceedings in case of doubt. However, the appeal

[65] It is essential (valuable) for the general public that the invention is available as soon as possible. The applicant is also interested in obtaining his monopoly right and, thus, in exploiting his invention commercially as soon as possible.

proceedings still need to be admissible, as weighing the finality of interest against the interest in granting shows that the latter, at least here, should prevail. Given the interest in granting as the reason for instituting patent granting proceedings in the first place, all other interests, particularly the finality interest, can only be taken into account once this first interest in granting has been satisfied.

The predominance of the interest in granting over the finality interest also results from the law allowing the involvement of personal opposing interests through the possibility of filling an opposition followed by an appeal. Since that delays the proceedings, it proves that the law places the interest in granting above the finality interest, at least at these procedural stages. This predominance is also shown by the institution of an action for annulment: the interest in granting is so powerful that any party can reopen the finally concluded proceedings. Even notable disadvantages of this result, that is, other interests directed against it, cannot undermine it. Even if the patent office itself is burdened with additional work (compared to the previous practice) by the obligation to continue the appeal proceedings irrespective of the withdrawal of the appeal, there is no doubt that the additional work is necessary in the interest of granting. Suppose additional work becomes necessary in the first place. In that case, this is already a sign that the claim to grant a patent is not simply justified yet and, therefore, requires further examination in the interest of granting.

Longer duration and additional costs (financial interests) must be accepted, and the fact that the Treasury incurs additional costs cannot be challenged since the interest in granting them outweighs them. That shows that the causal interests in the patent law require continuing the substantive examination despite the opponent's withdrawal of the complaint. According to Sohn, dogmatic considerations that explain and deepen the results above can be made at this stage. The appeal procedure cannot be an appeal procedure proper because a second-instance procedure that can continue regardless of whether the application initiating it is withdrawn cannot be seen as an appeal procedure in the sense of procedural dogmatics. Furthermore, Sohn is aware that the opponent is not entitled to a "withdrawal" in the true sense of the word. The idea of a "withdrawal" of the appeal is based on a material view. A declaration as such cannot be "withdrawn." Only a second, subsequent declaration could mean that the effects of the first declaration should cease in the future. A procedure started by an "appeal" that cannot be "withdrawn" can not be seen as an appeal proper according to dogmatics but as a request to continue the examination proceedings.

Appellate Division I also rejects the analogy with civil procedure if it leads to an unsatisfactory result and hence aligns with the Interessenjurisprudenz theory that analogy is only admissible if the interests are equal.[66] Thus, according to *Interessenjurisprudenz* developments, one should recognize the Imperial Patent Office's result as correct.

The Grand Senate decision

The Appellate Division I decision was endorsed by the Grand Senate of the Imperial Patent Office in a decision of October 18, 1932.[67] The Grand Senate assumes that the answer to the question "can be only derived from the nature of the patent grant procedure," whereby "the particular nature of the procedure must be taken into account decisively." It, therefore, examines the "aim and purpose" of the patent grant procedure and finds them in the "grant or revocation of the patent that meets the statutory requirements."

The opponent cannot prevent this objective due to his position in the patent granting procedure. In this procedure, the "patent seeker" and the "patent granting state authority" are facing each other. The "opponent's intervention after the publication" is, in contrast, "something merely additional, incidental." The opponent is, therefore, only an "assistant to the Patent Office in preventing the granting of an unallowable property right." Hence, the opponent cannot be itself a "party," even if he "may occupy a position similar to that of a party." Consequently, he cannot "bring about the granting of non-grantable protective rights by arbitrarily withdrawing the appeal lodged."

66 In civil procedure, the appeal and the civil process are generally matters of the two private parties with individual procedural interests. At the same time, as we have seen above, in the patent granting procedure, we have a collision of collective or public interests, more precisely, the interest in granting and the finality interest. The two groups of interests are dissimilar; therefore, no analogy with Civil Procedure Appeal (that could fill an eventual gap in the patent procedure) is possible.

67 Sohn, "Ïnteressenjurisprudenz," 347.

Sohn approached this second decision through the *Interessenjurisprudenz* lenses by identifying the relevant interests and their relative weight under the manifest reasoning. The Grand Senate examines the "aim" and "purpose" of the patent grant procedure and, thus, arrives to understand the interest in granting and its meaning. The Grand Senate is not looking for a term (concept) under which the examination procedure could be subsumed to find a solution to the question from the elements of that concept.[68] Neither does the Grand Senate establish a "theory of official proceedings" that "culminates in the principle of equality of the first and second instance parts of the proceedings" to obtain a result from it,[69] but rather, it mentions the essential equality of the two instances only insofar as it exists between the undisputed details of the respective proceedings. Furthermore, the Grand Senate does not build an analogy of the case at hand with the treatment of the withdrawal of the opposition in the proceedings of the first instance.[70]

The Grand Senate determines the causal interests to refute the assertion that the Appellate Division is an appeal instance by correctly grasping the "aim" of the Appellate Division. It states explicitly that the "aim" of the Appellate Division is different from that which "in proceedings of a different kind [Civil Procedure, our note] are assigned to an appeal instance."[71] When considering the "position of the opponent," the Grand Senate follows the *Interessenjurisprudenz* method, too. It examines the general interests situation by contrasting the "patent seeker" and the "state patent granting authority," that is, the applicant and the general public, as the opposing parties. The Grand Senate also examines the legislator's assessment of interests[72] in question when it characterizes the opponent as an "assistant" of the patent office, that is, when it states that he belongs to the general public's circle of interests and, therefore, cannot act against the interests of the general public. Accordingly, the Grand Senate rightly concludes that the opponent

---

68 That would be an interpretation according to the revived *Begriffsjurisprudenz*, identified by Heck in the first case of this paper.

69 That would be an interpretation using classificatory concepts according to the original *Begriffsjurisprudenz*.

70 That would be another example of a revived *Begriffsjurisprudenz* interpretation.

71 Sohn, "Interessenjurisprudenz," 357.

72 ibid., 357.

who withdraws his appeal can, at most, exclude himself from the appeal proceedings but cannot thereby terminate them.[73]

The Grand Senate does not reach this conclusion based on legal concepts by a logical operation of thought[74] but by researching the interests that are causal for the opponent's institution in the first place and their evaluation by the legislator. To Sohn, the Appellate Division I and Grand Senate decisions demonstrated a cogent application of *Interessenjurisprudenz* methodology, even if the theory went uncited explicitly. Neither ruling was primarily driven by deductive reasoning from codified legal concepts or analogies to other areas of law. Instead, the patent office deliberately examined the context-specific purposes, interests, and policies underlying the patent system's statutory scheme and procedures. The interpretation was derived from ascertaining the relative prioritization of the interests inherent in the legislative act and then applying that weighing to the specific circumstances. This unconscious yet insightful balancing vindicates *Interessenjurisprudenz* as the proper method for legal interpretation[75] and its continuing relevance for calibrating the law to life's complexities.

Conclusion

In the first two decisions, Heck's critique and proposed solution using *Interessenjurisprudenz* offered a compelling alternative to Reichsgericht's (RG's) approach. RG's methodological arguments shifted from *Begriffsjurisprudenz* in the first case of 1917 to interests considerations in the second case of 1923, even if the interests were not correctly identified and were only meant to hide a pretorian elaboration by the court acting as a legislator. We chose the examples of decisions reelaborated *ex cathedra* by the exceptional methodological acumen of Heck to hint at the difficulties and the extreme power of solving complex cases that *Interesenjurisprudenz* possesses. We have to wait for the final two cases of 1932 analyzed by Sohn to see the eventual adoption of the Interessenjurisprudenz by the German courts, even if in a simplified and hidden form, correlated with an abandonment of *Begriffsjurisprudenz's*

73 ibid., 357.

74 By *Begriffsjurisprudenz*.

75 Sohn, "Interessenjurisprudenz," 357.

arguments. This later embrace of *Interessenjurisprudenz* is acknowledged by German authors, underlining that the interpretative doctrine and Heck's teachings have become the core of many modern interpretations.[76]

[76] "By instructing the judge to understand the value judgments contained in the law with regard to the case being judged, interest jurisprudence has drawn on a generation of lawyers raised in formal thinking and strict legal positivism - without to really break through the barriers of positivism - had a liberating and fruitful effect. This is all the more so since it also recommends the same procedure for filling gaps in the law and thus gives the judge the opportunity to develop the law in a way that is "law-abiding" and yet still in accordance with the needs of life." Karl Larenz, *Methodenlehre der Rechtswissenschaft* (Berlin: Springer, 1991), 53.

Remarques à propos de l'interprétation des textes de droit civil et pénal par le juge français

Didier Guével et Luc-Michel Nivôse
Université Sorbonne-Paris-Nord

« L'interprétation de la loi n'est pas [...] différente de celle d'un testament ».
Jean Carbonnier [1]

Ce document propose une analyse approfondie des méthodes d'interprétation juridique en droit prive français. L'étude s'ouvre sur une Introduction détaillée des concepts fondamentaux de l'interprétation juridique. Une première partie du document se consacre à l'examen détaillé des différentes méthodes traditionnelles d'interprétation employées par les juges dans le système juridique français. L'analyse s'organise autour de deux grands axes: d'une part, une étude des principes souples applicables en droit civil et commercial, où l'interprétation peut s'avérer plus flexible, et d'autre part une étude approfondie des principes spécifiques au droit pénal, caractérisés par leur rigueur et leur stricte interprétation. La seconde partie explore la dynamique complexe des relations entre le pouvoir législatif et le pouvoir judiciaire. Cette section analyse en profondeur comment la jurisprudence et la loi s'influencent mutuellement dans un dialogue constant, façonnant ainsi l'évolution du droit. Elle examine également comment les décisions judiciaires peuvent parfois conduire à des modifications législatives, créant ainsi un cercle vertueux d'amélioration continue du droit. Cette deuxième partie différencie les situations en Droit civil (*lato sensu*) et les situations en Droit pénal.

Introduction: aspects terminologiques

Il y a, au demeurant, fort à parier que les remarques ici présentées seront communes à tous les pays de Droit romano-germanique (tels ceux d'Eurasie), même si l'on peut rencontrer des problématiques voisines dans les pays de

1 Jean Carbonnier, «Droit civil, Tome premier, coll. Thémis », *Puf*, 7, no. 37 (1967): 129.

Common Law.[2] L'ouvrage qui contient cette contribution se voulant pluridisciplinaire, les juristes voudront bien ne pas nous tenir rigueur de présenter parfois ici des propos qui pourront leur paraître constituer des banalités.

L'interprétation, c'est selon le Dictionnaire de l'Académie française dans sa neuvième édition[3] l' «éxplication du sens qu'on peut donner à un texte». En musique comme en Droit, l'interprète apporte nécessairement quelque chose à l'œuvre initiale. Mais, aujourd'hui, son rôle est probablement différent et moins important que celui d'un traducteur,[4] le passage d'une langue à l'autre impliquant plus évidemment une part de création. En Droit, le mot suppose en sus un défaut initial du document sur lequel le juge est appelé à travailler. Selon le dictionnaire juridique de référence, il s'agit de l' «opération qui consiste à discerner le véritable sens d'un texte obscur ».[5] Pour le juge, si un texte est complet et clairement rédigé, il se doit de l'appliquer. Il ne peut dans ce cas recourir à une interprétation exégétique et à une recherche des intentions effectives du rédacteur. Il doit s'en tenir à une interprétation littérale.

Un texte peut être clair et cependant avoir un sens caché. Pour l'interprétation par les juristes, l'obscurité du texte est donc un présupposé. Des auteurs contemporains évoquent une nécessaire expression «incomplète, obscure ou ambiguë».[6] Le mot loi sera bien sûr entendu ici principalement au sens strict de texte émanant du Parlement. Mais, en France, la Constitution nous conduit à devoir prendre en compte également les ordonnances[7] et même les règlements dans la mesure où les textes parlementaires ne peuvent contenir que des règles générales et ont un domaine limité.[8] Enfin, on doit parfois savoir tenir compte de normes supranationales. Nous avons retenu ici l'occurrence de textes, mais il pourrait encore s'agir de coutumes (voire de décisions juridictionnelles, susceptibles de générer une jurisprudence, expliquées *a posteriori* par l'interprète).

---

2 Ronan Cormacain, *The Form of Legislation and the Rule of Law* (London: Bloomsbury, 2022).

3 < http://www.dictionnaire-academie.fr/article/A9I1758> (consulté le 19 janvier 2023).

4 Autrefois «interprétation» était synonyme de notre moderne «traduction».

5 Gérard Cornu, «Association Henri Capitant», *Puf*, 1 (1987).

6 Pierre Voirin par Gilles Goubeaux, «Droit civil, Tome 1, Introduction au Droit, 42ème éditio », *LGDJ* 1067 (2022): 474.

7 Art. 38 de la Constitution

8 Art. 34 de la Constitution.

Le juge sera logiquement dans ces développements principalement le magistrat judiciaire, le juge du siège de Droit privé (juges des tribunaux judiciaires, conseillers des cours d'appel et Hauts Conseillers à la Cour de cassation). Mais, là encore, on pourra être amené à entendre l'expression dans un sens plus large de toute personne ou institution ayant une mission de *juris dictio* de « dire le Droit » principalement à l'occasion d'un contentieux en Droit privé. Rappelons pour les non-juristes que le Droit privé est constitué des règles relatives à la vie des particuliers, personnes physiques et personnes morales. À ce titre, on peut même être amené à appréhender, comme on le verra, des décisions du Conseil constitutionnel.

Si nous évoquons ici le rôle d'interprète du juge dans le cadre d'une décision contentieuse ou sur procédure consultative[9], il ne faut pas oublier, même si le référé législatif a depuis longtemps disparu,[10] que le législateur (*lato sensu*) peut lui aussi avoir cette fonction, notamment lorsqu'il transpose (*a minima* ou *a maxima*) une directive européenne ou lorsque l'on est en présence d'une loi interprétative censée se contenter d'expliquer un texte antérieur.[11] La doctrine, ce que Aubry et Rau appelaient l'interprétation privée[12] et qui aujourd'hui peut englober les avis de bien des organismes au-delà du seul monde universitaire, a aussi pour mission d'expliquer le Droit positif et les méthodes qu'elle peut utiliser sont identiques à celles retenues par les juges. Nous ne prétendons pas ici reprendre les longs et célèbres débats qui ont pu, à ce propos, agiter la doctrine juridique au fil des siècles. Il serait bel et bon de renvoyer aux ouvrages classiques consacrés au sujet.[13]

---

9 V. Le Code civil enrichi, *Méthodes contemporaines d'interprétation législative hors litige. Journée franco-italienne de droit comparé*, dir. Naiara Posenato et Gustavo Cerqueira (Nice: GREDEG-SLC10, 2022).

10 Existant sous l'Ancien Régime, réinstauré en 1790 puis, sous une autre forme, en 1807 et supprimé en 1837.

11 Sauf détournement hypocrite du procédé utilisé pour aboutir à une rétroactivité de la loi (comme à propos de la promotion immobilière et de l'article L. 110-1 du Code de commerce (achat pour revendre les immeubles); V., à ce propos, Didier Guével, *Droit du commerce et des affaires, LGDJ*, no. 67 (2017): 44.

12 Charles Aubry et Charles Rau, *Cours de droit civil français, Tome premier, 4ème édit.* (Paris: Marchal, Billard et Cie, 1869), Sec. 38, 124.

13 Gény, «Méthode d'interprétation et sources en droit privé positif», *LGDJ* (2016); Jean Carbonnier, *Droit civil, Tome premier*, coll. Thémis, *Puf*, 7, no. 37 (1967): 128.

Enfin, il semble aller de soi que, dans une législation laïcisée, les interprétations divinatoires ou magiques n'ont pas leur place, quel que soit le rôle éminent qu'elles aient pu jouer dans des cadres différents. L'interprétation juridique peut concerner des textes législatifs et réglementaires, « opération consistant à déterminer le sens et la portée d'une norme, qu'elle soit légale ou contractuelle »,[14] mais aussi des stipulations contractuelles.[15] Pour l'interprétation des contrats, le Code civil a prévu des aides, des guides pour le juge,[16] pas pour l'interprétation des lois. Notre propos, on l'a compris, portera ici exclusivement sur la première problématique. On l'a dit, il peut souvent s'agir de l'interprétation par le juge national d'une norme supranationale.[17] La Cour de cassation peut, au demeurant, n'être saisie que pour interprétation d'un texte. Plus généralement, les procédures des (mal nommés) renvois préjudiciels ont ce but.[18] Donc, ne semble rentrer dans la compétence du juge que l'intervention à propos d'un texte manquant de clarté. Selon Aubry et Rau, « il peut y avoir lieu à interprétation dans deux hypothèses distinctes: 1° Lorsque la rédaction employée par le législateur ne présente pas par elle-même un sens clair et complet, soit à raison de la signification plus ou moins vague des termes, soit à raison d'une construction de phrase plus ou moins vicieuse. 2° Lorsque cette rédaction, quoique présentant un sens nettement déterminé, n'exprime pas exactement la pensée du législateur ».[19]

---

14 Romain Boffa, «Droit civil, 1ère année, 5ème édition», *LGDJ* (2022): 73.

15 En matière contractuelle, le Code civil donne des indications pour aider le juge (art. 1188); Cf *infra* n. 15.

16 Actuels art. 1188 et s. et, à la rigueur, art. 515-14 et s. C. civ.; V. Jacques Dupichot, «Pour un retour aux textes: Défense et illustration du petit «guide-âne» des articles 1156 à 1164 du Code civil», in «Études offertes à Jacques Flour, Defrénois», réédit. *LGDJ* (2013), 179.

17 Jean-Jacques Daigre, «Rapport du HCJP sur 'Les dispositifs de signalement, de prévention et de transparence relatifs aux risques extra-financiers des grandes sociétés», *D.* (2022): 1604 ; Michel Mahieu, «L'interprétation du droit communautaire», <https://books.openedition.org/pusl/8921?lang=fr> (consulté le 23 janvier 2023); Auriane Taveau, *L'interprétation du champ d'application de la Charte des droits fondamentaux de l'Union européenne. Analyse comparée franco-allemande* (Paris: Mare & Martin, 2023). On peut aussi songer à la LUVI (Convention portant loi uniforme sur la vente internationale des objets mobiliers corporels).

18 V., tout spécialement: art. 267 TFUE.

19 Charles Aubry et Charles Rau, *Cours de droit civil français, Tome premier, 4ème édit.* (Paris: Marchal, Billard et Cie, 1869), Sec. 40, 129.

Or les textes législatifs et réglementaires français actuels sont particulièrement mal rédigés, faute de présence suffisante de juristes au sein des ministères (projets de lois et propositions de lois suggérées par l'Exécutif) et faute d'enseignement généralisé de la légistique. C'est ainsi par exemple que, récemment, le législateur français a cru bon de prévoir des dispositions très proches dans plusieurs Codes sans que l'un soit présenté nécessairement comme Code suiveur. Tel est le cas à propos de l'appréhension juridique des clauses dites abusives,[20] ce qui a contraint la Cour de cassation à rechercher l'intention (hypothétique) du législateur.[21] Parfois, les textes sont d'une telle complexité que les professionnels en viennent à profiter de leur supplétivité pour tout faire contractuellement pour éviter leur éventuelle application,[22] le juge ne pouvant plus, dès lors, que rarement en connaître.[23] Les récentes réformes et projets de réforme du Code civil français ont d'ailleurs été prétexte à diverses interrogations rédactionnelles, par exemple en matière de responsabilité.[24]

---

20 Art. L. 212-1 et s. C. consom., 1171 C. civ. et L. 442-6 C. com.

21 Cass. com., 26 janv. 2022, no. 20-16.782: «Il ressort des travaux parlementaires de la loi du 20 avril 2018 ratifiant ladite ordonnance, que l'intention du législateur était que l'article 1171 du code civil, qui régit le droit commun des contrats, sanctionne les clauses abusives dans les contrats ne relevant pas des dispositions spéciales des articles L. 442-6 du code de commerce et L. 212-1 du code de la consommation».

22 Didier Guével, «L'imprévision dans le Code civil français: l'équilibre au prix de la complexité, La revisión para imprevisión», in *La réforme du droit des contrats, La reforma del derecho de los contratos: Miradas cruzadas Francia-México*, Viernes, Octubre 21, 2016 (ITAM, IRDA, Paris 12), Mexico City, Mexique, 21 octobre 2016 et 24 octobre 2016 à Santiago (Chili), publié en espagnol, 2017; *L'imprévision dans le Code civil français: une réforme, deux révolutions, in La réforme du Droit des contrats: regards croisés franco-péruviens*, Pontifica Universidad del Perù (J. Espinoza Espinoza), IRDA, MIL, Lima, 9 juin 2017; *La réforme du droit des contrats. Regards croisés franco-argentin*, 23 oct. 2017, Mendoza, coorganisé par A. Kemelmajer, Fr. Bicheron (MIL) et M. Mekki (IRDA), *La imprevisiòn en el Còdigo Civil francés: une reforma, dos revoluciones, La imprevisiòn en el Còdigo Civil francés: une reforma, dos revoluciones in* <Revista de responsabilidad civil y seguros : *publicación mensual de doctrina, jurisprudencia y legislación*, Año 21, nº. Extra 3, 2019> (Ejemplar dedicado a : III Jornadas franco-argentinas de Derecho (Mendoza, 2017), 64–84.

23 V., cependant, T. com. Paris 14 décembre 2022: *D.* 2023, 5, obs. Julien Dubarry.

24 V., p. ex., *Méthode d'interprétation et réforme du droit des contrat* - Du Code civil à la réforme de 2016, colloque 17 novembre 2022, Paris-Cité; Didier Guével, *Faits générateurs et responsabilité extracontractuelle (réflexions autour du projet de réforme*

Il semble utile de présenter les différents procédés d'interprétation mis à la disposition du juge même si, comme l'écrivait Jean Carbonnier, évoquant la ratio legis, «Toutes nos méthodes d'interprétation procèdent, au fond, d'une même conception: que la loi est volonté, volonté humaine et raisonnable, ce qui permet toujours à l'interprète de la retrouver à travers sa propre volonté, car les hommes s'entendent toujours entre eux».[25] Dans un second temps, il peut paraître pertinent de s'interroger sur les relations entre le juge et le parlement, entre la jurisprudence et la loi, dans l'interprétation de la règle.

Les modes d'interprétation

Il faut rappeler qu'en Droit français, le Droit pénal relève du Droit privé parce que faisant prévaloir la protection des individus sur la répression publique, comme il se doit en démocratie. Par ailleurs en simplifiant, on assimilera ici au Droit civil, les autres branches du droit privé non répressif et, notamment, le Droit du commerce et des affaires. Les modes d'interprétation sont très largement différents en Droit civil et en Droit pénal.[26]

Les modes d'interprétation en Droit civil

Il semble que, dans ce cadre, trois catégories de méthodes peuvent être distinguées: littérales, exégétiques et mixtes, étant entendu que tout le monde s'accorde pour laisser au juge le choix de la méthode qu'il entend utiliser, notamment quand ces procédés déductifs entrent en concurrence (sous la réserve, bien entendu, de la prohibition des arrêts de règlement).[27]

---

français), Colloque, *La réforme de la responsabilité* (dir. Bernard Haftel), 13–14 septembre 2019, Université de Monterrey, Mexique, <https://www.linkedin.com/posts/mustapha-mekki-0a342025_coloquio-franco-mexicano-sobre-responsabilidad-activity-6594857255852662784-eo5p>; <https://drive.google.com/file/d/18Z00IOCY8AeU7rrFiWLzWOmFEuMZ8Y7Y/view?pli=1%E2%80%AC>.

25 Jean Carbonnier, «Droit civil, Tome premier, coll. Thémis», *Puf*, 7, no. 39 (1967), 133.

26 Pour le Droit fiscal, Daniel Gutmann, « Sources et ressources de l'interprétation juridique. Étude de droit fiscal», *LGDJ* (2023).

27 Art. 5 C. civ.

Des interprétations littérales et de leur portée

L'interprétation littérale, comme son qualificatif l'indique, consiste à appliquer une loi à la lettre. Ceci étant, en cas d'obscurité d'un texte, notamment hélas quand il y a une erreur dans les substantifs utilisés, une faute de grammaire ou de ponctuation, le juge peut être désarmé. On se souvient de cas de virgules intempestives. Ainsi, par exemple, en matière successorale, les héritiers *ab intestat* peuvent bénéficier, au titre des articles 831 et suivants du Code civil, d'une attribution préférentielle de certains biens successoraux. Mais l'article 833 du Code civil dispose que l'attribution peut être accordée «au conjoint ou à tout héritier, qu'il soit copropriétaire en pleine propriété ou en nue-propriété». La présence de la virgule implique que le conjoint survivant ne puisse pas demander l'attribution préférentielle lorsqu'il ne vient qu'en usufruit, ce qui n'était probablement pas l'intention profonde du législateur. Le juge a été contraint de respecter le sens que la rigueur grammaticale imposait.[28]

Identiquement, et l'occurrence est plus connue, le nantissement d'un fonds de commerce doit faire l'objet d'un écrit et d'un enregistrement. Le premier alinéa de l'article L. 142-3 du Code de commerce disposait: «Le contrat de nantissement est constaté par un acte authentique ou par un acte sous seing privé, dûment enregistré»; l'ajout intempestif de la virgule avait contraint ici à l'enregistrement des actes authentiques qui n'est pourtant normalement pas nécessaire[29] et était inutilement coûteux. Une ordonnance est venue heureusement modifier ledit texte,[30] les protestations du monde des affaires ayant sans doute été finalement entendues par le pouvoir exécutif. Mais entre-temps le monde du commerce avait été contraint d'appliquer une disposition absurde.

Le raisonnement *a contrario* n'est souvent, finalement, que le prolongement d'une interprétation littérale. Il peut au demeurant, ici encore, amener le juge à montrer des effets délétères auxquels le législateur n'avait pas songé. Il en

---

28 Cass. civ. 1re 10 mai 1966: *D.*1966 467, note A.B. ; Cass. civ. 1re 27 juin 2000: no. 98-17.177, *Bull. civ.* I, no. 201, 130. V., p. ex., Didier Guével, «Droit des successions et des libéralités, 3ème édit.», *LGDJ*, no. 616, 252.

29 V. p. ex., Didier Guével, «Droit du Commerce et des affaires, 5ème édit.», *LGDJ*, 299 (2017), 146.

30 Ordonnance no. 2021-1192 du 15 septembre 2021.

va probablement de même pour une autre méthode issue de la rhétorique, le raisonnement *a fortiori*.

Des méthodes exégétiques et extensives

Si le juge veut aller au-delà de la lettre du texte qu'il a à appliquer, les approches à sa disposition sont nombreuses.

Des méthodes exégétiques

L'exégèse peut conduire fort loin, à condition, en principe, de ne pas statuer *extra* ou *ultra legem*.

On le sait, ce procédé prend sa source dans les commentaires des textes sacrés.[31] On apprend au début des études juridiques ce que furent, dès le Moyen-Âge, les glossateurs et postglossateurs et, au XIXème siècle, les tenants de l'École de l'exégèse. Comme Hermès pouvait traduire la pensée de Jupiter, le juge va devoir comprendre et exprimer la pensée de la loi. Il s'agit alors de rechercher et de tenter de se conformer à l'esprit du texte.[32] L'esprit d'un texte, c'est d'abord son but. Il faut éviter qu'un texte aboutisse à des résultats factuels différents (voire contraires) de ceux espérés et recherchés par ses rédacteurs.[33]

Récemment, le conseil constitutionnel a pu ainsi se méprendre sur le sens d'un texte, faute, peut-être, de connaissance suffisante du droit privé et ce, à propos de l'article L. 116-4 du Code de l'action sociale instituant une incapacité spéciale de recevoir pour les «personnes physiques propriétaires, gestionnaires, administrateurs ou employés d'un établissement ou service soumis à autorisation ou à déclaration en application du présent code, ainsi que les bénévoles ou les volontaires qui agissent en leur sein ou y exercent une responsabilité». Le but de cette disposition est de protéger des personnes accueillies (en situation de faiblesse) pour qu'elles ne se dépouillent pas de

31 Sachant que «la loi» au sens religieux peut être contenue ailleurs que dans les textes sacrés. On pense à la *sunnat Allâh* pour le Coran, à l'herméneutique pour la Bible à l'*Agada* hébraïque. Pour le Tao et les commentaires des textes taoïstes, V., p. ex., *Le livre de la contemplation intérieure et autres textes taoïstes*, préface de Catherine Despeux, Rivages Poche, no. 1014 édit. *Payot et Rivages*, 2022, not. p. 22. V. aussi Alfonso Alibrandi, *La maîtrise de l'interprétation de la loi. L'apport doctrinal de la Sacrée Congrégation du Concile au XVII*ème *siècle*, *Historia et Ius* 2022.

32 On ne peut que songer ici à *L'esprit des lois* de Montesquieu.

33 C'est l'interprétation que l'on appelle généralement «téléologique» et qui va au-delà de l'exégèse. Mais le procédé ne va pas sans interroger l'observateur.

leurs biens; l'on redoute en effet que certains de ces personnels profitent de leur situation pour influencer des personnes hébergées.

Or le conseil constitutionnel, dans une décision du 12 mars 2021,[34] déclare le texte inconstitutionnel au motif que «l'interdiction générale […] porte au droit de propriété une atteinte disproportionnée à l'objectif poursuivi», c'est le droit de propriété des personnes hébergées qui est ainsi évoqué. C'est donc une incapacité de donner qui est condamnée comme excessive, alors que le but du texte était bien de prévoir une incapacité de recevoir. On le voit, parfois interprétation, comme traduction peut rimer avec trahison. En Droit commercial cette fois, le Conseil constitutionnel, le 5 mars 2021,[35] a estimé que l'indemnité d'éviction, dont doit bénéficier le preneur à bail commercial lorsque son contrat n'est pas renouvelé,[36] ne portait pas une atteinte disproportionnée au droit de propriété du bailleur (même s'il est ainsi parfois contraint de verser une indemnité d'une valeur supérieure à celle des murs). Il semblait donc clair que l'on restait en présence d'un droit personnel. On se trompait.

Dans un arrêt du 11 mars 2021,[37] la troisième chambre civile de la cour de cassation, qui prend quand même soin de mettre l'expression entre guillemets, nous dit que la «propriété commerciale», qui, selon elle, «s'entend du droit au renouvellement du bail»[38] est protégée au titre de l'article premier du premier protocole additionnel de la Convention européenne de sauvegarde des droits de l'homme et des libertés fondamentales.[39]

Pour la cour de cassation, ce droit personnel est donc un droit de propriété au sens de la Convention européenne des droits de l'homme. Il est vrai que la Cour européenne des droits de l'homme entend, non pas la notion de propriété, mais le concept de "bien » de manière très large (une créance

34 no. 2020-888 QPC.

35 no. 2020-887 QPC.

36 Art. L.145-4 ets. C. com.

37 no. 20-13.639.

38 Alors qu'il ne s'agit en aucun cas d'un droit au renouvellement, mais d'un droit à indemnité et que l'expression a toujours été considérée comme un abus de langage et une simplification de praticiens.

39 Qui dispose: «Toute personne physique ou morale a droit au respect de ses biens. Nul ne peut être privé de sa propriété que pour cause d'utilité publique et dans les conditions prévues par la loi et les principes généraux du droit international».

pouvant être considérée comme un bien[40]). Notre Cour judiciaire suprême a donc choisi l'esprit du Droit européen plutôt que la *ratio legis* française. Ces nuances (pour le moins discutables) d'interprétation seraient complexes à enseigner en première année d'études juridiques. Il est également loisible au juge de puiser dans les principes généraux d'une spécialité. Mais l'on sait que si nul ne conteste qu'il peut y avoir des principes généraux du (ou des) Droits communs privés ou publics, il a toujours été plus délicat de se prononcer pour les Droits spéciaux (Cf. *infra* interpretation contextuelle).[41]

Les methodes extensives: la méthode dite créatrice

La méthode dite créatrice, chère à François Gény, peut aller encore plus loin, notamment en actualisant un texte et en recherchant, pour un texte un peu ancien, quelle pourrait être au moment de son interprétation, le sens que pourrait lui donner un rédacteur et, principalement, le législateur.

Des procédés intermédiaires ou mixtes

Interpretation contextuelle

Le juge peut aller au-delà de la lettre d'une formule, mais se limiter à tenir compte du contenant formel des syntagmes litigieux: la loi, le règlement ou le Code qui contient l'article reprenant la ou les phrases concernées (voire, au-delà, l'ensemble des règles écrites du Droit objectif, privé ou public).

C'est ainsi que, récemment, il a été proposé de tenir compte des intitulés du plan de ce contenant (argument dit *a rubrica*), ce qui peut être tout à fait pertinent.[42]

---

40 V., p. ex., Aida Grgiæ, Zvonimir Mataga, Matija Longar et Ana Vilfan, «Le droit à la propriété dans la Convention européenne des Droits de l'Homme», Précis du Conseil de l'Europe sur les droits de l'Homme no. 10, <https://rm.coe.int/168007ff64> (consulté le 27 mars 2021).

41 Même si la solution semble être entendue pour certains d'entre eux (considérés comme suffisamment autonomes), comme le Droit commercial V., p. ex., Didier Guével, «Droit du commerce et des affaires», *LGDJ*, 5, no. 14, 17.

42 V. Charlotte Dubois, «Le plan du code pénal, outil d'interprétation des incriminations? De la pertinence de l'argument a rubrica en droit pénal», *D.* (2022) : 1477.

Les raisonnements par analogie

On va retrouver les raisonnements par analogie (*a pari, a simili*). Les rapports entre les Droits communs et les Droits spéciaux vont être là encore convoqués. La question est d'autant plus complexe que, non seulement le nombre des règles spéciales ne cesse de croître, mais que, parallèlement, des Droits communs nouveaux se constituent.[43] Le juge a une tâche simplifiée mais étrange lorsque, anormalement, des textes spéciaux reprennent des règles générales.[44]

L'interprétation extensive

L'interprétation dite extensive constitue un raisonnement par analogie, non plus par rapport directement à un autre texte, mais par rapport à des situations identiques. Il est de plus en plus fréquent qu'un texte ancien soit interprété à la lumière d'une disposition nouvelle,[45] voire du contenu d'un projet en cours d'élaboration ou d'un nouveau texte non applicable en l'espèce.[46]

La méthode d'interprétation dite de l'effet utile

On peut également accorder ici une place à la méthode d'interprétation dite de l'effet utile selon laquelle, en quelque sorte, lorsqu'un texte paraît vain, on part du principe que le législateur n'a pas pu écrire et voter pour ne rien exprimer; le juge doit alors en rechercher le sens profond.[47] La prise en compte de la date d'un texte peut se révéler essentielle. Par exemple les textes concernant la location des murs des commerces sont très favorables aux locataires et, à l'inverse, les juges qui interprètent ces textes sont, à tort ou à raison, taxés de favoritisme au profit des propriétaires loueurs. Ceci s'explique si l'on replace

---

43 V., p. ex., Didier Guével, *Droit commun et droit spécial des contrats spéciaux (introduction)*, IRDA/ARIDA, Osaka (Japon), Séminaire IRDA-ARIDA, 22 octobre 2022, actes à paraitre.

44 Comme en matière de contrats spéciaux.

45 Même s'il peut y avoir des contre-exemples: Cass. 3e civ., 6 décembre 2018, no.17-21.170 et no. 17-21.171.

46 V., p. ex., Cass. 3° civ., 23 juillet 2022: no. 21-16.407.

47 V. *L'effet utile: méthode d'interprétation ou outil d'émancipation du juge?* (dir. Sophie Monnier) Actes du colloque éponyme du 24 septembre 2021 (CREDESPO, Université de Bourgogne), *Institut Francophone pour la Justice et la Démocratie*, 2023. Et pour le Droit québécois: Stéphane Beaulac et Frédéric Bérard, *Précis d'interprétation législative*, 2ème édit. Montréal, *LexisNexis* Canada, 2014.

les articles concernés dans leur époque de rédaction:[48] ces textes ont été établis après la seconde guerre mondiale, moment où il fallait tout reconstruire et où les immeubles commerciaux étaient rares; les propriétaires des rares locaux existants avaient donc tendance à en profiter. D'où un texte qui leur était très défavorable. Mais aujourd'hui, en matière commerciale, ce sont souvent les locataires qui sont en position de force compte tenu de l'abondance de locaux vides. Il est donc logique que les juges interprètent actuellement les textes en faveur des propriétaires.

À la limite du raisonnement, on peut penser qu'il y a souvent une part nécessaire d'interprétation dans les contrôles de proportionnalité, de conventionalité et de constitutionnalité (notamment de la part du Conseil d'État, de la Cour de cassation et, bien sûr, du Conseil constitutionnel dans le cadre des Questions Prioritaires de Constitutionnalité (QPC)).

Les modes d'interprétation en Droit pénal

Contrairement au juge civil qui doit toujours apporter une solution au litige qui lui est soumis, éventuellement après avoir ordonné des mesures d'instructions civiles, pour être éclairé, le juge répressif doit respecter le principe de la légalité et la présomption d'innocence. Il ne peut pas condamner une personne poursuivie en l'absence de loi réprimant un tel comportement ou, s'il n'ya pas la certitude de la réalité matérielle des faits commis par le délinquant, il devra le «renvoyer des fins de la poursuite».

Le juge pénal doit d'abord rechercher la loi qui détermine le crime ou le délit applicable au fait poursuivi,[49] en respectant le principe de la légalité,[50] lequel impose celui de l'interprétation stricte de la loi pénale.[51] Dès lors, le juge répressif doit appliquer la loi pénale sans extension ni restriction. Si le comportement d'une personne poursuivie n'est pas expressément prévu par la loi, ou bien si le juge n'a pas la preuve matérielle évidente de sa culpabilité, il devra prononcer une décision de relaxe pour les prévenus, jugés par le tribunal correctionnel ou d'acquittement pour les accusés renvoyés devant une

48 Toute codification efface la chronologie.
49 Article 111-2 du code pénal.
50 Article 111-3 du code pénal.
51 Article 111-4 du code pénal.

cour d'assises. Les juges répressifs ne peuvent prononcer une condamnation que si le fait poursuivi constitue une infraction punissable.[52] Le principe de la légalité impose au juge de bien choisir la loi d'incrimination applicable au litige. Dans sa décision de condamnation, le juge doit constater l'existence des éléments constitutifs exigées par la loi pour déclarer le fait poursuivi punissable. Le juge doit appliquer la bonne qualification et respecter certaines règles qu'impose le principe de la légalité. En cas de concours de qualifications, le juge doit choisir la qualification la plus sévère.[53] Si une qualification est une circonstance aggravante d'une autre, il n'est pas possible de retenir les deux qualifications indépendamment l'une de l'autre : exemple du vol et du port d'arme, il faut retenir le vol avec arme;[54] si un viol est accompagné de tortures et actes de barbarie, il faut retenir le viol avec actes de tortures et de barbarie.[55]

Si deux qualifications sont applicables l'une générale et l'autre spéciale, la règle *specialia generalibus derogant* impose de choisir la qualification spéciale au lieu de la qualification générale.[56] Cependant, en cas de correctionnalisation judiciaire, le juge omet sciemment une circonstance qui permet d'oublier que l'infraction commise est un crime pour la juger comme un délit. Cette pratique, contraire au principe de la légalité, n'est possible qu'avec le consentement du magistrat du Parquet, du prévenu et de son avocat, de la partie civile et de son avocat, et des magistrats du siège chargés du jugement de l'affaire. Cette pratique irrégulière a été permise par l'article 469, alinéa 4 du code de procédure pénale, issu de la loi du 9 mars 2004, qui dispose que, si les parties n'ont pas contesté la qualification correctionnelle retenue

---

52 Crim. 24 novembre 1993, Bull. crim. no. 353; Ass. plen. 29 juin 2001, Bull. crim. no.165; l'article 5 de la Déclaration des Droits de l'Homme de 1789 dispose que: Tout ce qui n'est pas défendu par la Loi ne peut être empêché, et nul ne peut être contraint à faire ce qu'elle n'ordonne pas."

53 Retour critique sur le principe d'unicité de qualification des faits en droit pénal par Paul Cazalbou dans la Revue de science criminelle et de droit pénal comparé 2018/2 (no. 2), 387-407.

54 Crim. 29 juin 1994, pourvoi no. 93-85.322, Publié au bulletin.

55 Crim. 14 mars 2001, pourvoi no. 00-85.011; Crim. 17 janvier 2001, pourvoi no. 00-82.380.

56 Crim. 8 février 2006, pourvoi no. 05-82.894.

au moment du renvoi de l'affaire par le juge d'instruction, elles ne pourront plus le faire devant le tribunal.

Le juge ne peut donc jamais suppléer la carence de la loi et tout ce qui n'est pas interdit par la loi pénale ne constitue pas une infraction. L'exemple très classique est celui de la filouterie d'aliments,[57] étendue à l'hôtellerie, à la distribution d'essence et de lubrifiants, et aux transports.[58] La filouterie qui n'est pas un vol en l'absence de soustraction frauduleuse, ni une escroquerie en l'absence de stratagème, ni un abus de confiance, est une infraction autonome, définie comme le fait pour une personne qui sait être dans l'impossibilité de payer, ou qui est déterminée à ne pas payer, de se faire servir, un repas, du carburant, se faire attribuer une chambre d'hôtel ou se faire transporter gratuitement. L'adoption d'une loi a été nécessaire pour punir ce type de comportements.

Dans un autre domaine, le législateur a dû intervenir en 1987[59] pour interdire l'utilisation des décodeurs dits «pirates», qui permettaient d'accéder à des chaînes cryptées sans abonnement. Enfin, le titulaire d'un compte bancaire et d'une carte de crédit, qui retire des billets dans un distributeur sachant que son solde est négatif, ne commet aucune infraction.[60] Les mêmes règles s'appliquent aux conditions de la prescription pénale. Les juges ne peuvent pas se fonder sur une prétendue erreur du législateur qui a manifesté une volonté constante de favoriser la répression des infractions sexuelles sur les mineurs en allongeant les délais de prescription, pour retenir une prescription de vingt ans à compter de la majorité pour le délit d'agression sexuelle sur mineur de quinze ans, alors que les articles 222-29-1 du code pénal et 8 du code de procédure pénale mentionnent un délai de dix ans.[61]

La loi se doit d'être claire et précise pour exclure toute appréciation arbitraire mais le législateur peut parfois laisser au juge un large pouvoir d'interprétation. C'est le cas lorsque la loi prévoit des incriminations pénales, sans en donner une définition exacte. Voir à titre d'exemples: les violences

---

57 Crim. 5 novembre 1847: DP 1847, 1, p. 510; Loi du 26 juillet 1873, introduite à l'article 401, alinéa 3 du code pénal de 1810.

58 Article 315-5 du code pénal.

59 Article 429-1 du code pénal créé par la loi n. 87-520 du 10 juillet 1987; Crim. 27 février 2018, pourvoi n. 16-86.881, Publié au bulletin.

60 Crim. 24 novembre 1983, pourvoi n. 82-90.672, Publié au bulletin.

61 Crim. 29 juin 2022, pourvoi n. 21-83.342.

(articles 222-7, 222-9, 222-11, 222-13 du code pénal), les atteintes, les agressions sexuelles et le viol (articles 222-22, 222-23 et 222-27 du code pénal), la participation délictueuse à un attroupement (articles 431-3 à 431-8-1 du code pénal), l'association de malfaiteurs (article 450-1 du code pénal[62]) et la bande organisée (article 132-71 du code pénal), les actes de terrorisme (articles 421-1 et suivants du code pénal), les délits d'entrave (articles L. 2146-1, 2317-1, du code du travail[63]).

La Cour européenne des droits de l'homme considère que la condition de prévisibilité est remplie lorsqu'un individu peut savoir, à l'aide de l'interprétation donnée par la jurisprudence quels actes et omissions engagent sa responsabilité.[64] C'est ce qu'elle a décidé pour les écoutes téléphoniques.[65]

Le Conseil constitutionnel, saisi d'une QPC a décidé que le harcèlement sexuel, prévu par l'article 222-23, alors en vigueur, du code pénal, n'était pas défini de façon suffisante et méconnaissait le principe de la légalité.[66] Le juge peut, en interprétant la loi, l'adapter à la vie actuelle. Ainsi, la Cour de cassation a décidé que l'électricité était une chose, susceptible de soustraction, au sens de l'article 379, ancien, du code pénal.[67] La chambre criminelle a pu définir, au fil des années ce qui caractérisait les manœuvres frauduleuses, constitutives d'escroquerie[68] et retenir que le délit d'escroquerie pouvait porter sur un immeuble, lequel constitue un bien au sens de l'article 313-1 du code pénal.[69]

---

62 «Tout groupement formé ou entente établie en vue de la préparation, caractérisée par un ou plusieurs faits matériels, d'un ou plusieurs crimes ou d'un ou plusieurs délits punis d'au moins cinq ans d'emprisonnement».

63 Le fait d'apporter une entrave à l'exercice du droit syndical, défini par les articles L. 2141-4, L. 2141-9 et L. 2141-11 à L. 2143-22, est puni d'un emprisonnement d'un an et d'une amende de 3 750 euros.

64 CEDH, 25 mai 1993, no.14307/88, Kokkinakis c/ Grèce, série A, n. 260-A, Sec 52.

65 Jean Pradel, «Un contrôle très strict des écoutes téléphoniques par la Cour de Strasbourg», *Recueil Dalloz* (2005), 1755.

66 Cons. const., décision n. 2012-240 QPC du 4 mai 2012.

67 Crim. 3 août 2012: S 1913, 1, p. 337.

68 Crim. 18 janv. 2017, pourvoi no. 15-85.209 et pourvoi no. 16-80.200: le mensonge peut devenir une manœuvre et justifier une condamnation du chef d'escroquerie. (Y. Mayaud, La crédibilité, critère du mensonge punissable en droit pénal, AJ pénal 2008. 111).

69 Crim. 28 sept. 2016, pourvoi no. 15-84.485.

Le délit de contrefaçon est réalisé par toute reproduction, représentation ou diffusion, par quelque moyen que ce soit, d'une œuvre de l'esprit en violation des droits de l'auteur;[70] cette rédaction a donc permis à la Cour de cassation de retenir que «tout service de communication au public en ligne d'œuvres protégées, sans qu'aient été obtenues les autorisations requises et toute mise à disposition d'un logiciel ayant cette finalité, entre dans les prévisions de l'article L. 335-2-1 du code de la propriété intellectuelle.[71]

Les échanges d'interprétations entre le législateur et son interprète judiciaire

On a parlé parfois de dialogue entre le législateur et son interprète judiciaire. L'expression est probablement abusive, sauf à accepter qu'il ait pu s'agir fréquemment d'un dialogue de sourds. Nous sommes souvent plutôt en présence d'échanges à distance comme peuvent les pratiquer, non pas deux adversaires mais deux concurrents, lors d'une compétition amicale de tennis. Là encore on pourra distinguer selon que l'on se trouve en Droit civil (*lato sensu*) ou en Droit répressif.

Les échanges d'interprétations en Droit civil

La Cour de cassation utilise parfois le procédé de l'interprétation littérale pour mettre le législateur devant ses responsabilités lorsqu'un texte, bien que clair, a en réalité été mal conçu et, selon les travaux préparatoires, devait signifier autre chose. Le problème est que souvent le législateur, par indifférence ou méconnaissance de la jurisprudence, ne modifie pas son texte en conséquence, et C'est dans ce cas le justiciable qui en pâtit.

Tel fut le cas à propos de l'article L. 110-3 du Code de commerce.[72] Cet article, issu de l'élaboration du nouveau Code de commerce en 2000, est la reprise à Droit constant de l'ancien article 109. Malheureusement, l'ancien article 109 avait été déjà mal rédigé lors d'une précédente réforme en 1980. Alors que la liberté de preuve devrait s'appliquer soit en présence d'actes de

---

70 Article L. 335-3 du code de la propriété littéraire, loi no. 92-597 du 1er juillet 1992.

71 Crim. 27 février 2018, pourvoi no. 16-86.881, Publié au bulletin.

72 V. Didier Guével, «Plaidoyer en faveur de la réforme d'un texte en matière de preuve», *D.*, 39 (2022): 1961; Jean-Christophe Roda, «Que reste-t-il de la liberté de la preuve en droit commercial?», *Rev. Jurisp. Com*, no. 6 (2022): 475.

commerce, soit dans des rapports entre commerçants, le législateur a choisi la formule «à l'égard des commerçants, les actes de commerce…». En bon français, la phrase exige deux conditions cumulatives pour que le plaideur puisse accéder à la preuve commerciale: la présence d'actes de commerce et celle de commerçants. Les conditions alternatives étaient devenues cumulatives. C'est ce que la Cour de cassation a naturellement conclu,[73] faisant ainsi une analyse et une application littérales du texte issu de la réforme maladroite de 1980. Malheureusement, le Parlement n'a pas entendu le message et les deux conditions demeurent exigées du plaideur qui ne dispose pas d'un écrit.

Les échanges d'interprétations en Droit pénal

Le législateur a accordé une confiance grandissante au juge judiciaire

L'évolution du droit pénal permet de comprendre que le législateur a accordé une confiance grandissante au juge judiciaire. Le code de 1791 prévoyait des peines fixes pour chaque infraction, sans laisser de pouvoir d'appréciation au juge, celui de 1810 a mis en place une fourchette des peines en laissant au juge le soin de prononcer une sanction comprise entre un minimum et un maximum. Sous la Monarchie de juillet, une loi de 1837 a mis en place les circonstances atténuantes qui, accordées par le juge, lui permettaient de condamner à une peine inférieure au minimum. Le nouveau code pénal'entré en vigueur le 1er mars 1994 a prévu un maximum des peines encourues, supprimant les minima, sauf en matière criminelle[74] et laissant au juge la possibilité de fixer librement la sanction sans pouvoir dépasser la limite supérieure. C'est dans cette logique qu'ont été supprimées les circonstances atténuantes, devenues inutiles. En 2007, le législateur a rétabli les peines plancher en cas de récidive, supprimées en 2014.[75]

---

73 Cass. com. 12 octobre 1982: no. 81-11.812. Pour des décisions dans le même sens, Guével, «Droit du commerce et des affaires, 5ème édit.», *Lextenso*, no. 202 (2017): 104.

74 Article 132-18 du code pénal: lorsque la réclusion criminelle à perpétuité est encourue, la peine minimale est fixée à deux ans d'emprisonnement et ce minimum est d'un an d'emprisonnement pour les infractions qui encourent une peine de 30 ans de réclusion.

75 La loi no. 2007-1198 du 10 août 2007, renforçant la lutte contre la récidive des majeurs et des mineurs, introduit dans le code pénal les articles 132-18-1et 132-19-1, abrogés par la loi no. 2014-896 du 15 août 2014.

Le code pénal, entré en vigueur en 1994, ayant adopté la numérotation des codes modernes, a fait œuvre de continuité en reprenant dans le livre 1er, consacré aux dispositions générales, la plupart des principes et des définitions dégagées par la jurisprudence du Conseil constitutionnel[76] et de la Chambre criminelle de la Cour de cassation.[77] Mais, la nouvelle formulation du principe de la responsabilité pénale,[78] exigeant la preuve de la faute pénale, a conduit les juges, pour admettre le délit d'abandon de famille, à exiger la preuve de la volonté du prévenu de ne pas payer la pension alimentaire.[79]

Va-et-vient entre le législateur et les juges

Le Conseil constitutionnel, qui est chargé du contrôle de la loi *a priori* et *a posteriori* depuis la QPC, exerce ses pleins pouvoirs lorsqu'il est face à un législateur laxiste. Le délit de harcèlement sexuel, donne un exemple clair d'un va-et-vient entre le législateur et les juges constitutionnel et judiciaire. En mai 1992, le Conseil constitutionnel, saisi d'une QPC par la Chambre criminelle de la Cour de cassation, a décidé que la définition du harcèlement sexuel, prévue à l'article 222-23 du code pénal,[80] n'étant pas suffisamment

---

76 Voir par exemple l'interdiction de prononcer des peines privatives de liberté en matière correctionnelle: décision du Conseil constitutionnel no. 73-80 L du 28 novembre 1973 «la détermination des contraventions et des peines qui leur sont applicables est du domaine réglementaire lorsque lesdites peines ne comportent pas de mesures privatives de liberté» et article 131-13 du code pénal, entré en vigueur dès la promulgation de la loi du 19 juillet 1993.

77 L'article 111-5 du code pénal de 1994, qui donne au juge pénal compétence pour contrôler la légalité des actes administratifs règlementaires ou individuels, a entériné a posteriori la jurisprudence de la chambre criminelle de la Cour de cassation (Dame Le Roux 21 décembre 1961) qui permettait le contrôle de la légalité des actes administratifs individuels, base des poursuites pénales en s'opposant au Tribunal des conflits (arrêt Avranches et Desmaret, 5 juillet 1951).

78 Article 121-1 du code pénal: «Nul n'est responsable pénalement que de son propre fait» et article 121-3 du code pénal: «Il n'y a point de crime ou de délit sans intention de le commettre."

79 Crim., 10 décembre 2008, pourvoi no. 08-83.663, Publié au bulletin; Crim., 19 janv. 2022, pourvoi no. 20-84.287.

80 Article 222-23 du code pénal abrogé : «Le fait de harceler autrui dans le but d'obtenir des faveurs de nature sexuelle est puni d'un an d'emprisonnement et de 15 000 euros d'amende.»

précise, méconnaissait le principe de la légalité, et il a abrogé cet article dès la publication de sa décision.

Le législateur est intervenu rapidement pour donner une nouvelle définition de l'infraction en juillet 1992,[81] qu'il précise en juin 1998.[82] Mais, sans raison apparente, la loi du 17 janvier 2002 reprend la définition initiale,[83] laquelle est à nouveau abrogée par le Conseil constitutionnel le 4 mai 2012.[84] La loi du 6 août 2012 a redonné une définition précise du harcèlement sexuel.[85]

---

81 Loi no. 92-684 du 22 juillet 1992 portant réforme des dispositions du code pénal relatives à la répression des crimes et délits contre les personnes a défini le harcèlement sexuel comme: «Le fait de harceler autrui en usant d'ordres, de menaces ou de contraintes, dans le but d'obtenir des faveurs de nature sexuelle, par une personne abusant de l'autorité que lui confèrent ses fonctions, est puni d'un an d'emprisonnement et de 100 000 F d'amende.»

82 L'article 222-33 du code pénal, modifié par la loi no.98-468 du 17 juin 1998, dispose: «Le fait de harceler autrui en donnant des ordres, proférant des menaces, imposant des contraintes ou exerçant des pressions graves dans le but d'obtenir des faveurs de nature sexuelle, par une personne abusant de l'autorité que lui confèrent ses fonctions, est puni d'un an d'emprisonnement et de 100 000 F d'amende.» L'ordonnance no. 2000-916 du 19 septembre 2000 qui adapte les peines encourues à l'euro prévoit une amende de 15 000 euros.

83 Article 222-33 modifié par la loi no.2002-73 du 17 janvier 2002, en vigueur du 18 janvier 2002 au 5 mai 2012: «Le fait de harceler autrui dans le but d'obtenir des faveurs de nature sexuelle est puni d'un an d'emprisonnement et de 15 000 euros d'amende».

84 Décision du Conseil constitutionnel no.2012-240 QPC du 4 mai 2012, (NOR : CSCX1222762S): 4. Considérant que, dans sa rédaction résultant de la loi du 22 juillet 1992 susvisée, le harcèlement sexuel, prévu et réprimé par l'article 222-33 du nouveau code pénal, était défini comme «le fait de harceler autrui en usant d'ordres, de menaces ou de contraintes, dans le but d'obtenir des faveurs de nature sexuelle, par une personne abusant de l'autorité que lui confèrent ses fonctions» que l'article 11 de la loi du 17 juin 1998 susvisée a donné une nouvelle définition de ce délit en substituant aux mots: «en usant d'ordres, de menaces ou de contraintes» les mots: «en donnant des ordres, proférant des menaces, imposant des contraintes ou exerçant des pressions graves» ; que l'article 179 de la loi du 17 janvier 2002 susvisée a de nouveau modifié la définition du délit de harcèlement sexuel en conférant à l'article 222-33 du code pénal la rédaction contestée. 5. Considérant qu'il résulte de ce qui précède que l'article 222-33 du code pénal permet que le délit de harcèlement sexuel soit punissable sans que les éléments constitutifs de l'infraction soient suffisamment définis; qu'ainsi ces dispositions méconnaissent le principe de légalité des délits et des peines et doivent être déclarées contraires à la Constitution».

85 L'article 222-33, créé par la loi no. 2012-954 du 6 août 2012 en vigueur du 8 août 2012 au 6 août 2018 définit le harcèlement sexuel comme le fait d'imposer à une personne,

Le juge pénal interprète la loi pénale, sous la surveillance du législateur

Le juge pénal interprète la loi pénale, sous la surveillance du législateur. Un premier exemple peut être pris avec la loi 10 juillet 2000, dite «le loi Fauchon». Selon le premier président Guy Canivet, «cette loi offre un exemple considérable de coopération positive et utile au bien public, entre le législateur, qui a très clairement annoncé et énoncé l'intention de la loi, et des juges, qui se sont efforcés de l'interpréter loyalement».[86]

L'article 121-3, alinéa 3 du code pénal entré en vigueur en 1994 définissait la faute d'imprudence d'un auteur, comme le fait de ne pas avoir accompli les diligences normales découlant de sa mission et le «nouveau code pénal n'avait pas remis en cause le principe de l'unité des fautes pénale et civile.[87] Les juridictions pénales, appliquant la loi, ont condamné des maires et des responsables publics ou privés. M. Fauchon, sénateur, a soutenu le projet de réforme en expliquant qu'il fallait mettre fin à la confusion entre la responsabilité civile et la responsabilité pénale.

La loi nouvelle, plus douce dès lors qu'il était plus difficile de mettre en œuvre la responsabilité de l'auteur d'une faute d'imprudence et d'application

---

de façon répétée, des propos ou comportements à connotation sexuelle qui soit portent atteinte à sa dignité en raison de leur caractère dégradant ou humiliant, soit créent à son encontre une situation intimidante, hostile ou offensante.

La loi no.2018-703 du 3 août 2018 précise que «le harcèlement sexuel est le fait d'imposer à une personne, de façon répétée, des propos ou comportements à connotation sexuelle ou sexiste qui soit portent atteinte à sa dignité en raison de leur caractère dégradant ou humiliant, soit créent à son encontre une situation intimidante, hostile ou offensante». Et que l'infraction est également constituée:

> «1° Lorsque ces propos ou comportements sont imposés à une même victime par plusieurs personnes, de manière concertée ou à l'instigation de l'une d'elles, alors même que chacune de ces personnes n'a pas agi de façon répétée; 2° Lorsque ces propos ou comportements sont imposés à une même victime, successivement, par plusieurs personnes qui, même en l'absence de concertation, savent que ces propos ou comportements caractérisent une répétition».

86 Guy Canivet, premier président de la Cour de cassation in Actes du colloque au Palais du Luxembourg , 1er mars 2006, «Les délits non intentionnels - La loi Fauchon : 5 ans après».

87 Arrêt de la Cour de cassation, chambre civile du 18 décembre 1912, Brochet et Deschamps et l'arrêt Gouron de la Chambre criminelle en 1934 en déduit l'autorité de la chose jugée au pénal sur le civil.

immédiate, rompait avec le droit antérieur.[88] Elle a imposé un réexamen des affaires qui n'étaient pas définitivement jugées et une application des nouvelles dispositions de l'article 121-3 du Code pénal. Dans l'affaire dite du DRAC, dans laquelle de jeunes élèves en classe de découverte avaient été surpris par la brusque montée des eaux de la rivière, les responsables qui avaient été condamnés devant la cour d'appel, sur le fondement de la loi ancienne, ont obtenu l'annulation de leur condamnation par la Cour de cassation qui a statué après l'entrée en vigueur de la loi nouvelle.[89]

L'évolution des définitions proposées par la loi et des interprétations retenues par la jurisprudence

Les différents abus sexuels, sont un autre exemple de l'évolution des définitions proposées par la loi et des interprétations retenues par la jurisprudence. Sur un plan théorique, les parlementaires, élus par les citoyens, votent la loi qui doit être l'expression de la volonté générale et les juges, indépendants, prennent des décisions au nom du peuple français. Mais les relations des parlementaires, des juges et des citoyens sont sources de fluctuations liées à l'actualité.

Avant 1980,[90] le viol était une infraction formelle, constituée dès lors qu'une femme était la victime d'un rapport sexuel non consenti de nature à la mettre enceinte.[91] Le viol et les attentats à la pudeur étaient des délits qui devenaient des crimes en présence de circonstances aggravantes. Mais, une femme mariée, tenue au devoir conjugal était censée consentir aux ardeurs de son époux.

Selon l'article 332 du code pénal, devenu l'article 222-23 du code de 1994: «Tout acte de pénétration sexuelle, de quelque nature qu'il soit, commis sur la personne d'autrui par violence, contrainte, ou surprise est un viol.» Depuis lors, le viol est un crime, les agressions et les atteintes sexuelles sont des délits. La jurisprudence a dû préciser les conditions de l'absence de consentement de la victime et le contenu des éléments matériels du viol.

---

88 Bruno Cotte in Actes du colloque au Palais du Luxembourg, 1er mars 2006, «Les délits non intentionnels - La loi Fauchon : 5 ans après».

89 Crim., 12 décembre 2000, pourvoi no. 98-83.969, Publié.

90 Loi no. 80-1041 du 23 décembre 1980 relative à la répression du viol et de certains attentats aux mœurs.

91 Crim., 10 juillet 1973, pourvoi no. 73-90.104, publié.

Depuis 1990, dans des décisions largement commentées, la chambre criminelle de la Cour de cassation a admis le viol entre époux,[92] «afin de protéger la liberté de chacun» et parce que «la présomption de consentement des époux aux actes sexuels accomplis dans l'intimité de la vie conjugale ne vaut que jusqu'à preuve du contraire». Mais, cette présomption de consentement des époux a été supprimée par la loi n° 2010-769 du 9 juillet 2010. La Cour européenne des droits de l'homme a décidé dans le même sens que «l'abandon de l'idée inacceptable qu'un mari ne pourrait être poursuivi pour le viol de sa femme était conforme non seulement à une notion civilisée du mariage mais encore et surtout aux objectifs fondamentaux de la Convention dont l'essence même est le respect de la dignité et de la liberté humaines».[93]

Le législateur de 2006 [94] a entériné cette vision des relations de couple et fait du mariage, du PACS ou du concubinage, une circonstance aggravante du viol. En 2018, le législateur a ajouté la menace aux trois autres circonstances[95] et il a précisé à l'article 222-22-1 du code pénal que la contrainte peut être physique ou morale, que la contrainte morale sur un mineur peut résulter de la différence d'âge existant entre la victime et l'auteur des faits et que la contrainte ou la surprise sur un mineur de 15 ans est caractérisée par l'abus de la vulnérabilité de la victime ne disposant pas du discernement nécessaire pour ces actes.

La chambre criminelle jugeait déjà que la menace est une forme de la contrainte [96] et que la menace peut provenir d'une arme ou d'une forte pression psychologique.[97] Pour les éléments matériels du viol et des agressions sexuelles, la chambre criminelle a dû définir ce qui est constitutif d'une atteinte sexuelle, d'une agression sexuelle et un acte de pénétration sexuelle de quelque nature qu'il soit. La chambre criminelle admet que les atteintes à l'intimité sexuelle d'une personne rentrent dans le champ de la loi pénale:

---

92 Crim., 5 septembre 1990, pourvoi no. 90-83.786, publié; Crim., 11 juin 1992, pourvoi no. 90-83.786, publié.

93 CEDH 22 novembre 1995, requête no. 20166/92 SW c/ Royaume-Uni.

94 Loi no. 2006-399 du 4 avril 2006, renforçant la prévention et la répression des violences au sein du couple ou commises contre les mineurs (article 222-22 alinéa 2 du code pénal).

95 Loi Schiappa no. 2018-703 du 3 août 2018.

96 Crim. 14 octobre 1998, pourvoi no. 97-84.730, publié.

97 Crim., 7 décembre 1988, pourvoi no. 88-81.895, publié.

une pénétration sexuelle, vaginale ou anal, avec le sexe, la main, la bouche ou un objet quelconque. L'infraction peut être commise par un homme ou par une femme, sur un homme ou sur une femme. Une fellation est un viol, qu'elle soit subie par la victime ou pratiquée sur l'auteur du viol.

La chambre criminelle a parfois été hésitante pour des pénétrations anales commises avec un objet. Elle retient la qualification de viol pour des actes «à connotation sexuelle»[98] mais non pour d'autres qui se rapprochent des tortures. C'est ce qu'elle a jugé pour une pénétration anale avec un bâton dans le but d'extorquer à la victime une somme d'argent.[99] Depuis 1988, les cours d'assises ont considéré de façon constante que l'excision était une mutilation volontaire criminelle, ces décisions ont été confirmées par la chambre criminelle[100] et le législateur est intervenu en 2013 et 2021 pour faire disparaître cette pratique sur le territoire français.[101]

Des caresses peuvent avoir un caractère sexuel en raison de la manière dont elles ont été effectuées et des circonstances dans lesquelles les faits se sont déroulés.[102] Par ailleurs, selon la jurisprudence constante de la chambre criminelle, la poitrine d'une femme est sexuelle par nature: le fait de caresser les seins d'une femme est une agression sexuelle,[103] comme le fait d'exhiber sa poitrine est une exhibition sexuelle.[104] Pour les militantes Femen, l'infraction est bien constituée, mais le comportement s'inscrivant dans une démarche de protestation politique, la sanction constituerait une ingérence

---

98 Crim. 6 décembre 1995, pourvoi no. 95-84.881, publié; «les personnes mises en examen avaient la volonté d'accomplir un acte de nature sexuelle ; que l'humiliation particulière infligée à Y... par l'introduction d'un corps étranger dans l'anus n'est pas de la même espèce que les autres sévices qu'il a endurés; qu'il s'agissait alors d'attenter à son intimité sexuelle; qu'à cet égard l'utilisation d'un préservatif pour recouvrir le morceau de bois est significative».

99 Crim., 9 décembre 1993, pourvoi no. 93-81.044, publié.

100 Crim., 20 août 1983, pourvoi no. 83-92.616.

101 Loi no. 2013-711 du 5 août 2013, l'article 227-24-1 du code pénal réprime le fait d'inciter un ou une mineur à subir une mutilation sexuelle par des offres, promesses ou en exerçant des pressions ou contraintes de toute nature, la peine encourue a été portée de 5 à 7 années d'emprisonnement par la loi no.2021-478 du 21 avril 2021.

102 Crim., 3 mars 2021, pourvoi no. 20-82.399, publié.

103 Crim., 4 novembre 1998, pourvoi no. 97-85.394.

104 Crim., 10 janvier 2018, pourvoi no.17-80.816; Crim. 9 janvier 2019, pourvoi no. 17-81.618; Crim. 26 février 2020, pourvoi no. 19-81.827, publié.

disproportionnée dans l'exercice de la liberté d'expression.[105] Ainsi, le dialogue entre le législateur, le juge pénal, et le Conseil constitutionnel est permanent et permet une évolution de la matière pénale.

Quel avenir pour les pratiques interpretative a la lumiere des technologies du numériques?

Enfin, les technologies du numériques pourraient modifier les pratiques interpretatives. La question peut ainsi se poser de savoir si les données juridictionnelles ouvertes sont susceptibles de faire évoluer les méthodes d'interprétation.[106] La liberté du juge risque d'être limitée par la connaissance de solutions interprétatives statistiquement majoritaires et très largement diffusées par des entreprises privées.

Par ailleurs, de plus en plus souvent, lors de l'élaboration des projets de lois, les citoyens sont amenés à apporter leur contribution par le biais de l'Internet. Il serait sans doute souhaitable que les magistrats soient en premier lieu invités à participer à ce type de consultations pour, en quelque sorte, permettre, en amont, une plus grande facilité d'abord, pour les interprétations futures. Comment mieux achever ces quelques pages qu'en écoutant la sagesse de nos anciens maîtres: «le ministère des juges est d'appliquer les lois avec discernement et fidélité; de juger suivant la loi, et non pas de juger la loi: Meminisse debet judex ne aliter judicet quàm legibus proditum est. Mais il est souvent nécessaire d'interpréter la loi, c'est-à-dire d'en fixer le sens lorsqu'il est incertain».[107]

---

105 CEDH 13 octobre 2022, no. 22636/19; Crim. 26 février 2020, pourvoi no. 19-81.827, publié.

106 Autour de cette question: Quel avenir pour la jurisprudence à l'ère de l'open data des décisions judiciaires? Réflexions à partir du rapport sur la diffusion des données décisionnelles et la jurisprudence, Université Lyon 3 Jean Moulin, 26 janvier 2023: https://univ-droit.fr/actualites-de-la-recherche/manifestations/46820-quel-avenir-pour-la-jurisprudence-a-l-ere-de-l-open-data-des-decisions-judiciaires.

107 C. B. M. Toullier, *Le droit civil français, suivant l'ordre du code, Tome premier* (Paris, *Warée*, 1824), no. 135, 104.

Normative Resolutions of Interpretation by the Supreme Court of Kazakhstan

Zhuldyz Sairambayeva
Al-Farabi Kazakh National University

In the modern legal system of the Republic of Kazakhstan, the Supreme Court has jurisdiction to adopt normative resolutions of interpretation to solve various legal issues, including analyzing laws, filling gaps in legislation, and regulating legal relations. After an introduction focusing on factors relevant to interpretation in general, the article examines the nature, object, and specificity of the Supreme Court's normative interpretative resolutions. The paper further illustrates the application of such normative resolutions to elucidate the meaning of norms belonging to civil law, civil procedure, and criminal law. The paper's conclusion underlines the significance of such resolutions in ensuring the consistent application of laws and contributing to the fairness and efficiency of justice in Kazakhstan.

Introduction: Interpretation in general

Defining and understanding the interpretation of legal norms is one of the most important and widely discussed topics in legal science. Some scholars view it as the process of grasping the meaning of a legal norm (Denisov A.P., Vilnyansky S.I., Shchetinin B.V.), while others see interpretation as explaining the content of these norms (Golunsky S.A., Strogovich M.S., Tkachenko Yu.G.). Still, others believe that interpretation entails both aspects – understanding and explaining the meaning of legal norms (Alexandrov N.G., Nedbaylo P.E., Pigolkin A.S).[1]

This third perspective seems preferable, as it acknowledges interpretation as a multifaceted process. Indeed, in applying the law, it is often necessary to comprehend the meaning of a norm or statute and clarify it to others. Therefore, it is logical to assume that to clarify the meaning and content of a rule of law, one must first understand it. Moreover, interpretation plays a

1 T.N. Radko, *Theory of Government and Rights* (Moscow: Unity, 2004), 396.

crucial role in legal qualification and decision-making in a case. This process requires both in-depth legal knowledge and legal culture, as well as expertise in jurisprudence.[2] Interpretation aims to achieve an accurate, uniform, and correct understanding and application of the law and to identify its true essence, as articulated by the legislator. Importantly, interpretation does not imply changes or additions to existing norms; it is limited solely to explaining and clarifying the law's content. Due to their abstract nature, regulatory legal acts rarely address comprehensively all aspects of social relations. Therefore, legal professionals such as judges, prosecutors, investigators, or other law enforcement officers face the challenge of resolving certain situations. If interpretation is confined solely to elucidating the literal meaning of the norm, the Court may encounter difficulties arising from the absence of a specific regulation governing the dispute. Therefore, for law enforcement and the process of interpretation, the creative aspect of "logical development" of the norms under scrutiny is also crucial.[3]

The efficiency of the interpretation process relates to various factors, including the technical and legal precision of the interpreted legislation and the interpreter's level of professional expertise.[4] Indeed, interpretation seems optional when laws are easily understood from a direct reading. However, upon closer analysis, what initially appears clear and understandable can become further ambiguous and perplexing. Herein lies a reference to a subjective viewpoint or perception since what is clear to someone may be unclear to another. Moreover, interpretation becomes imperative to ascertain whether the legislator's intent is clearly articulated in a legal norm. Sometimes, the missing interpretation seems apparent: the seasoned lawyer might effortlessly grasp the abstract meaning of a rule and apply it to specific situations. This transparency of the interpretative process correlates here with the legal acumen of the interpreter. However, one must note that even clear norms

---

2 S.S. Alekseev, *State and Law* (Moscow: Prospekt, 2006), 134.

3 N.A. Vasilenko, "Concretization and Interpretation of Law as the Creative Content of Judicial Practice," *Journal of Russian Law*, 8 (2016): 43–57.

4 Zh.S. Elyubaev, "Correct Interpretation of Legislative and Contractual Provisions to Form Uniform Law Enforcement Practice," *IX International Atyrau Legal Conference* <https://online.zakon.kz/Document/?doc_id=31101093&pos=3;-54#pos=3;-54>, accessed 04.05.2024.

are subject to interpretation, as the determination of a rule (norm) as being clear or unclear stems from a preliminary interpretation.[5]

Defining the normative resolutions of interpretation by the Supreme Court

The importance and the role of the normative resolutions

By Paragraph 1 of Article 4 and Article 81 of the Constitution of Kazakhstan, the Supreme Court of the Republic is empowered to issue normative resolutions of interpretation.[6] These resolutions serve to provide clarifications on issues of judicial practice and offer proposals for the improvement of legislation.[7] Moreover, these normative resolutions of the Supreme Court pertain to the primary regulatory acts[8] and hold a position outside the hierarchy of legal acts.[9]

Such resolutions are adopted during a plenary session of the Court, requiring at least two-thirds of the votes of the present judges and a quorum of at least three-quarters of the total number of Supreme Court judges.[10] The primary objective of the Court's interpretation is to elucidate the content and meaning of the law in specific situations and its application to individual cases, considering the circumstances and legislative intent. Within Russian and domestic legal doctrine, there are varying opinions regarding the role and significance of these Supreme Court resolutions.

According to A.V. Fomina, as the culmination of meticulous study, analysis, and synthesis of substantial judicial information and information from

---

5 O.M. Belyaeva, *Interpretation of Legal norms. Scientific Notes of Kazan State University. Volume 149* (Moscow: 2007), 39–47.

6 Constitution of the Republic of Kazakhstan, dated August 30, 1995. <https://adilet.zan.kz/rus/docs/K950001000>, accessed 02.05.2024.

7 Constitutional Law of the Republic of Kazakhstan dated December 25, 2000, N 132 "On the Judicial System and Status of Judges of the Republic of Kazakhstan," paragraph 1 of Art. 17. <https://adilet.zan.kz/rus/docs/Z000000132>, accessed 03.05.2024.

8 Law of the Republic of Kazakhstan dated April 6, 2016, No. 480-V ZRK "On Legal Acts," Paragraph 5 of Article 10. <https://adilet.zan.kz/rus/docs/Z1600000480>, accessed 03.05.2024.

9 Law of the Republic of Kazakhstan "On Legal Acts," Paragraph 5 of Article 10.

10 Constitutional Law of the Republic of Kazakhstan "On the Judicial System and Status of Judges of the Republic of Kazakhstan," Paragraph 3 of Article 22.

specific areas of judicial proceedings, the court provides clarifications that address gaps and conflicts in the law. Thus, this normative interpretation by the Plenums of the Court serves as foundational elements for the operations of judicial bodies. They are directed toward clarity in legal interpretation, fostering uniformity in judicial practice, and preventing the occurrence of judicial errors.[11] G.A. Vasilevich asserts that the role of normative resolutions made by the Supreme Court is crucial in interpretation, as alterations in law interpretation can markedly broaden or restrict the scope of law enforcement practices or maintain inertial influence after new criminal laws adoption. Moreover, when necessary, judicial practice can follow new trends.[12]

In "Sources of Law and Decisions of the Plenum of the Supreme Court of the Russian Federation," S.V. Perov and M.A. Panfilov argue that the normative interpretation provided by the Supreme Court is essential precisely as a guarantee for the proper implementation of legislative norms by the courts. Otherwise, the Supreme Court's mandate of ensuring uniformity in judicial practice would become problematic. Therefore, such clarifications should be mandatory for courts or other participants in legal proceedings. Furthermore, the failure to apply them should imply the cancelation of a decision adopted without considering the explanations provided by the Plenum of the Supreme Court.[13]

According to the analysis of V.V. Sorokin, normative resolutions fill gaps in legislation and react flexibly to the dynamics of social relations. They offer a system of stable guidelines for a transitional society, ensuring continuous legal regulation.[14] S. Udartsev observes that these decisions of the Supreme Court often include provisions aimed at resolving conflicts between legal norms. These decisions may also empower courts to determine the applicability of specific provisions of law, drawing upon constitutional provisions and

---

11 A.V. Fomin, "The role of the Resolutions of the Plenum of the Supreme Court of the Russian Federation," *International Journal of Humanities and Natural Sciences*, 4-4, no. 55 (2021): 185–188.

12 G.A. Vasilevich, "Interpretation (explanation) of Normative Legal Acts: Theory and Practice," *Law Enforcement* 1, no. 1 (2017), 19–27.

13 S.V. Perov and M.A. Panfilov, "Sources of Law and Decisions of the Plenum of the Supreme Court of the Russian Federation," *Studium*, 4 (2013): 14.

14 V.V. Sorokin, "Judicial Practice as a Source of Law: Pros and Cons," *Siberian Legal Bulletin*, 3 (2002): 9–122

current laws.[15] D.A. Kerimov argues that the need for normative clarifications of legal regulations by the Supreme Court arises from an objective necessity, given that the dispositions of the law are formulated as general, typical rules of conduct and, therefore, cannot account for all the specific circumstances in their implementation.[16]

In "The Role and Significance of Normative Resolutions of the Supreme Court of the Republic of Kazakhstan," G.Zh. Suleimenova underlines that law enforcers need to clearly and correctly understand the meaning and content of regulations contained in statutes due to their variable formulations, imperfections of legal technique, inconsistencies and gaps, vagueness and ambiguity of legal definitions and formulations, terminological ambiguity, or insufficient regulation of individual provisions, along with difficulties in interpreting evaluative concepts.[17] The viewpoints presented by these various authors underscore the critical importance and role of the Supreme Court's normative resolutions of interpretation for law enforcement agents.

The specificity of normative interpretative resolutions of the Supreme Court

To differentiate the normative interpretative resolutions of the Supreme Court from classical normative legal acts, one must underline the following characteristics:

- Limited structure: normative resolutions often lack all the structural elements of legal norms (hypotheses, dispositions, sanctions) and focus only on specific aspects of the legal norm.
- An alternative expression of normativity: normative resolutions do not adhere to the classical structure of a legal norm to express normativity. Instead, they rely on other features like general applicability, application

15 S. Udartsev, "Court and lawmaking. Materials of the International Scientific and Practical Conference, Legislative Process in the Republic of Kazakhstan: Status and Problems," March 27-28, 1997 - Almaty, 1997, 181–193.

16 D.A. Kerimov, "Interpretation of Legislation," *Law and Education*, 3 (2002): 88.

17 G.Zh Suleimenova, "The Role and Significance of Normative Decisions of the Supreme Court of the Republic of Kazakhstan," <https://online.zakon.kz/Document/?doc_id=38018571&pos=5;-111#pos=5;-111> accessed 02.05.2024.

to multiple cases rather than a single case, and application to multiple individuals rather than a specific person.

- Dependence on the main act: rules formulated in normative resolutions typically cannot stand alone and require a primary normative legal act for context and specification.
- Temporal limitation: normative resolutions hold validity and significance only within the timeframe of the applied norms. Upon repeal of the primary act, they lose their validity.[18]

In conclusion, the normative resolutions of the Supreme Court exhibit distinct characteristics that set them apart from other normative legal acts. However, some scholars argue that resolutions of the Supreme Courts are formal sources of law, and as such, they not only possess an interpretative nature but can also establish new legal norms.[19] Conversely, opponents object to the idea of the creation of new legal norms through judicial rulings, contending that judicial lawmaking contradicts the principle of separation of powers and is incompatible with the principle of legality.[20]

In answering this problem, it is necessary to clearly define the relationship between lawmaking and interpretation, given the widely accepted thesis that in the process of interpretation, new legal norms should not be created.[21] Interpretation is recognized in some studies with the functions of legal correction and law creation, compensating for technical ambiguities and inaccuracies and filling in the gaps of legal norms. Within this approach, a corrective interpretation of legal norms is allowed, which can change their

---

18 M.T. Alimbekov, "Normative decisions of the Supreme Court as official acts of judicial lawmaking," *Collection of materials from the international scientific and practical conference*, *Legal Nature of Normative Decisions of the Supreme Court of the Republic of Kazakhstan and their Role in the Effectiveness of the Administration of Justice*, May 12, 2009, Almaty, 2009, 6–12.

19 V.M. Zhuikov, *On the Issue of Judicial Practice as a Source Of Law: Judicial Practice as a Source of Law* (Moscow, 2000), 78–90.

20 V.S. Nersesyants, Russian Courts Do Not Have Lawmaking Powers: Judicial Practice as a Source of Law (Moscow, 2000), 107–112.

21 A.S. Pigolkin, *Interpretation of Legal Norms and Lawmaking: Problems of Correlation Law: Creation and Interpretation*, ed. A.S. Pigolkina (Moscow: Spark, 1998), 69.

content without making changes to the text of the normative legal act.[22] The result of interpretation is only the emergence of new understandings and interpretations of the legal norm, which stem from its content.[23]

Consequently, establishing mandatory provisions for subsequent law enforcement that do not follow existing legal norms cannot be considered interpretation but represents lawmaking. Considering all that, today, as the highest interpreter of the law, the Supreme Court of the Republic of Kazakhstan faces the challenge of maintaining the unity of judicial practice across all areas of Kazakhstani legislation applied by lower courts. When resolving cases, lower courts must strictly adhere to the requirements of the Constitution of Kazakhstan, procedural laws, and other normative legal acts. Thus, the principle of legality in the field of legal proceedings is manifested in the legislator's requirement, primarily addressed to the Court.

Under the current legislation of Kazakhstan, the Supreme Court has the authority to issue normative resolutions that hold nationwide binding force and elucidate judicial practice derived from case law and experience. The Supreme Court scrutinizes the norm, assessing its alignment with the Constitution and other legislative acts of superior legal authority or identifying potential conflicts with normative acts of comparable legal standing. Judicial interpretation through these resolutions aids in resolving ambiguities or obscurities in legislation, ensuring compliance with laws in the judicial process.

Normative resolutions of the Supreme Court of Kazakhstan in matters of civil law and civil procedure

According to Subpart 1 and 2 of Article 2 of the Code of Civil Procedure, the legislation governing civil proceedings to be applied and complied with by courts in civil cases includes constitutional laws and the Civil Procedure Code of Kazakhstan. Generally recognized principles and norms of international law, international treaties, and other obligations of the republic, normative resolutions of the Constitutional Council and the Supreme Court. Provisions

---

22 D.A. Gavrilov, "Law Enforcement Interpretation: Author's aAbstract. Dis. .c.l.s.," *Saratov* (2000): 5–6.

23 A.F. Cherdantsev, "Questions of Interpretation of Soviet Law," *Sverdlovsk* (1972): 42–43.

of other laws regulating civil proceedings are subject to incorporation into the Code of Civil Procedure.[24]

Let us consider the normative resolutions of civil procedure, which explain individual provisions of the Civil Procedure Code and reveal the content of individual legal norms. Gaps in legal regulation are overcome using the analogy of law or legal principles. Gaps in legal regulation prompted consideration of the possibility of overcoming this phenomenon through judicial practice.

A gap in civil procedural law is understood as the unsettled or insufficient regulation of a specific norm of the Civil Procedure Code or another source of procedural law. The gap can be filled only with the help of the law enforcement process since no new norms are created here, but a recourse to analogy of law or legal precedent. Thus, the civil procedural legislation reserves the courts the right to interpret laws by deciding on the application of legal analogy.[25]

The role of the Supreme Court is especially significant due to the complexity of civil legislation, which contains vague concepts and terms that need definitions. Formulating definitions and explaining the meaning of civil law requires considerable effort and is often underestimated. New laws require precise definitions of legal phenomena, which must be carried out through the Supreme Court normative resolutions. Faced with this element of novelty, the understanding and commenting become meaningful.[26]

For example, the Normative Resolution of the Supreme Court of Kazakhstan of April 28, 2000, No. 5 "On the application of legislation by courts when considering cases of divorce (matrimony)"[27] explains the correct application

---

[24] G. Suleimenova, "Legality in Civil Proceedings: Commentary on Article 6 of the Civil Procedure Code of the Republic of Kazakhstan," <https://online.zakon.kz/Document/?doc_id=32497044&pos=4;-111#pos=4;-111> accessed 05.02.2024.

[25] G.Kh Yusupova, "Judicial Practice: Interpretation and Explanation of the Law," *Bulletin of the Institute of Legislation of the Republic of Kazakhstan*, 2, no. 18 (2010): 127-129.

[26] Mentioned above. Cf. M.T. Alimbekov, "Normative Decisions of the Supreme Court as Official Acts of Judicial Lawmaking."

[27] Regulatory Resolution of the Supreme Court of the Republic of Kazakhstan dated April 28, 2000, No. 5 "On the Application of Legislation by Courts When Considering Cases of Divorce (Matrimony)." < https://adilet.zan.kz/rus/docs/P00000005S> accessed 05.02.2024.

of the norms of the Code "On Marriage and Family." This resolution clarifies the rules governing the termination of a marriage, its recognition as invalid, and the property relations of spouses.

Also, the resolution has a rule regarding the procedure for collecting alimony for the past period. Courts should consider that alimony for the past period can be recovered within three years from the date of application to the court if it is established that the plaintiff took measures to obtain funds for maintenance but did not receive alimony due to the defendant's evasion of payment. The defendant must present evidence refuting the plaintiff's accusations of evading alimony payment and confirming payment within the specified period.

These rules are not mentioned in the Code "On Marriage and Family," or in the Civil Code. Therefore, the courts must be guided by this resolution when considering issues of alimony payment. In addition, this resolution explains the correct application of the rules on the termination of a marriage, its recognition as invalid and the property relations between spouses. It also provides detailed instructions regarding the judicial process. It equally contains detailed instructions regarding the information that must be present in the operative part of the decision to satisfy the divorce claim and the court decision as a whole. For example, the operative part must reflect the court's findings regarding all the parties" claims specified in paragraph 2 of Article 22 of the Code. That includes related claims intended for joint consideration. The marriage certificate states that the decision must include the spouses" surnames. The maiden surname must also be indicated if a surname was changed upon marriage.

The decision must also reflect the moment of termination of the marriage, from the moment the decision enters into force. The content of the court hearing protocol in divorce cases must comply with the requirements set out in Article 282 of the Code of Civil Procedure. It must reflect all the essential aspects of the trial, including information about the plaintiff and defendant, details about children and their ages, explanations of the claim's merits, witness testimony, the Court's examination of other evidence and actions taken to reconcile the spouses. This resolution is based on the norms of the Civil Code, Civil Procedure Code and Code "On Marriage and Family." It reveals the core of the norms governing the termination and invalidation of marriage and property relations between spouses. Moreover, this interpretation is binding for the country's judicial authorities when considering cases specified in the Resolution.

Normative resolutions of the Supreme Court of Kazakhstan in the matters of criminal law

According to paragraph 2 of Article 1 of the Criminal Code, normative resolutions of the Supreme Court of Kazakhstan constitute an integral part of the country's criminal legislation. That is because the Criminal Code of the Republic is characterized by a high degree of abstraction of norms, general and reference norms, legal regulations containing evaluative characteristics, norms offering several behavioral options and specific terms and concepts. Additionally, legal norms do not function in isolation but within a system. Only in conjunction with one another can they be interpreted correctly.[28] Moreover, criminal law cannot be deemed complete and perfect. The continuous amendments, which have become customary legal practice, prove that.

Scholars rightfully observe that not all articles of the Criminal Code of Kazakhstan possess sufficient certainty, hence necessitating interpretation. One must also refrain from harboring illusions about the possibility of achieving an ideal legal level. Undeniably, gaps and conflicts or rules have always existed and will exist within criminal law. The imperfections within the law and the ambiguity of specific provisions compel law enforcement officials to seek solutions independently, hence a clear need for uniformity.[29] In this regard, normative resolutions adopted by the Supreme Court and based on judicial practice play a significant role in law enforcement activities concerning the regulation of criminal legal relations. Recognizing the precedent nature of decisions by the highest judicial body is mandated by the Constitution's requirement for the uniform application of the Criminal Code. It is also essential for implementing its principles – legality, equality of

---

28 O.A. Savelyeva, "The Role of Judicial Interpretation in the Application of Criminal Law: Abstract for the Degree of Candidate of Legal Sciences," (Moscow, 2008). <https://www.dissercat.com/content/rol-sudebnogo-tolkovaniya-v-primenenii-ugolovnogo-zakona> accessed 06.02.2024.

29 Yu.S. Pestereva, I.G. Ragozina, E.I. Chekmezova, "The Role of the Plenum of the Supreme Court of the Russian Federation in Forming Judicial Practice," *Law Enforcement*, 5, no. 4 (2021): 209–25.

citizens before the law and justice. These normative resolutions are generally binding for subsequent application of criminal law sources.

For instance, Article 268 of the Criminal Code of Kazakhstan, which addresses "Banditry," does not fully explain the terms "arming" and "weapons."

Therefore, to properly apply the norms of the Criminal Code, particularly in qualifying this crime, one should refer to the Normative Resolution of the Supreme Court of June 21, 2001, No. 2.[30] The Resolutions provides detailed criteria for defining "banditry," including interpretations of "weapons" and the arming of gang members, the identification of accomplices and distinctions between banditry and extortion, among other aspects. Furthermore, the resolution specifies that when determining whether items used by gang members during an attack qualify as weapons, one should adhere to the provisions outlined in the Law of the Republic of Kazakhstan of December 30, 1998, No. 339, "On State Control over the Circulation of Certain Types of Weapons." The presence of weapons among at least one gang member and the awareness of other members constitute armedness. However, if participants use weapons or replicas unsuitable for their intended use, they need to meet the criteria of being armed. In such cases, an examination may be necessary to determine the nature of the used items.

Clause 10 of the Resolution clarifies that armedness is a mandatory characteristic of a gang. Therefore, the actions of the organizer, leader or member involving illegal trafficking of weapons, ammunition, explosives and explosive devices related to the organization and functioning of the gang do not require additional qualification under Article 287 of the Criminal Code. That is because these actions are fully covered by the mandatory criterion of armedness for a gang. Actions by gang members related to the illegal trafficking of weapons for other purposes, such as arms sales or theft of weapons, should be classified according to the range of criminal offenses outlined in Article 268 of the Criminal Code and relevant articles in the Special Part of the Criminal Code. This interpretation is provided in the Resolution of the Supreme Court of Kazakhstan of June 21, 2001, No. 2, titled "On some

---

30 Normative Resolution of the Supreme Court of June 21, 2001, No. 2 "On Some Issues of the Application by Courts of Legislation on Liability for Banditry and other Criminal Offenses Committed in Complicity," <https://adilet.zan.kz/rus/docs/P01000002S> accessed 05.02.2024.

issues of the application by courts of legislation on liability for banditry and other criminal offenses committed in complicity."

This interpretation by the Supreme Court, in the form of a resolution, contributes to a consistent and uniform application of Article 268 of the Criminal Code of the Republic of Kazakhstan. That is crucial for distinguishing this crime from other types of offenses. Additionally, this interpretation guides investigative authorities conducting criminal proceedings. It is to be noted that this June 21, 2001 Supreme Court Resolution does not create new norms. It only clarifies the concept of "banditry" and how this criminal act should be qualified. Furthermore, the resolution does not introduce amendments or additions to the Criminal Code. It simply explains and clarifies what is already formulated in the law. Nevertheless, it provides detailed instructions to investigating authorities and the courts when considering such cases.

The following example is a Normative Resolution of the Supreme Court of the Republic of Kazakhstan, of July 11, 2003, No. 8, titled "On judicial practice in cases of theft," which provides detailed explanations regarding judicial practices related to the qualification of criminal offenses encroaching on someone else's property.[31] Paragraph 4 of this Resolution notes that courts must focus on the perpetrator's perception of the situation when determining the nature of theft as a secret act. For example, in Article 188 of the Criminal Code of the Republic of Kazakhstan, "theft is understood as the secret taking of someone else's property." However, if a person stole a phone on public transport and other passengers on the bus noticed this incident, the question arises about how to classify such an act. According to the Normative Resolutions of the Supreme Court of the Republic of Kazakhstan dated July 11, 2003, No. 8, this act will be classified as theft since the person committing it thought that no one would notice his action.

If the perpetrator acted believing that his actions went unnoticed by others, then the act should be classified as theft, even if the owner or another person was watching. Likewise, if one of these persons noticed the process of taking property but did not realize its criminal nature, the act should also be classified as theft. Suppose the theft occurred in the presence of relatives,

---

31 Normative Resolution of the Supreme Court of the Republic of Kazakhstan dated July 11, 2003, No. 8 "On judicial practice in cases of theft" <https://adilet.zan.kz/rus/docs/P03000008S> accessed 05.02.2024.

friends or other persons with whom the perpetrator maintains personal relationships, and he relied on their silence and non-interference. In that case, the act should also be qualified as theft. However, if these persons prevented the theft, the culprit will be liable for attempted theft. The above Supreme Court normative resolution is an example of an essential regulatory document that elaborates on judicial practice related to the qualification of criminal offenses encroaching on someone else's property. Implementing this Resolution plays a crucial role in law enforcement practice and helps ensure fairness and legality in the work of investigative authorities.

Conclusion

For modern law enforcement, interpreting laws normatively by the Supreme Court is essential. However, the provision of paragraph 1 of Article 4 and Article 81 of the Constitution of the Republic[32] does not grant the Supreme Court the right to amend or supplement legislation and other normative regulatory acts with new norms. It does not allow the Supreme Court to evaluate the interpreted norms when explaining them in resolutions. The Supreme Court has only the right to explicate the content of the interpreted norms of law for their correct and uniform understanding and application, but not to make amendments or additions. That is why these normative resolutions of the Supreme Court belong to their specific category.[33]

The article's examples show how these resolutions guide the courts when considering cases and help ensure the uniform application of laws, as well as the legality and fairness of the judicial system. Considering the points above, the question arises: If a law enforcement official, judge or other civil servant fails to consider the normative resolutions of the Plenum of the Supreme Court in their activities, would their decision be legal and fair? The answer is negative. A judicial ruling deviating from the legal positions outlined in the resolutions of the Plenum of the Supreme Court is subject to annulment. Therefore, the decisions of the Plenum, regardless of personal preferences

---

32 As mentioned above. Constitution of the Republic of Kazakhstan, dated August 30, 1995.

33 V.A. Petrushev, "Legal nature of acts of judicial interpretation of law," *Bulletin of Omsk University*, vol. 3 (1997): 100–01.

or whether the legislature explicitly mandates their binding nature, hold a precedent value and must be considered by judges and other law enforcement officials when adjudicating cases. Consistent with the analysis above, we emphasize the enormous practical significance of the interpretation provided by the Supreme Court of Kazakhstan in the context of law enforcement and ensuring justice within the judicial system. Through detailed clarifications and guidance, the Supreme Court aids courts, investigative bodies and law enforcement agencies in applying the law accurately and consistently, thereby reducing errors and bolstering public trust in the judicial system.

PART II

Transitions in the Constitutional Control by the Courts

Nouveau regard sur les réserves (d'interprétation) transitoires du Conseil constitutionnel

Maxime Charité
Université Le Havre Normandie

La présente contribution propose de dépeindre les traits fondamentaux d'une technique décisionnelle nouvelle du Conseil constitutionnel : les réserves d'interprétation transitoires. Le contentieux de la question prioritaire de constitutionnalité (QPC) voit le Conseil constitutionnel user, depuis 2014, d'une technique décisionnelle nouvelle: les réserves d'interprétation transitoires, qui consistent, au soutien d'une décision d'abrogation à effet différé de la disposition législative contestée, en son interprétation conforme à la Constitution entre la date de la décision et la date de prise d'effet de l'abrogation. Le «nouveau regard » que nous portons sur elles nous permettra de démontrer qu'elles sont une technique non seulement consubstantielle au report dans le temps des effets de l'abrogation, mais également une technique matériellement législative.

Introduction

La décision du Conseil constitutionnel n° 2023-1062 QPC du 28 septembre 2023 fait l'actualité non seulement compte tenu de l'identité du requérant, un certain M. François F. (pour François Fillon, Premier ministre de 2007 à 2012 et candidat à l'élection présidentielle de 2017), ainsi que celle de l'un des intervenants, le non moins fameux M. Nicolas S. (pour Nicolas Sarkozy, Président de la République de 2007 à 2012), mais également en raison de l'abstention de siéger subséquente de trois des neuf membres (nommés) du Conseil constitutionnel,[1] MM. Alain Juppé, François Pillet et François Séners,

[1] Aujourd'hui, les «membres nommés» constituent l'ensemble des membres du Conseil constitutionnel, la catégorie des «membres de droit» étant, en l'état actuel, une coquille vide depuis le décès du Président Giscard d'Estaing le 2 décembre 2020; les actuels

qui a eu pour effet que le Conseil juge cette question prioritaire de constitutionnalité (ci-après QPC) à six membres, «cas de force majeure » permettant de déroger à la règle posée par l'article 14 de l'ordonnance n° 58-1067 du 7 novembre 1958 portant loi organique sur le Conseil constitutionnel d'après laquelle « les décisions et les avis du Conseil constitutionnel sont rendus par sept conseillers au moins»?[2]

Le cœur de ladite décision réside pourtant moins dans ces éléments que dans la déclaration d'inconstitutionnalité des mots «sauf lorsqu'il est saisi par le renvoi ordonné par le juge d'instruction ou la chambre de l'instruction» figurant au premier alinéa de l'article 385 du code de procédure pénale, dans sa rédaction résultant de la loi n° 2000-516 du 15 juin 2000 renforçant la présomption d'innocence et les droits des victimes, la considération d'après laquelle «il y a lieu de reporter au 1er octobre 2024 la date de leur abrogation», ainsi que celle selon laquelle, «en revanche, afin de faire cesser l'inconstitutionnalité constatée à compter de la publication de la présente décision, il y a lieu de juger que, jusqu'à l'entrée en vigueur d'une nouvelle loi ou, au plus tard, au 1er octobre 2024, la déclaration d'inconstitutionnalité peut être invoquée dans les instances en cours ou à venir lorsque la purge des nullités a été ou est opposée à un moyen de nullité qui n'a pu être connu avant la

---

anciens Présidents de la République, Nicolas Sarkozy et François Hollande, ayant depuis longtemps et pour des raisons différentes renoncé à siéger rue de Montpensier, de même, plus récemment, qu'Emmanuel Macron», (Nicolas Sarkozy ayant, le 4 juillet 2013, après la décision du Conseil constitutionnel invalidant ses comptes de campagne) CC, no. 2013-156 PDR, 4 juill. 2013, Décision du Conseil constitutionnel sur un recours de M. Nicolas Sarkozy dirigé contre la décision du 19 déc. 2012 de la Commission nationale des comptes de campagnes et des financements politiques, Rec. p. 865), «démissionné» immédiatement « afin de retrouver sa liberté de parole»; François Hollande et Emmanuel Macron ayant, quant à eux, les 12 décembre 2014 et 21 décembre 2019, renoncé au préalable à siéger rue de Montpensier).

2 Art. 14 de l'ord. no. 58-1067 du 7 nov. 1958 portant loi organique Conseil constitutionnel, *JORF* (1958): 10129. Le choix de l'interrogation plutôt que de l'affirmation s'explique par le fait que ladite «*force majeur* » doit être «dûment constatée au procès-verbal», qui n'est communicable de plein droit qu'à l'expiration d'un délai de vingt-cinq ans à compter de sa date conformément aux dispositions de l'article L. 213-2 du code du patrimoine.

clôture de l'instruction» et qu'«il reviendra alors à la juridiction compétente de statuer sur ce moyen de nullité».[3]

Ce faisant, le Conseil a formulé une nouvelle réserve d'interprétation transitoire. Depuis 2014, le Conseil constitutionnel pratique cette technique décisionnelle dans le cadre de la procédure prévue à l'article 61-1 de la Constitution française du 4 octobre 1958, la QPC. Cette procédure a été instaurée avec la loi constitutionnelle n° 2008-724 du 23 juillet 2008 de modernisation des institutions de la Ve République, dont l'article 29 a inséré, après l'article 61 de la Constitution, un article 61-1 ainsi rédigé: «Lorsque, à l'occasion d'une instance en cours devant une juridiction, il est soutenu qu'une disposition législative porte atteinte aux droits et libertés que la Constitution garantit, le Conseil constitutionnel peut être saisi de cette question sur renvoi du Conseil d'État ou de la Cour de cassation qui se prononce dans un délai déterminé. Une loi organique détermine les conditions d'application du présent article».[4] Sur ce fondement, ladite loi organique a été élaborée et votée par le Parlement, déclarée conforme à la Constitution par le Conseil constitutionnel.[5] promulguée par le Président de la République,[6] et la procédure de QPC est entrée en vigueur le 1er mars 2010. Comme l'a considéré le Conseil par la suite, «en posant une question prioritaire de constitutionnalité, tout justiciable a le droit de contester la constitutionnalité de la portée effective qu'une interprétation jurisprudentielle constante confère à cette disposition».[7] La doctrine, tant organique qu'universitaire, s'est rapidement et massivement approprié ce nouvel objet

---

3 CC, no. 2023-1062 QPC, 28 sept. 2023, M. François F., *JORF* no. 226 du 29 sept. 2023, texte no. 65.

4 Art. 29 de la loi constitutionnelle no. 2008-724 du 23 juill. 2008 de modernisation des institutions de la Ve République, *JORF* no. 171 du 24 juill. 2008, texte no. 2.

5 CC, no. 2009-595 DC, 3 déc. 2009, «Loi organique relative à l'application de l'article 61-1 de la Constitution, Rec.», 206.

6 LO no. no. 2009-1523 du 10 décembre 2009 relative à l'application de l'article 61-1 de la Constitution, JORF no. 287 du 11 déc. 2009, texte no. 1.

7 V., pour la première fois, CC, no. 2010-39 QPC, 6 oct. 2010, «Mmes Isabelle D. et Isabelle B., Rec », 265.

d'étude.[8] Au 30 septembre 2023, le Conseil constitutionnel a rendu 951 décisions siglées QPC.

Les réserves d'interprétation transitoires sont une technique décisionnelle propre à ce contentieux. Originaire d'Allemagne,[9] cette technique lui permet, au soutien d'une abrogation reportée dans le temps, de neutraliser « les effets inconstitutionnels de la disposition en cause jusqu'à son remplacement par une loi nouvelle».[10] Elle participe, plus généralement, à «l'émergence d'un droit transitoire constitutionnel».[11]

Alors qu'une telle technique célèbre, en 2024, son dixième anniversaire dans la jurisprudence QPC du Conseil constitutionnel, peu d'études générales y ont été spécifiquement consacrées.[12] Le présent ouvrage collectif, intitulé

---

8 V., not., D. Rousseau, «La question prioritaire de constitutionnalité», *Gazette du Palais-Lextens* (2012), 259; X. Magnon (dir.), «QPC: la question prioritaire de constitutionnalité: principes généraux, pratique et droit du contentieux, 2e éd.», LexisNexis, 2013, 454; G. Carcassonne, O. Duhamel, «QPC: la question prioritaire de constitutionnalité, 2e éd.», Dalloz, 2015, 207; Maugüé C., Stahl J.-H., La question prioritaire de constitutionnalité, 3e éd., Dalloz, 2017, 352; M. Disant, «Droit de la question prioritaire de constitutionnalité: cadre juridique, pratiques jurisprudentielles», (Lamy, 2011), 420; S. Giumarra, M. Guerrini, «Le contentieux de la question prioritaire de constitutionnalité», (Puam, 2012), 149; P. Belloir, «La question prioritaire de constitutionnalité,» (l'Harmattan, 2012), 106; Mathieu B., Rousseau D., Cassard-Valembois A.-L., Gahdoun P.-Y., «Les grandes décisions de la question prioritaire de constitutionnalité», *LGDJ*-Lextenso éditions, 2013, 365; M. Verpeaux, *La question prioritaire de constitutionnalité* (Hachette, 2013), 165; J. Bonnet, P.-Y Gahdoun, «La question prioritaire de constitutionnalité,» *PUF* (2014): 127; M. Guillaume, «Question prioritaire de constitutionnalité» *Dalloz* (2019), 193.

9 V., not., O. Jouanjan, «La modulation des effets des décisions des juridictions constitutionnelle et administratives en droit allemand», *RFDA* (2004) : 680-83 ; C. Behrendt, «Quelques réflexions sur l'activité du juge constitutionnel comme législateur-cadre», *CCC*, 20 (2006): 168; O. Jouanjan, «Les effets dans le temps des décisions de la Cour constitutionnelle fédérale d'Allemagne», *NCCC*, 47 (2015): 91-97.

10 CC, «Les effets dans le temps des décisions QPC (septembre 2014)» <https://qpc360.conseil-constitutionnel.fr/la-qpc/septembre-2014-les-effets-dans-le-temps-des-decisions-qpc>

11 P.-Y Gahdoun, «L'émergence d'un droit transitoire constitutionnel», *RDP* (2016): 149-184.

12 N. Jacquinot, «Regard critique sur la notion de réserve transitoire dans la jurisprudence du Conseil constitutionnel», *AJDA* (2018): 2007-2012. V. égal., S. Benzina, «L'effectivité des décisions QPC du Conseil constitutionnel», *LGDJ* (2017) : 329-336; T. Ducharme, «Le bénéfice des décisions d'inconstitutionnalité: quelle(s) application(s) en fonction

«Les méthodes interprétatives et les Cours en Eurasie», nous donne l'occasion de porter sur ces réserves d'interprétation transitoires un «nouveau regard». Préalable indispensable à ce nouveau regard, l'identification des décisions QPC du Conseil constitutionnel dans lesquelles ce dernier a formulé une réserve d'interprétation transitoire est brouillé par le recensement établi par le Conseil lui-même. Au 30 septembre 2023, son site Internet recense 24 décisions de ce type. Ce recensement est néanmoins doublement inexact. D'une part, y figure par erreur la décision n° 2021-900 QPC du 23 avril 2021 dans laquelle le Conseil constitutionnel a considéré, d'une part, qu'«il y a lieu de reporter au 31 décembre 2021 la date de l'abrogation des dispositions contestées», d'autre part, que «la déclaration d'inconstitutionnalité peut être invoquée dans les instances en cours ou à venir lorsque la purge des nullités a été ou est opposée à un accusé…en cas de défaut d'information de l'intéressé ne lui ayant pas permis de contester utilement les irrégularités de procédure et alors même que cette défaillance ne procède pas d'une manœuvre de sa part ou de sa négligence».[13]

Cette combinaison ne permet ainsi pas au Conseil constitutionnel de neutraliser les effets inconstitutionnels desdites dispositions jusqu'à leur remplacement par une loi nouvelle, mais simplement de déterminer les instances dans lesquelles la déclaration d'inconstitutionnalité peut être invoquée en dépit du report dans le temps de l'abrogation. Ladite décision se rapproche cependant de la décision n° 2023-1062 QPC du 28 septembre 2023 dans la mesure où, au-delà de leur objet commun, la purge des nullités, en matière criminelle dans la première, en matière correctionnelle dans la seconde, la technique décisionnelle pratiquée par le Conseil en l'espèce est essentiellement

---

des droits et libertés méconnus?», *RDLF*, no. 7 (2022). Qu'il soit aussi permis de renvoyer à notre étude: M. Charité «Réserves d'interprétation transitoires dans la jurisprudence QPC," *AJDA* (2015): 1622-25. Les décisions dans lesquelles le Conseil constitutionnel a formulé une réserve d'interprétation transitoire ont, quant à elles, fait l'objet de nombreuses notes, commentaires, chroniques et études particulières, dont les références sont disponibles à la liste des commentaires des Recueils des décisions du Conseil constitutionnel 2014 et 2015 ainsi que, pour l'ensemble des décisions du Conseil constitutionnel concernées, aux onglets «Références doctrinales» situés, sur son site Internet, à gauche de la page de chaque décision ayant fait l'objet d'annotations par la doctrine.

13 CC, no. 2021-900 QPC, 23 avr. 2021, *M. Vladimir M.*, *JORF*, no. 97 du 24 avr. 2021, texte no. 80.

la même et permet l'invocation de la déclaration d'inconstitutionnalité dans certaines instances malgré le report dans le temps de l'abrogation. La décision du 28 septembre 2023 se détache néanmoins de celle du 23 avril 2021, non seulement en ce que la technique décisionnelle pratiquée l'est expressément «afin de faire cesser l'inconstitutionnalité constatée à compter la date de la publication de la [...] décision»,[14] considération utilisée quasi exclusivement pour justifier la formulation d'une réserve d'interprétation transitoire,[15] mais également en ce que la formule retenue est très légèrement plus précise, le Conseil constitutionnel ajoutant qu'«il reviendra alors à la juridiction compétente de statuer sur ce moyen de nullité».[16]

La comparaison de ces deux décisions montre toutefois la porosité de la frontière séparant ces deux techniques décisionnelles. D'autre part, n'y figurent pas par omission 6 décisions manifestant pourtant l'expression d'une telle technique.[17] 24 – 1 + 6: au total, ce sont donc, en réalité, au 30 septembre 2023, 29 décisions du Conseil constitutionnel qui formulent une réserve d'interprétation transitoire.[18] Avec Théo Ducharme, nous constatons que

---

14 CC, no. 2023-1062 QPC, déc. préc.

15 À l'exception de la décision du Conseil constitutionnel no. 2021-892 QPC du 26 mars 2021, *Société Akka technologies et autres*, dans laquelle ce dernier l'a utilisée afin de motiver la détermination des instances dans lesquelles la déclaration d'inconstitutionnalité peut être invoquée en dépit du report dans le temps de l'abrogation (CC, no. 2021-892 QPC, 26 mars 2021, *Société Akka technologies et a.*, *JORF* no. 74 du 27 mars 2021, texte no. 70).

16 CC, no. 2023-1062 QPC, déc. préc.

17 CC, no. 2017-651 QPC, 31 mai 2017, Association En Marche!, *JORF* no. 128 du 1 juin 2017, texte no. 25; CC, no. 2018-715 QPC, 22 juin 2018, Section française de l'Observatoire international des prisons, *JORF* no. 143 du 23 juin 2018, texte no. 76; CC, no. 2018-717/718 QPC, 6 juill. 2018, *M. Cédric H. et a.*, *JORF* no. 155 du 7 juill. 2018, texte no. 107 ; CC, no. 2021-934 QPC, 30 sept. 2021, *M. Djibril D.*, *JORF* no. 229 du 1 oct. 2021, texte no. 74; CC, no. 2021-935 QPC, 30 sept. 2021, *M. Rabah D.*, *JORF* no. 229 du 1 oct. 2021, texte no. 75; CC, no. 2021-978 QPC, 11 mars 2022, *Mme Pascale G.*, *JORF* no. 60 du 12 mars 2022, texte no. 94.

18 CC, no. 2014-400 QPC, 6 juin 2014, *Société Orange SA*, *Rec.* p. 310 ; CC, no. 2014-404 QPC, 20 juin 2014, Époux M., *Rec.* p. 323; CC, no. 2014-420/421 QPC, 9 oct. 2014, *M. Maurice L. et a.*, *Rec.* p. 453; CC, no. 2014-453/454 QPC et 2015-462 QPC, 18 mars 2015, *M. John L. et a.*, *Rec.* p. 179; CC, no. 2014-457 QPC, 20 mars 2015, *Mme Valérie C., épouse D.*, *Rec.* p. 193; CC, no. 2015-506 QPC, 4 déc. 2015, *M. Gilbert A.*, *Rec.* p. 618 ; CC, no. 2015-566 QPC, 16 sept. 2016, *Mme Marie-Lou B. et a.*, *JORF* no. 218 du 18 sept. 2016, texte no. 38 ; CC, no. 2016-590 QPC, 21 oct. 2016, *La Quadrature du Net*

« ces réserves transitoires s'appliquent principalement à deux hypothèses de méconnaissance des droits et libertés : la procédure pénale et le principe d'égalité».[19]

Technique décisionnelle du Conseil constitutionnel propre au contentieux de la QPC, les réserves d'interprétation transitoires sont constituées de deux éléments: le report dans le temps des effets de l'abrogation et la réserve d'interprétation en tant que telle. Le «nouveau regard» que nous portons sur elles nous permettra de démontrer qu'elles sont une technique non seulement consubstantielle au report dans le temps des effets de l'abrogation, mais également matériellement législative, et avec, montrer que le rattachement de cette technique à quelconque méthode interprétative est autant trompeur que stratégique.

Une technique consubstantielle au report dans le temps des effets de l'abrogation

Premier élément constitutif des réserves d'interprétation transitoires du Conseil constitutionnel, le report dans le temps des effets de l'abrogation de la

et a., *JORF* no. 248 du 23 oct. 2016, texte no. 37; CC, no. 2017-651 QPC, déc. préc.; CC, no. 2017-688 QPC, 2 févr. 2018, *M. Axel N.*, *JORF* no. 30 du 6 févr. 2018, texte no. 46; CC, no. 2017-694 QPC, 2 mars 2018, *M. Ousmane K. et a.*, *JORF* no. 52 du 3 mars 2018, texte no. 55; CC, no. 2018-715 QPC, déc. préc.; CC, no. 2018-717/718 QPC, déc. préc. ; CC, no. 2018-739 QPC, 12 oct. 2018, *Société Dom Com Invest*, *JORF* no. 237 du 13 oct. 2018, texte no. 83; CC, no. 2018-763 QPC, 8 févr. 2019, *Section française de l'Observatoire international des prisons*, *JORF* no. 34 du 9 févr. 2019, texte no. 69; CC, no. 2019-773 QPC, 5 avr. 2019, *Société Uber B.V. et a.*, *JORF* no. 82 du 6 avr. 2019, texte no. 91 ; CC, no. 2019-786 QPC, 24 mai 2019, *Association Sea Shepherd*, *JORF* no. 121 du 25 mai 2019, texte no. 127; CC, no. 2019-815 QPC, 29 nov. 2019, *Mme Carole L.*, *JORF* no. 278 du 30 nov. 2019, texte no. 106; CC, no. 2020-886 QPC, 4 mars 2021, *M. Oussama C.*, *JORF* no. 55 du 5 mars 2021, texte no. 96; CC, no. 2021-893 QPC, 26 mars 2021, *M. Brahim N.*, *JORF* no. 74 du 27 mars 2021, texte no. 71; CC, no. 2021-894 QPC, 9 avr. 2021, *M. Mohamed H.*, *JORF* no. 85 du 10 avr. 2021, texte no. 83; CC, no. 2021-895/901/902/903 QPC, 9 avr. 2021, *M. Francis S. et a.*, *JORF* no. 85 du 10 avr. 2021, texte no. 84; CC, no. 2021-909 QPC, 26 mai 2021, *Mme Line M.*, *JORF* no. 121 du 27 mai 2021, texte no. 112; CC, no. 2021-910 QPC, 26 mai 2021, *Mme Line M.*, *JORF* no. 121 du 27 mai 2021, texte no. 113; CC, no. 2021-920 QPC, 18 juin 2021, *M. Al Hassane S.*, *JORF* no. 141 du 19 juin 2021, texte no. 61; CC, no. 2021-934 QPC, déc. préc.; CC, no. 2021-935 QPC, déc. préc.; CC, no. 2021-978 QPC, déc. préc.; CC, no. 2023-1062 QPC, déc. préc.

19 T. Ducharmet, *loc. cit.*

disposition déclarée inconstitutionnelle sur le fondement de l'article 61-1 de la Constitution en constitue le cadre. À ce titre, la Professeure Nathalie Jacquinot écrit que «les réserves transitoires prononcées sont consubstantielles des hypothèses d'abrogation différée permise par l'article 62 de la Constitution».[20] Si elle poursuit que «de façon exceptionnelle, une réserve transitoire a pu accompagner une décision de conformité»,[21] à travers l'exemple de la décision du Conseil constitutionnel n° 2015-473 QPC du 26 juin 2015 dans laquelle ce dernier a déclaré des dispositions du code général des impôts conformes à la Constitution sous une réserve «qui n'est applicable qu'aux impositions contestées avant la date de publication de la [...] décision»,[22] cette décision ne formule toutefois pas de réserve d'interprétation transitoire à proprement parler, mais, en réalité, énonce une réserve d'interprétation «classique», dont les effets temporels sont simplement modulés.

Apparu dans le cadre du contrôle de constitutionnalité *a priori*, le contrôle de constitutionnalité selon l'article 61 de la Constitution,[23] le report dans le temps des effets de la décision du Conseil constitutionnel est cependant essentiellement pratiqué dans le cadre du contrôle de constitutionnalité *a posteriori*, la procédure de QPC,[24] dans la mesure où, contrairement au premier, cette dernière porte sur «une disposition législative qui a déjà vécu».[25]

---

20 N. Jacquinot, *op. cit.*, p. 2008.

21 ibid.

22 CC, no. 2015-473 QPC, 26 juin 2015, Époux P., *Rec.* p. 345.

23 CC, no. 2008-564 DC, 19 juin 2008, *Loi relative aux organismes génétiquement modifiés*, *Rec.* p. 313. V. égal., CC, no. 2011-635 DC, 4 août 2011, *Loi sur la participation des citoyens au fonctionnement de la justice pénale et le jugement des mineurs*, *Rec.* p. 407.

24 V., pour la première fois, CC, no. 2010-1 QPC, 28 mai 2010, *Consorts L.*, *Rec.* p. 91. V., not., S. Brimo , «Les conséquences de la modulation dans le temps des effets des décisions QPC», *RDP* (2011) : 1189-1212; R. Tilli, «La modulation dans le temps des effets des décisions d'inconstitutionnalité *a posteriori*," *RDP* (2011) : 1591-1612; S. Benzina, « Les déclarations d'inconstitutionnalité à effet différé du Conseil constitutionnel », mém., Paris 2, 2012, dactyl., 105; M. Disant, «Les effets dans le temps des décisions QPC. Le Conseil constitutionnel, 'maître du temps'? Le législateur, bouche du Conseil constitutionnel?», *NCCC*, 40. (2013), 63-82; T. Ducharmet, «Les effets dans le temps des décisions du Conseil constitutionnel», mém., Paris 1, 2014, dactyl., 142; P. Deumier, «Les effets dans le temps des décisions QPC: un droit des conséquences des décisions constitutionnelles," *NCCC*, no. 47 (2015): 65-77.

25 A. Vidal-Naquet, «Quelles techniques juridictionnelles pour la QPC?», in *La question prioritaire de constitutionnalité: Approche de droit comparé*, dir. L. Gay (Paris: Bruylant, 2014), 197.

L'article 62 de la Constitution du 4 octobre 1958, dans sa version modifiée par la loi constitutionnelle n° 2008-724 du 23 juillet 2008 de modernisation des institutions de la Ve République, dispose en effet: «Une disposition déclarée inconstitutionnelle sur le fondement de l'article 61-1 est abrogée à compter de la publication de la décision du Conseil constitutionnel ou d'une date ultérieure fixée par cette décision. Le Conseil constitutionnel détermine les conditions et limites dans lesquelles les effets que la disposition a produits sont susceptibles d'être remis en cause».

En 2011, le Conseil constitutionnel a considéré que «les dispositions de l'article 62 de la Constitution réservent à ce dernier le pouvoir … de fixer la date de l'abrogation et de reporter dans le temps ses effets».[26] Au 30 septembre 2023, on recense 117 décisions à effet différé dans la jurisprudence QPC du Conseil constitutionnel (951 décisions), soit environ 40 % de ses décisions de non-conformité (294 décisions). En principe, le report dans le temps des effets de l'abrogation «déroge au principe selon lequel la déclaration d'inconstitutionnalité doit bénéficier au justiciable qui a présenté une question prioritaire de constitutionnalité».[27] Ce principe, l'effet utile des QPC, a été défini ainsi par le Conseil constitutionnel: «la déclaration d'inconstitutionnalité doit bénéficier à l'auteur de la question prioritaire de constitutionnalité et la disposition déclarée contraire à la Constitution ne peut être appliquée dans les instances en cours à la date de la publication de la décision du Conseil constitutionnel».[28] Compte tenu de l'importance de la proportion de décisions de non-conformité à effet différé parmi les décisions de non-conformité, «l'effet inutile des QPC» serait néanmoins « une exception devenue le principe».[29] Cette affirmation, contestable en tant qu'elle est trop catégorique, révèle pourtant une tendance réelle. Le report dans le temps des effets de l'abrogation de la disposition déclarée inconstitutionnelle sur le fondement de l'article 61-1 a pour conséquence, d'une part, qu'elle peut être appliquée dans les instances en cours à la date

---

26 V., pour la première fois, CC, no. 2010-108 QPC, 25 mars 2011, *Mme Marie-Christine D.*, *Rec.* p. 155; CC, no. 2010-110 QPC, 25 mars 2011, *M. Jean-Pierre B.*, *Rec.*, 162.

27 CC, comm. off. de CC, no. 2010-14/22 QPC, 30 juill. 2010, M. Daniel W. et a., 21.

28 CC, no. 2010-108 QPC, déc. préc.; CC, no. 2010-110 QPC, déc. préc.

29 T. Ducharmet,, «L'effet inutile des QPC confronté aux droits européens», *RDP* (2019): 122-27.

de la publication de la décision du Conseil constitutionnel, en particulier celle de l'auteur de la QPC, contrairement à ce qu'exige le principe de l'effet utile des QPC. Ici, les réserves d'interprétation transitoires constituent un palliatif à ce premier inconvénient. Dans 4 décisions sur 29 (soit environ 14%), notamment les deux premières, C'est d'ailleurs «afin de préserver l'effet utile de la [...] décision» que le Conseil constitutionnel décide de formuler une réserve d'interprétation transitoire.[30] La capacité des réserves d'interprétation transitoires à préserver l'effet utile des décisions QPC n'est toutefois pas systématique en ce que le Conseil constitutionnel peut les combiner avec le pouvoir que lui réserve également l'article 62 de la Constitution « de prévoir la remise en cause des effets que la disposition a produits avant l'intervention de cette déclaration » pour maintenir, tout ou en partie, les effets produits par la disposition abrogée.[31]

Le report dans le temps des effets de l'abrogation de la disposition déclarée inconstitutionnelle sur le fondement de l'article 61-1 de la Constitution déroge également au principe de constitutionnalité, d'après lequel les actes juridiques subordonnés à la Constitution dans la hiérarchie des normes, notamment les lois, doivent lui être « conformes », à tout le moins être compatibles avec elle. Ce report a pour conséquence, d'autre part, que ladite disposition est maintenue en vigueur dans l'ordre juridique jusqu'à la date de l'abrogation fixée par le Conseil constitutionnel. Là aussi, les réserves d'interprétation transitoires constituent un palliatif à ce second inconvénient. Dans 25 décisions sur 29 (soit environ 86 %), C'est précisément «afin de faire cesser l'inconstitutionnalité constatée à compter la date de la publication de la...décision» que le Conseil constitutionnel décide de formuler une réserve d'interprétation transitoire.[32]

---

30 CC, no. 2014-400 QPC, déc. préc., p. 312 ; CC, no. 2014-404 QPC, déc. préc., p. 325; CC, no. 2019-815 QPC, déc. préc.; CC, no. 2021-893 QPC, déc. préc.

31 CC, no. 2014-420/421 QPC, déc. préc.; CC, no. 2014-457 QPC, déc. préc.; CC, no. 2015-506 QPC, déc. préc.; CC, no. 2017-688 QPC, déc. préc.; CC, no. 2017-694 QPC, déc. préc.; CC, no. 2019-786 QPC, déc. préc.

32 CC, no. 2014-420/421 QPC, déc. préc., p. 460; CC, no. 2014-453/454 QPC et 2015-462 QPC, déc. préc., p. 191; CC, no. 2014-457 QPC, déc. préc., p. 196; CC, no. 2015-506 QPC, déc. préc., p. 624 ; CC, no. 2015-566 QPC, déc. préc. ; CC, no. 2016-590 QPC, déc. préc.; CC, no. 2017-651 QPC, déc. préc.; CC, no. 2017-688 QPC, déc. préc.; CC, no. 2017-694 QPC, déc. préc.; CC, no. 2018-715 QPC, déc. préc.; CC, no. 2018-717/718 QPC, déc. préc. ; CC, no. 2018-739 QPC, déc. préc.; CC, no. 2018-763 QPC, déc. préc.; CC, no. 2019-773 QPC, déc. préc. ; CC, no. 2019-786 QPC, déc. préc.; CC, no. 2020-886

Si les réserves d'interprétation transitoires ont un «effet correctif» des deux grands inconvénients du report dans le temps des effets de l'abrogation,[33] une autre technique le permet également: le «pouvoir d'injonction que le Conseil constitutionnel se reconnaît à l'égard du Parlement pour l'exécution de ses décisions d'abrogation différée».[34] Dans ce cas, le Conseil constitutionnel considère, dans sa formulation la plus moderne, qu'«il appartient aux … juridictions saisies de surseoir à statuer jusqu'à l'entrée en vigueur de la nouvelle loi ou, au plus tard, jusqu'à … une certaine date dans les procédures en cours ou à venir dont l'issue dépend de l'application des dispositions déclarées inconstitutionnelles».[35]

Comme les réserves d'interprétation transitoires, c'est «afin de préserver l'effet utile de… décision» que cette technique est utilisée.[36] Dans la mesure où les injonctions prononcées sont aussi consubstantielles des hypothèses d'abrogation différée permise par l'article 62 de la Constitution, elles permettent également au législateur de «remédier à l'inconstitutionnalité constatée» pour reprendre la formule utilisée par le Conseil constitutionnel depuis sa première décision QPC dite «Cristallisation des pensions».[37] Dans la poursuite de ces deux grands objectifs, le pouvoir d'injonction est néanmoins plus efficace que les réserves d'interprétation transitoires: dans le premier cas, le législateur peut remédier pleinement à l'inconstitutionnalité constatée et le bénéficie n'en est que plus grand pour les justiciables. Dans la seconde hypothèse, les

---

QPC, déc. préc.; CC, no. 2021-894 QPC, déc. préc.; CC, no. 2021-895/901/902/903 QPC, déc. préc.; CC, no. 2021-909 QPC, déc. préc.; CC, no. 2021-910 QPC, déc. préc.; CC, no. 2021-920 QPC, déc. préc.; CC, no. 2021-934 QPC, déc. préc.; CC, no. 2021-935 QPC, déc. préc.; CC, no. 2021-978 QPC, déc. préc. ; CC, no. 2023-1062 QPC, déc. préc.

33 S. Benzina, *op. cit.*, 330-33.

34 O. Dord, «La QPC et le Parlement: une bienveillance réciproque?» *NCCC*, no. 38 (2013): 33-34.

35 CC, no. 2014-413 QPC, 19 sept. 2014, *Société PV-CP Distribution*, *Rec.* p. 407 ; CC, no. 2017-669 QPC, 27 oct. 2017, *Société EDI-TV*, *JORF* no. 254 du 29 oct. 2017, texte no. 37. Antérieurement, v. CC, no. 2010-1 QPC, déc. préc.; CC, no. 2010-83 QPC, 13 janv. 2011, *M. Claude G.*, *Rec.* p. 57 ; CC, no. 2013-343 QPC, 27 sept. 2013, Époux L., *Rec.* p. 942. V. égal., CC, no. 2015-492 QPC, 16 oct. 2015, *Association Communauté rwandaise de France*, *Rec.* p. 536.

36 CC, no. 2010-1 QPC, déc. préc.; CC, no. 2010-83 QPC, déc. préc. ; CC, no. 2013-343 QPC, déc. préc.; CC, no. 2014-413 QPC, déc. préc. ; CC, no. 2017-669 QPC, déc. préc.; CC, comm. off. de CC, no. 2015-492 QPC, déc. préc., p. 15.

37 CC, no. 2010-1 QPC, déc. préc., p. 96.

réserves d'interprétation transitoires formulées par le Conseil constitutionnel ne permettent que de neutraliser «les effets inconstitutionnels de la disposition en cause jusqu'à son remplacement par une loi nouvelle».[38] Le pouvoir d'injonction est, de surcroît, plus respectueux du pouvoir d'appréciation et de décision du Parlement en ce qu'il implique que ce soit le législateur, et non le Conseil lui-même, qui fixe la règle applicable durant la période transitoire. Seul inconvénient majeur d'une telle technique, la lourdeur de la procédure législative explique sans doute la parcimonie avec laquelle le Conseil constitutionnel y recourt (au 30 septembre 2023, on recense en effet seulement 5 injonctions de ce type contre 29 réserves d'interprétation transitoires).

Consubstantielle au report des effets dans le temps de l'abrogation, les réserves d'interprétation transitoires constituent également une technique matériellement législative.

Une technique matériellement législative

Second élément constitutif des réserves d'interprétation transitoires, la réserve d'interprétation en tant que telle en caractériserait la nature. Dès la décision pionnière *Société Orange SA* du 6 juin 2014, cette technique est ainsi qualifiée, dans le commentaire officiel de ladite décision, de «réserve d'interprétation».[39] Au fil du temps et décisions QPC du Conseil constitutionnel ayant formulé une réserve d'interprétation transitoire, cette qualification a progressivement évolué: «réserve d'interprétation permettant l'application du régime le plus favorable»,[40] «réserve, qui a vocation à s"appliquer à titre transitoire»,[41] «réserve d'interprétation transitoire»,[42] «réserve transitoire».[43] Cette dernière qualification est finalement celle qui a été retenue par le Conseil constitutionnel pour identifier ce type de décisions, ses tables analytiques utilisant

[38] CC, «Les effets…» *loc. cit.*
[39] CC, comm. off. de CC, no. 2014-400 QPC, déc. préc., p. 12.
[40] CC, comm. off. de CC, no. 2014-404 QPC, déc. préc., p. 11.
[41] CC, comm. off. de CC, no. 2014-420/421 QPC, déc. préc., p. 15.
[42] V., pour la première fois, CC, «Les effets…» *loc. cit.*
[43] V., pour la première fois dans un commentaire officiel de décision, CC, comm. off. de CC, no. 2015-506 QPC, déc. préc., p. 19.

celle de «réserve transitoire avant abrogation»,[44] par opposition à la «réserve pérenne»,[45] la réserve d'interprétation «traditionnelle». Ce passage de la qualification de «réserve d'interprétation» à celle de «réserve transitoire» est également observable en doctrine: avec les réserves transitoires, nous serions passés d'une « nouvelle catégorie de réserves d'interprétation»,[46] à «une notion indûment assimilée aux réserves d'interprétation».[47] Cette évolution soulève la question de savoir si les réserves d'interprétation transitoires constituent un nouveau type de réserves d'interprétation ou une technique *sui generis*? Pour poser la question autrement, y-a-t-il entre elles une simple différence de degré ou bien une véritable différence de nature?

La réserve d'interprétation est une technique par laquelle le Conseil constitutionnel, lorsqu'un «texte est susceptible d'au moins deux interprétations»,[48] choisit celle qui le rend conforme à la Constitution. Là encore apparue dans le cadre du contrôle de constitutionnalité selon l'article 61 de la Constitution,[49] cette technique a été transposée à la procédure de QPC.[50] À la suite du Doyen Louis Favoreu, la doctrine constitutionnaliste distingue trois grands types de réserves d'interprétation: tout d'abord, les réserves constructives par lesquelles «le juge constitutionnel ajoute au texte ce qui lui manque pour être

---

44 V., pour la première fois, *Rec.* 2014, p. 774.

45 CC, *Tables d'analyse du 4 octobre 1958 au 31 décembre 2022*, p. 5306-5307 <https://www.conseil-constitutionnel.fr/sites/default/files/2023-04/1958-2022_tables_analytiques-v2.pdf>.

46 D. Rousseau, P.-Y Gahdoun, J. Bonnet, «Chronique de jurisprudence constitutionnelle 2014», *RDP* (2015) : 253.

47 JACQUINOT N., op. cit., p. 2010-2011.

48 CC, n° 85-191 DC, 10 juill. 1985, Loi portant diverses dispositions d'ordre économique et financier, Rec. p. 47.

49 V., pour la première fois, CC, no. 59-2 DC, 24 juin 1959, *Règlement de l'Assemblée nationale*, *Rec.*, 58.

50 V., pour la première fois, CC, no. 2010-8 QPC, 18 juin 2010, Époux L., *Rec.* p. 117. V., not., MODERNE F., «La déclaration de conformité sous réserve», in *Le Conseil constitutionnel et les partis politiques*, ed. L. Favoreau, *PUAM-Economica* (1988): 93-118 ; T. Di Mannot, «Le juge constitutionnel et la technique des décisions "interprétatives" en France et en Italie», *Economica* (1997) : 617; A. Viala, «Les réserves d'interprétation dans la jurisprudence du Conseil constitutionnel», *LGDJ* (1999): 318; A. Viala, «Les réserves d'interprétations: un outil de «resserrement» de la contrainte de constitutionnalité», *RDP* (1997): 1048-67; T. Di Manno, «L'influence des réserves d'interprétation», in «La légitimité de la jurisprudence du Conseil constitutionnel», *Economica* (1999): 189-272.

conforme, sous couleur de l'interpréter»;[51] ensuite, les réserves neutralisantes « ont pour effet de gommer l'effet nocif de certaines dispositions en affirmant qu'elles n'ont pas la signification qui semble découler du texte ou qu'elles sont dépourvues d'effet juridique».[52] Enfin, les réserves directives «ont pour objet de tracer une ligne de conduite à ceux qui auront à appliquer la loi déclarée conforme sous réserve, et notamment aux tribunaux».[53] Indépendamment de cette classification tripartite, d'ailleurs moins rigoureuse scientifiquement que pédagogique,[54] les réserves d'interprétation énoncées par le Conseil constitutionnel sont limitées par la considération selon laquelle ce dernier ne dispose pas d'«un pouvoir général d'appréciation et de décision de même nature que celui du Parlement».[55] Comme le souligne le Secrétariat général du Conseil constitutionnel, «les réserves sont limitées par des garde-fous que s"impose le Conseil constitutionnel par refus de faire œuvre de colégislateur ».[56]

---

51 L. Favoreu, «La décision de constitutionnalité,» *RIDC* (1986): 622.

52 ibid., 622-23.

53 ibid., 622-23.

54 Elle est, en effet, doublement critiquable. D'une part, elle n'est pas exhaustive comme en témoigne l'existence de «réserves inclassables.» A. Viala, «Les réserves… », *op. cit.*, 85-89, et de «réserves implicites.» A. Viala, « Les réserves… », *op. cit.*, 89-92. D'autre part, elle est poreusenon seulement dans la mesure où «toutes les réserves ont en fait une nature directive. A. Viala., Les réserves…, *op. cit.*, p. 74, mais également en ce que la distinction entre les réserves constructives et les réserves neutralisantes est «délicate.» A. VIALA, *Les réserves*, *op. cit.*, p. 74, les caractères constructif et neutralisant d'une réserve d'interprétation constituant parfois les deux faces de la même médaille. V., par ex., CC, no. 83-167 DC, 19 janv. 1984, *Loi relative à l'activité et au contrôle des établissements de crédit*, *Rec.* p. 23. V. MODERNE F., *loc. cit.*, p. 105).

55 V., pour la première fois, CC, no. 2000-433 DC, 27 juill. 2000, *Loi modifiant la loi no. 86-1067 du 30 septembre 1986 relative à la liberté de communication*, *Rec.* p. 129. Avant, le Conseil constitutionnel employait le vocable «*identique*» à la place de l'expression «de même nature» (v., pour la première fois, CC, no. 74-54 DC, 15 janvier 1975, *Examen de la loi relative à l'interruption volontaire de la grossesse*, *Rec.* p. 19). V., not., M. Talon, «Le Conseil constitutionnel ne dispose pas d'un pouvoir général d'appréciation et de décision de même nature que celui du Parlement : un mythe du droit constitutionnel », *RDP* (2020): 137-69.

56 Secrétariat général du Conseil constitutionnel, *Les réserves d'interprétation du Conseil constitutionnel*, 2002, p. 8 <https://www.conseil-constitutionnel.fr/sites/default/files/as/root/bank_mm/pdf/Conseil/reserves2002.pdf>

En particulier, cette technique ne doit «pas aboutir à donner au texte soumis à son examen une interprétation qui en contredirait ouvertement la lettre».[57]

En apparence, les réserves d'interprétation transitoires semblent s'inscrire dans le cadre classique des réserves d'interprétation, comme en témoigne l'usage occasionnel de la formule d'après laquelle les dispositions contestées « ne sauraient être interprétées comme»,[58] «doivent être interprétées comme».[59] De manière exceptionnelle, le Conseil constitutionnel a même intégré une réserve d'interprétation transitoire au dispositif de sa décision selon lequel «la déclaration d'inconstitutionnalité de l'article 1er prend effet sous la réserve énoncée au considérant 26 et dans les conditions prévues aux considérants 25 et 27».[60] En l'absence de fondement textuel explicite, cette assimilation permet au Conseil constitutionnel de justifier le recours à une telle technique.

En réalité, les réserves d'interprétation transitoires diffèrent sur trois points des réserves d'interprétation traditionnelles. La première différence est d'ordre temporel. Alors que les réserves d'interprétation classiques sont «pérennes» et ont vocation à «faire corps» avec le texte interprété, les réserves d'interprétations transitoires « ont vocation à disparaître, soit parce que la situation visée s'est éteinte – par exemple l'instance en cours est terminée – soit parce que la nouvelle législation a finalement été adoptée».[61] Comme le remarque le commentaire officiel de la décision pionnière *Société Orange SA* du 6 juin 2014 précité, cette technique est «circonscrite temporellement».[62]

La deuxième différence est d'ordre matériel. Si les réserves d'interprétation traditionnelles se rattachent à l'interprétation à proprement parler, entendu comme l'acte consistant à «indiquer» ou «déterminer la signification» d'un texte,[63] dans la mesure où cette technique est, pour reprendre une formule utilisée

---

57 B. Genevois, « Un universitaire au Conseil constitutionnel: le Doyen Georges Vedel», *RFDA* (2004): 222.

58 CC, no. 2014-420/421 QPC, déc. préc.; CC, no. 2015-506 QPC, déc. préc.; CC, no. 2015-566 QPC, déc. préc.

59 CC, no. 2017-694 QPC, déc. préc.; CC, no. 2019-773 QPC, déc. préc.

60 CC, no. 2014-420/421 QPC, déc. préc.

61 G. Rousseau, P.-Y Gahdoun, J. Bonnet, *loc. cit.*

62 CC, comm. off. de CC, no. 2014-400 QPC préc.

63 M. Troper, «La théorie du droit, le droit, l'État», *PUF* (2001): 69.

par le Conseil constitutionnel depuis 1991, «nécessaire à l'appréciation de sa constitutionnalité»,[64] les réserves d'interprétation transitoires s'en détachent et «constituent une réglementation transitoire».[65] Comme le souligne la Professeure Nathalie Jacquinot, «en réalité c'est bien parce que le juge constitutionnel a conscience qu'il franchit les garde-fous sus-évoqués qu'il décide de ne pas prononcer de déclaration de conformité sous réserve et opte pour une abrogation»; «s'il s'agissait de simples réserves neutralisantes par exemple, le juge n'aurait justement pas eu besoin de censurer lesdites dispositions pour assurer le respect de la Constitution».[66] Le lien entre cette «législation provisoire», qualification préférée par Samy Benzina,[67] et le texte est donc plus distendu, pour ne pas dire rompu: «la réserve d'interprétation n'intervient donc pas, comme c'est normalement le cas, au stade du correctif à appliquer à l'inconstitutionnalité constatée, mais à celui des effets de la déclaration d'inconstitutionnalité».[68]

La troisième différence, moins importante que les deux premières, est d'ordre formel. Tandis que les réserves d'interprétation pérennes sont intégrées au dispositif des décisions du Conseil constitutionnel d'après lequel, dans sa formulation la plus moderne, telle disposition législative est conforme à la Constitution «sous la réserve énoncée au» considérant, dorénavant paragraphe X,[69] les réserves d'interprétations transitoires, exception faite de l'exemple sus-évoqué[70] sont généralement confinées dans les motifs des décisions; leur dispositif se bornant à énoncer que la déclaration d'inconstitutionnalité

64 CC, no. 91-298 DC, 24 juill. 1991, *Loi portant diverses dispositions d'ordre économique et financier*, *Rec.* p. 89.

65 N. Jacquinot, *op. cit.*, 2010-11.

66 ibid., 2011.

67 S. Benzina, *op. cit.*, 333-36.

68 ibid., 334.

69 V., pour la première fois, CC, no. 2001-454 DC, 17 janv. 2002, *Loi relative à la Corse*, *Rec.* p. 79.

70 CC, no. 2014-420/421 QPC, déc. préc.

«prend effet dans les conditions fixées aux»[71] «par les»[72] «prévues aux» considérants/paragraphes X et/à Y.[73]

Plus ou moins essentielles, ces trois différences particulières sont constitutives d'une différence générale, laquelle n'est pas une simple différence de degré, mais qui est une véritable différence de nature, entre les réserves d'interprétation transitoires et les réserves d'interprétation classiques. Il résulte de cette différence globale que les premières sont finalement une technique moins interprétative que matériellement législative.

À ce titre, elles se rapprochent du pouvoir dont, «grâce à l'article 62 de la Constitution, le Conseil est investi, lorsqu'il constate … [une] inconstitutionnalité … de déterminer des règles transitoires dans l'attente de l'adoption d'une éventuelle réforme destinée à remédier à l'inconstitutionnalité».[74] Ce pouvoir lui permet, après avoir constaté l'inconstitutionnalité de dispositions législatives, de les abroger immédiatement en même temps que de fixer une

---

71 CC, no. 2014-400 QPC, déc. préc. ; CC, no. 2014-420/421 QPC, déc. préc., p. 461; CC, no. 2014-453/454 QPC et 2015-462 QPC, déc. préc., p. 192; CC, no. 2017-688 QPC, déc. préc.; CC, no. 2017-694 QPC, déc. préc.; CC, no. 2018-715 QPC, déc. préc.; CC, no. 2018-717/718 QPC, déc. préc. ; CC, no. 2018-739 QPC, déc. préc.; CC, no. 2018-763 QPC, déc. préc.; CC, no. 2019-773 QPC, déc. préc. ; CC, no. 2019-786 QPC, déc. préc.; CC, no. 2019-815 QPC, déc. préc.; CC, no. 2020-886 QPC, déc. préc.; CC, no. 2021-893 QPC, déc. préc.; CC, no. 2021-894 QPC, déc. préc.; CC, no. 2021-895/901/902/903 QPC, déc. préc.; CC, no. 2021-909 QPC, déc. préc.; CC, no. 2021-910 QPC, déc. préc.; CC, no. 2021-920 QPC, déc. préc.; CC, no. 2021-934 QPC, déc. préc.; CC, no. 2021-935 QPC, déc. préc.; CC, no. 2021-978 QPC, déc. préc. ; CC, no. 2023-1062 QPC, déc. préc.

72 CC, no. 2014-404 QPC, déc. préc., p. 326; CC, no. 2017-651 QPC, déc. préc.

73 CC, no. 2014-457 QPC, déc. préc.; CC, no. 2015-506 QPC, déc. préc. ; CC, no. 2015-566 QPC, déc. préc. ; CC, no. 2016-590 QPC, déc. préc.

74 CC, «Juillet-Août 2010: Les effets dans le temps des décisions QPC du Conseil constitutionnel» <https://qpc360.conseil-constitutionnel.fr/la-qpc/juillet-aout-2010-les-effets-dans-le-temps-des-decisions-qpc-du-conseil-constitutionnel> V., not., B. Mathieu, «Question prioritaire de constitutionnalité. Jurisprudence du 1er mars au 2 juillet 2010», *JCP* (2010): 1485; J. Boudon, «Le Conseil constitutionnel s'est-il trompé de Constitution ? À propos de ce que devrait être la modulation dans le temps des effets de ses décisions», *JCP* (2010): 1826 ; J. Benetti, «Les incidences de la question prioritaire de constitutionnalité sur le travail législatif. D'une logique de prévention à une logique de correction des inconstitutionnalités», *Constitutions* (2011): 44-45; J. Boudon, «Lorsque le Conseil constitutionnel pré-légifère: les avertissements adressés au législateur dans les décisions QPC de censure», *VIIIe Congrès français de droit constitutionnel*, Nancy, 16-18 juin 2011, p. 1 ; G. Drago, « L'influence de la QPC sur le Parlement ou la loi sous la dictée du Conseil constitutionnel,» *JP*, no. 6 (2011), 6.

nouvelle règle applicable jusqu'à l'intervention éventuelle du législateur.[75] Ce pouvoir peut être rapproché des réserves d'interprétation transitoires dans la mesure où ils consistent tous les deux, pour le Conseil constitutionnel, dans la fixation d'une nouvelle règle de droit applicable consécutivement à une déclaration d'inconstitutionnalité. Il s'en différencie néanmoins, en ce qu'à titre officiel, il «s'origine dans les nouveaux pouvoirs que lui confère l'article 62 précité de la Constitution»,[76] ainsi qu'il accompagne une déclaration d'inconstitutionnalité immédiate (alors que les réserves d'interprétation transitoires assortissent des déclarations d'inconstitutionnalité différée), de même que la nouvelle règle de droit fixée l'est jusqu'à une éventuelle intervention du Parlement, tandis que les réserves d'interprétation transitoires sont circonscrites temporellement.[77] Un tel pouvoir est donc plus positif et constructif que les réserves d'interprétation transitoires, précisément parce que la disposition législative «réécrite» par le Conseil constitutionnel est potentiellement permanente. Ce pouvoir ne s"apparente toutefois pas à un authentique pouvoir de substitution au législateur, ce dernier restant, en tout état de cause, libre d'agir, de fixer une nouvelle règle de droit applicable ou de confirmer, à la suite de la décision du Conseil constitutionnel, celle décidée par lui.[78] C'est ainsi que pour se prémunir d'une critique de participation directe à la fonction législative, le Conseil constitutionnel précise occasionnellement qu'un tel pouvoir est utilisé « sans préjudice de modifications ultérieures».[79]

In fine, ce nouveau regard porté sur les réserves d'interprétation transitoires du Conseil constitutionnel en 2024, dix ans après leur apparition dans la jurisprudence QPC, nous permet de confirmer que, par-delà les apparences,

---

[75] CC, no. 2010-10 QPC, 2 juill. 2010, *Consorts C. et a.*, *Rec.* p. 131 ; CC, no. 2010-110 QPC, déc. préc.; CC, no. 2012-250 QPC, 8 juin 2012, M. Christian G., *Rec.* p. 281 ; CC, no. 2014-403 QPC, 13 juin 2014, *M. Laurent L.*, *Rec.* p. 320; CC, no. 2016-532 QPC, 1er avr. 2016, M. Jean-Marc E. et a., *JORF*, no. 81 du 6 avr. 2016, texte no. 55; CC, no. 2017-641 QPC, 30 juin 2017, Société Horizon OI et a., *JORF* no. 153 du 1 juill. 2017, texte no. 78.

[76] A. Borzeix, « La question prioritaire de constitutionnalité : quelle confiance légitime, quelle sécurité juridique?» *RDP* (2010) : 988.

[77] CC, comm. off. de CC, no. 2014-400 QPC préc.

[78] J. Benetti, «Les incidences de la question prioritaire de constitutionnalité sur le travail législatif. D'une logique de prévention à une logique de correction des inconstitutionnalités,» *Constitutions* (2011): 44-45.

[79] CC, no. 2010-110 QPC, déc. préc., p. 162; CC, no. 2012-250 QPC, déc. préc., p. 283.

cette technique est moins interprétative que matériellement législative, justifiant l'abandon du recours au champ sémantique de l'interprétation afin de la qualifier. Dans cette mesure et en l'absence de fondement textuel exprès, son assimilation aux réserves d'interprétation traditionnelles participe donc d'une stratégie justificative de sa pratique. Sous couvert d'interprétation, ainsi que de garantie des droits subjectifs des justiciables et des exigences inhérentes à la hiérarchie des normes en général, à la primauté de la Constitution en particulier, le Conseil constitutionnel, en formulant une réserve d'interprétation transitoire, participe à la fonction législative. Cette participation est toutefois limitée, ce qui permet à cette technique de continuer à se développer dans la jurisprudence QPC.

De la *rule of law* au *Human Rights Act*: Évolution des droits et libertés au Royaume-Uni

Louis-Philippe Gratton
LexFEIM

Ce chapitre examine l'évolution du contenu des droits et libertés considerées par le juge en s'attachant aux différences observées avant et après l'adoption du Human Rights Act 1998. La loi a incorporé en droit britannique les dispositions de la Convention européenne des droits de l'homme (CEDH) ouvrant aux individus un recours en cas de violation de leurs droits fondamentaux. Cette législation a profondément transformé le paysage juridique britannique et elle a entraîné des changements significatifs dans l'approche des juges lorsqu'ils abordent des affaires liées aux droits et libertés.

Avant la promulgation de la loi, ils s'appuyaient sur diverses méthodes d'interprétation influencées par la *common law* (jurisprudence ou *case law*), les principes d'interprétation des lois (*statutory interpretation*) et des références ponctuelles aux instruments internationaux. Le *Human Rights Act*, en fournissant un cadre statutaire pour la protection et la mise en oeuvre des droits et libertés, a modifié les méthodes interprétatives des juges. Ce chapitre se propose donc d'explorer ces changements, ainsi que l'impact de la loi sur le processus décisionnel des juges.

Introduction

Au Royaume-Uni, le contenu des droits et des libertés individuels a évolué avec l'adoption du Human Rights Act 1998.[1] La loi a incorporé en droit britannique les dispositions de la *Convention de sauvegarde des droits de l'homme et des libertés fondamentales*[2] (CEDH) ouvrant aux individus un recours en cas

---

1 Human Rights Act 1998, c. 42.

2 Convention de sauvegarde des droits de l'homme et des libertés fondamentales, 4 novembre 1950, 213 RTNU 223 (entrée en vigueur: 3 septembre 1953) [ci-après «Convention européenne des droits de l'homme» ou «CEDH». Le Human Rights Act est entré en vigueur le 2 octobre 2000: Human Rights Act 1998 (Commencement No. 2) Order 2000, SI 2000/1851, art. 2.

de violation de leurs droits fondamentaux. Cette intégration a eu un impact sur le travail d'interprétation du juge[3] lorsqu'il aborde des affaires liées aux droits et libertés et elle a affecté la hiérarchie des normes.

Avant l'entrée en vigueur de cette loi, la common law était perçue comme la principale – voire la seule – source des droits et des libertés individuels.[4] Le juge s'appuyait alors sur diverses méthodes d'interprétation tirées de la common law elle-même, sur les principes d'interprétation des lois (statutory interpretation)[5] et, ponctuellement, sur les dispositions d'instruments internationaux pour dégager le contenu matériel de ces droits et libertés et en appréhender la portée. Le Human Rights Act, en fournissant un cadre statutaire à la protection des droits fondamentaux, a toutefois modifié la substance de ces garanties, ainsi que les méthodes interprétatives et les pouvoirs du juge en la matière.

Traditionnellement, le rôle du juge dans l'interprétation de la loi est limité en raison du principe constitutionnel de la souveraineté parlementaire.[6] Le juge est entièrement subordonné à l'autorité du Parlement lorsqu'il interprète un texte législatif, devant donner effet à la volonté du législateur. Il adopte alors une approche dite raisonnée («purposive approach») consistant à rechercher le sens le plus cohérent avec l'objectif de la loi en cas de doute sur l'intention du législateur.[7] Si les termes de la législation sont clairs et sans ambiguïté, le juge doit leur donner plein effet même s'ils entrent en contradiction avec les obligations internationales du Royaume-Uni.[8] Ainsi, un traité qui n'a pas été incorporé en droit anglais ne peut être la source ni de droits ni d'obligations.[9]

---

3 Le travail d'interprétation du juge consiste à «dégager,sans appréciations personnelles,le sens de dispositions applicables au litige» en s'appuyant sur des sources formelles, telles que la loi: Remus Titiriga, «Le modèle standard de développement du droit par le juge en Allemagne», *Romanian Journal of Comparative Law* 4 (2013): 72, à la p. 74.

4 Emilio Santoro, «The Rule of Law and the "Liberties of the English: The Interpretation of Albert Venn Dicey,» in *The Rule of Law – History: Theory and Criticism*, dir. Pietro Costa et Danilo Zolo (Dordrecht: Springer, 2007), 153–55.

5 William D. Popkin, *Statutes in Court – The History and Theory of Statutory Interpretation* (Durham: Duke University Press, 1999), 9–30.

6 *R. (Miller) c. Secretary of State for Exiting the European Union*, [2017] UKSC 5, par. 42–43.

7 Sur la recherche de l'intention du législateur, *cf.* Remus Titiriga, «Le modèle standard de méthodologie interprétative allemande – Son évolution et sa signification actuelle,» (2012) 1 *Rom. J. Comp. L.* 27, à la p. 32.

8 *Salomon c. Commissioners of Customs and Excise*, [1967] 2 QB 116, à la p. 143 (LJ Diplock).

9 *J. H. Rayner (Mincing Lane) Ltd. c. Department of Trade and Industry*, [1990] 2 AC 418 (HL), à la p. 500 (LJ Oliver of Aylmerton); et *R. c. Secretary of State for the Home*

L'application en droit interne de ses dispositions par un juge équivaudrait à «une usurpation judiciaire de la fonction législative».[10]

Avec l'adoption de la loi de mise en œuvre de la Convention européenne des droits de l'homme, le Parlement a accordé au juge une plus grande marge de manœuvre, ce qui représente un changement significatif dans la répartition des pouvoirs entre les chambres législatives et les tribunaux. Une analyse du cadre juridique classique des droits fondamentaux au Royaume-Uni et des limites qui leur sont imposées permet de comprendre l'impact de l'entrée en vigueur du Human Rights Act sur le système juridique britannique, le travail du juge et la souveraineté du Parlement.

Le cadre juridique de la protection des droits et libertés

Le roi de Grande-Bretagne est un «ennemi invétéré de la liberté»,[11] écrivait Thomas Paine dans son pamphlet en faveur de l'indépendance des États-Unis. Alors qu'il croyait rejeter les institutions anglaises en affirmant plus avant que la loi est souveraine,[12] « law is king » en Amérique, Paine reformulait tout simplement un principe constitutionnel britannique essentiel.[13] Au Royaume-Uni, la constitution n'est pas la source des droits et des libertés.[14] Ils résultent plutôt d'une lente reconnaissance par le juge[15] aux individus de

Department, ex parte Brind, [1991] 1 AC 696 (HL), à la p. 761 (LJ Ackner). A contrario, les dispositions d'un traité international incorporées en droit interne sont source de droits et d'obligations: *R. (Miller) c. Secretary of State for Exiting the European Union* (SC), par. 86 et 90.

10 *R. c. Secretary of State for the Home Department, ex parte Brind*, ibid., p. 748 (LJ Bridge of Harwich, notre traduction).

11 Thomas Paine, *Common Sense*, in *The Complete Writings of Thomas Paine*, vol. 2 (New York: Citadel Press, 1945), 1–25.

12 T. Paine, *Common Sense*, 29.

13 Dicey estime que la *rule of law* est incompatible avec tout privilège ou prérogative: Albert V. Dicey, *Introduction to the Study of the Law of the Constitution* (Londres, Macmillan and Co., 1927), 198. *Cf. R. (Miller)* c. *Secretary of State for Exiting the European Union* (SC), *op. cit.*, par. 41.

14 A. V. Dicey, *Introduction to the Study of the Law of the Constitution* (Londres: Macmillan and Co., 1927), 198–99.

15 ibid., p. 191.

garanties spécifiques en application du principe de la *rule of law*[16] et de la consécration de certaines d'entre elles dans des instruments juridiques écrits.[17]

La rule of law: source jurisprudentielle des droits et libertés

Le Royaume-Uni est une démocratie constitutionnelle fondée sur la rule of law,[18] terme qu'il convient de traduire en français par primauté du droit.[19] Le législateur britannique a reconnu, en 2005, qu'il s'agit d'un «principe constitutionnel».[20] Il n'en a toutefois pas précisé les contours, laissant son interprétation au juge.[21] Il convient donc d'étudier le principe en tant que norme supérieure qui s'impose au juge, avant d'en décrire la dimension matérielle,[22] c'est-à-dire le contenu de la norme telle qu'élaborée par le juge.

Une approche formelle du principe: une norme supérieure s'imposant au juge

Alexis de Tocqueville avait constaté chez les Anglais un «respect profond du droit» et un «amour de la légalité».[23] Le philosophe français cernait là

16 E. Santoro, «The rule of law and the "liberties of the English"» in *The Rule of Law – History: Theory and Criticism*, dir. Pietro Costa et Danilo Zolo (Dordrecht: Springer, 2007), 160–61.

17 Hersch Lauterpacht, *An International Bill of the Rights of Man* (Oxford: OUP, 2013), 55–57.

18 *R. (Miller) c. Secretary of State for Exiting the European Union*, [2016] EWHC 2768 (Admin), par. 18.

19 Daniel Mockle, «Rule of law», in *Traité international de droit constitutionnel – Théorie de la constitution*, t. 1, dir. Dominique Chagnollaud et Michel Troper (Paris: Dalloz, 2012), 671, à la p. 672; et *Vocabulaire du droit* (liste de termes, expressions et définitions adoptés), *JORF* 3 (2011): 5964.

20 Constitutional Reform Act 2005, c. 4, art. 1(a).

21 Thomas Bingham, «The rule of Law», *Cambridge Law Journal* 66 (2007): 68.

22 Brian Z. Tamanaha, *On the Rule of Law: History, Politics, Theory* (Cambridge: CUP, 2004), 91-92; Brian Z. Tamanaha, *Law as a Means to an End: Threat to the rule of law* (Cambridge: CUP, 2006), 227–228.

23 Alexis de Tocqueville, *Voyage en Suisse, in Mélanges, fragments historiques et notes sur l'Ancien Régime, la Révolution et l'Empire – Voyages – Pensées* (Paris, Michel Lévy frères, 1865), 451–457.

l'un des principes élémentaires du système juridique anglais: la primauté du droit. «L'Angleterre est un pays régi par la rule of law»,[24] observait en effet Dicey dans son traité de droit constitutionnel. Il s'était appuyé sur l'étude de la jurisprudence et sur les observations de nombreux auteurs pour dégager le principe constitutionnel de la primauté du droit. Elle constitue, selon le juriste, l'un des deux traits caractéristiques des institutions anglaises avec la souveraineté parlementaire.[25]

La rule of law ne se traduit pas directement par des règles de droit contraignantes. Elle s'avère plutôt une notion abstraite qui s'incarne dans l'idée de la suprématie» ou de la «prédominance» de la loi ou du droit.[26] Il s'agit d'une loi «dobjectivement déterminée»,[27] qui ne tire donc sa source d'aucun texte écrit, et qui s'impose au juge. Le système juridique britannique reconnaît ainsi l'existence d'un droit supérieur aux normes adoptées par le Parlement ou dégagées par la jurisprudence.[28]

À l'instar du droit naturel ou du droit divin, la rule of law n'émane pas de la volonté des hommes.[29] Elle se rapproche à cet égard de la « loi véritable, la droite raison, conforme à la nature, universelle, immuable, éternelle»[30] défendue par Cicéron. Elle se présente comme un «idéal», une norme à laquelle les autres lois doivent se conformer.[31] Le principe de la primauté du droit se place au-dessus de tous les autres. Il ne peut pas être exprimé «sous la forme d'une règle de droit ordinaire»,[32] pour reprendre l'explication du chancelier Lord Falconer. Dicey définissait la rule of law comme «la garantie accordée

---

24 A. V. Dicey, *Introduction to the Study of the Law of the Constitution* (Londres: Macmillan and Co., 1927), 180 (notre traduction).

25 ibid., 179.

26 ibid., p. 179, 180, 182-183.

27 B. Z. Tamanaha, *Law as a Means to an End*, *op. cit.*, 11 (notre traduction).

28 Élisabeth Zoller, *Introduction au droit public*, 2e éd. (Paris, Dalloz, 2013), par. 93.

29 B. Z. Tamanaha, *Law as a Means to an End: Threat to the rule of law* (Cambridge: CUP, 2006), 11.

30 Cicéron, *La république* (Paris: Didier et cie, 1858), livre 3, 17, 184. Cf. Cicéron, *Des lois*, in Œuvres *complètes de Cicéron* (Paris: C.L.F. Panckoucke, 1835), livre 1, 6, 21–22.

31 Jeffrey Goldsworthy, *Parliamentary Sovereignty: Contemporary debates* (Cambridge: CUP, 2010), 58–61; et Joseph Raz, *The Authority of Law – Essays on law and morality* (Oxford: OUP, 2009), 223.

32 House of Lords, Parliamentary Debates, vol. 667 (7 décembre 2004), col. 738 (notre traduction).

aux droits des individus en vertu de la constitution anglaise».[33] William Blackstone, dans ses célèbres commentaires sur le droit anglais, écrivait à ce sujet que l'Angleterre est un pays dans lequel la «liberté politique ou civile» est l'objet même de la constitution.[34] Montesquieu avait affirmé en ce sens que l'«objet direct» de la constitution d'Angleterre est la «liberté politique».[35] Selon la conviction de nombreux auteurs anglo-saxons, l'Angleterre a tout simplement inventé la protection effective des droits et libertés à travers le principe de la rule of law.[36] Elle aménage l'autonomie de l'individu qui doit pouvoir organiser ses activités à l'aune de règles connues à l'avance.[37] La primauté du droit lui donne l'assurance de pouvoir poursuivre ses aspirations personnelles sans que l'État entrave délibérément ses efforts.[38]

La compréhension du principe privilégiée par de nombreux auteurs contemporains s"articule autour de garanties liées à la justice et à la liberté.[39] Ils retiennent principalement la «dimension libérale»[40] de la rule of law, un principe constitutionnel largement traversé par l'idée de «liberté et d'autonomie individuelle».[41] Hayek le perçoit d'ailleurs comme «l'incarnation juridique de la liberté».[42] Cette conception formelle de la primauté du droit

---

33 A. V. Dicey, *Introduction to the Study of the Law of the Constitution* (Londres: Macmillan and Co., 1927), 180 (notre traduction).

34 William Blackstone, *Commentaries on the Laws of England*, vol. 1 (Philadelphie: J.B. Lippincott Co., 1893), introd., 6 (notre traduction).

35 Montesquieu, *Esprit des lois* (Paris: Librairie de Firmin Didot frères, fils et cie, 1858), 128.

36 A. W. B. Simpson, «Human Rights, Fundamental Freedoms, and the World of the Common Law», in *Human Rights and the End of Empire: Britain and the Genesis of the European Convention*, dir. A. W. B. Simpson (Oxford: OUP, 2004), 1, aux p. 18–20.

37 Friedrich A. Hayek, *The Road to Serfdom* (Abingdon: Routledge, 2005), 75, 76, 78 et 84.

38 ibid., 76, 84.

39 Jeremy Waldron, «The rule of law in contemporary liberal theory», in *Liberalism – Critical concepts in political theory*, dir. G. W. Smith (Londres: Routledge, 2002), 93–95.

40 Daniel Mockle, «L'État de droit et la théorie de la rule of law», *Cahiers de droit* 35 (1994): 823–97.

41 Éric Carpano, État de droit et droits *européens – L'évolution du modèle de l'État de droit dans le cadre de l'européanisation des systèmes juridiques* (Paris: L'Harmattan, 2005), par. 289.

42 F. A. Hayek, *The Road to Serfdom* (Abingdon: Routledge, 2005), 85.

ne permet pas de dégager les principes matériels applicables, vers lesquels il faut maintenant se tourner.

Une approche matérielle du principe: le contenu de la norme établi par le juge

Dicey a reconnu lui-même «l'imprécision et l'ambiguïté»[43] du principe de la rule of law et souligné l'importance d'en déterminer le contenu normatif. Si la primauté du droit s"impose au juge, celui-ci en détermine en grande partie le contenu matériel dans un système de common law: «[L]e rôle du pouvoir judiciaire est de faire respecter et de promouvoir la rule of law».[44] L'élaboration des normes dans la tradition juridique anglo-saxonne n'est en effet pas réservée au législateur ou à l'exécutif. Les juges jouent aussi un rôle prépondérant dans leur définition. Le pouvoir du juge s'étend ainsi au-delà de la simple interprétation des lois: il crée du droit.[45]

Il appartient donc au juge de dégager le contenu matériel de la rule of law. Elle recouvre, selon Dicey, trois grands principes juridiques. Le premier, celui de la légalité, prévoit qu'aucun individu ne peut être puni sauf pour la violation d'une infraction prévue par la loi ordinaire et sanctionnée par un tribunal ordinaire.[46] La rule of law s'oppose ainsi à un système de gouvernement dans lequel le pouvoir de contrainte serait exercé de manière «large», «arbitraire» ou «discrétionnaire».[47]

Il s'agit du principe de légalité[48] que la Cour des plaids communs avait dégagé dans l'affaire Entick c. Carrington, dès 1795. Elle avait reconnu le caractère illicite d'une perquisition effectuée par des envoyés du roi puisqu'elle n'était prévue par aucune règle de droit.[49] La primauté du droit, dans cette acception, vise à réduire la discrétion laissée aux organes de l'exécutif lorsqu'ils exercent un pouvoir coercitif.[50] Le principe n'empêche pas l'exercice

---

43 A. V. Dicey, *Introduction to the Study of the Law of the Constitution*, *op. cit.*, p. 183 (notre traduction).

44 *R. (Miller)* c. *Secretary of State for Exiting the European Union* (SC), *op. cit.*, par. 42.

45 ibid., 42.

46 A. V. Dicey, *Introduction to the Study of the Law of the Constitution* (Londres: Macmillan and Co., 1927), 183.

47 ibid., p. 184 (notre traduction).

48 Élisabeth Zoller, *Introduction au droit public*, 2e éd. (Paris: Dalloz, 2013), par. 100.

49 *Entick c. Carrington*, (1765) 95 ER 807, à la p. 817.

50 F. A. Hayek, *The Road to Serfdom*, *op. cit.*, p. 76 et 87.

de pouvoirs discrétionnaires par les autorités, mais il en limite l'étendue.[51] L'État doit exercer ses pouvoirs conformément à la loi et dans les limites prescrites par celle-ci[52] vis-à-vis de l'ensemble des justiciables.

Le deuxième principe que recouvre la rule of law, celui de l'égalité devant la loi, veut qu'une personne soit soumise aux mêmes règles de droit et à la même justice, quel que soit son rang ou sa condition.[53] Ces exigences se concrétisent dans le principe de l'égalité devant la loi.[54] Il implique corolairement que personne n'est au-dessus des lois,[55] comme l'avait reconnu la Cour des plaids communs en faisant droit à la réclamation civile de la victime de la perquisition contre les représentants du pouvoir royal.[56] Les actions de l'État, de ses organes et de ses officiers sont ainsi soumises à la loi[57] comme celles de tout citoyen.

Le principe ne peut plus être affirmé en termes aussi absolus qu'à l'époque de Dicey. L'égalité devant la loi demeure un principe cardinal du droit anglais, mais il existe des exceptions à la règle.[58] Si la responsabilité délictuelle de la couronne est reconnue par la législation,[59] elle bénéficie aussi d'immunités qui s'étendent à ses représentants.[60] Ces immunités législatives demeurent limitées à leur tour par l'application rigoureuse de la rule of law par les tribunaux anglais.[61] Ainsi, la puissance publique ne se distingue généralement

51 Adam Tomkins et Colin Turpin, *British Government and the Constitution – Text and materials*, 6e éd. (Cambridge: CUP, 2010), 94–98; et J. Waldron, «The rule of law in contemporary liberal theory», op. cit., p. 95.

52 A. Tomkins et C. Turpin, *British Government and the Constitution – Text and materials*, 6e éd. (Cambridge: CUP, 2010), 77.

53 A. V. Dicey, *Introduction to the Study of the Law of the Constitution* (Londres: Macmillan and Co., 1927), 189.

54 Élisabeth Zoller, *Introduction au droit public*, 2e éd. (Paris: Dalloz, 2013), par. 101.

55 A. V. Dicey, *Introduction to the Study of the Law of the Constitution* (Londres: Macmillan and Co., 1927), 189–190.

56 *Entick c. Carrington*, (1765) 95 ER 807.

57 *M. c. Home Office*, [1994] 1 AC 377 (HL), à la p. 396.

58 A. Tomkins et C. Turpin, *British Government and the Constitution – Text and materials*, 6e éd. (Cambridge: CUP, 2010), 88–93.

59 Crown Proceedings Act 1947, 10 & 11 Geo. VI, c. 44, art. 1er et 2.

60 ibid., art. 21 (2).

61 *M. C. Home Office*, *op. cit.*

pas de l'individu quant à sa responsabilité et ses devoirs.[62] Le second principe se traduit donc toujours par un égal respect des lois par les individus et les autorités étatiques,[63] ce dont s'assure le juge.

Le dernier principe formulé par Dicey renvoie à l'importance de l'institution judiciaire face au pouvoir administratif pour assurer le respect des droits individuels.[64] Il s'agit d'un régime dans lequel la «prééminence du juge»[65] s"impose. Au Royaume-Uni, les principes de la rule of law sont dégagés par les juges lorsqu'ils se prononcent dans des cas particuliers portés devant eux.[66] Ils définissent les droits dans une affaire déterminée, puis les généralisent à l'ensemble des individus.[67]

La constitution anglaise n'est pas, rappelait Dicey, le fruit d'un effort législatif ou d'une assemblée constituante. Ses principes ont été définis au cas par cas par les cours appelées à entendre des affaires individuelles.[68] Aux côtés de l'exécutif et du Parlement, le juge est ainsi créateur de droit. La rule of law, bien que son champ matériel ait évolué avec la société et que sa définition se soit élargie,[69] s'avère insuffisante pour assurer seule la protection des libertés individuelles.[70] Elle est complétée par des droits et des libertés,

---

62 Tony Prosser, «Understanding the British Constitution», *Political Studies* 44 (1996): 473-75.

63 T. Bingham, «The Rule of Law», *Cambridge Law Journal*, 66 (2007): 225.

64 Élisabeth Zoller, *Introduction au droit public*, 2e éd. (Paris: Dalloz, 2013), par. 93 et 95.

65 Ibid., par. 95.

66 A. V. Dicey, *Introduction to the Study of the Law of the Constitution* (Londres: Macmillan and Co., 1927), 191.

67 ibid., 196.

68 ibid., 192.

69 T. Bingham, «The Rule of Law,» *Cambridge Law Journal* 66 (2007): 68–82; Joseph Raz, «The Politics of the Rule of Law», *Indian Journal of Constitutional Law* 2 (2008): 1, à la p. 9; Joseph Raz, *The Authority of Law – Essays on Law and Morality* (Oxford: OUP, 2009), 214–218; et Adam Tomkins et Colin Turpin, *British Government and the Constitution – Text and Materials*, 6e éd. (Cambridge: CUP, 2010), 98–102.

70 Joseph Raz, *The Authority of Law – Essays on Law and Morality* (Oxford: OUP, 2009), 226; et Jeremy Waldron, «The Rule of Law in Contemporary Liberal Theory», in *Liberalism – Critical Concepts in Political Theory*, dir. G. W. Smith (Londres: Routledge, 2002), 94.

reconnus expressément par le constituant ou le législateur, qui s"inscrivent dans l'esprit des principes découlant de la rule of law.[71]

Les droits et libertés: traduction textuelle de l'idéal de la rule of law

L'idéal de la rule of law s'est traduit par l'intégration à la loi de droits et libertés. L'Angleterre a ainsi inscrit dans des documents de caractère juridique, ensuite formellement adoptés par le Parlement sous la forme d'actes législatifs, un certain nombre de droits liés au principe constitutionnel.[72] Ces documents, négociés entre le souverain et ses sujets, ne constituaient pas la source de nouveaux droits, mais confirmaient l'existence de droits et de privilèges que détenaient déjà les Anglais en vertu de la common law.[73]

Avant la théorisation du principe de la rule of law, des droits avaient ainsi été concédés aux Anglais, dès le XIIIe siècle, dans un document écrit, la Magna Carta.[74] Elle constituait «la première déclaration générale … du principe de la primauté du droit»[75] et elle consignait les principales assises des « lois fondamentales de l'Angleterre».[76] Elle traduisait la volonté des représentants de la noblesse – les barons – de recourir à la loi pour contenir le pouvoir royal.[77]

---

71 William R. Lederman, «The Nature and Problems of a Bill of Rights», *Revue du Barreau canadien* 37 (1959): 4, à la p. 4.

72 *R. (Miller) c. Secretary of State for Exiting the European Union* (SC), [2017] UKSC 5, par. 41.

73 Jack N. Rakove, «Bill of Rights», in *The Princeton Encyclopedia of American Political History*, dir. Rebecca Edwards, Michael Kazin et Adam Rothman (Oxford: Princeton University Press, 2010), 64, à la p. 64.

74 Magna Carta (1215), in André Émond, *Constitution du Royaume-Uni – Des origines à nos jours* (Montréal: Wilson & Lafleur, 2009), 507.

75 *R. c. Secretary of State for Foreign and Commonwealth Affairs, ex parte Bancoult*, [2001] QB 1067, par. 36 (LJ Laws, notre traduction).

76 William Blackstone, *Commentaries on the Laws of England*, vol. 1 (Philadelphie: J.B. Lippincott Co., 1893), livre 1, p. 127 (notre traduction).

77 Hersch Lauterpacht, *An International Bill of the Rights of Man* (Oxford: OUP, 2013), 58; A. W. B. Simpson, «Human Rights, Fundamental Freedoms, and the World of the Common Law», in *Human Rights and the End of Empire: Britain and the Genesis of the European Convention*, dir. A. W. B. Simpson (Oxford: OUP, 2004), 20; et Brian Z. Tamanaha, *On the Rule of Law: History, Politics, Theory* (Cambridge: CUP, 2004), 15 et 25.

Il ne s'agissait pas à proprement parler d'une déclaration des droits de type révolutionnaire.[78] Elle consacrait plutôt des droits reconnus à tous les hommes par les coutumes féodales existantes, mais dont le contenu, l'interprétation et la portée demeuraient incertains.[79] La charte, révisée à plusieurs reprises et confirmée par les souverains successifs,[80] forme toujours une partie du droit constitutionnel écrit.[81]

À l'instar de la *Magna Carta*, les deux autres grands documents historiques relatifs aux droits et libertés des Anglais ne peuvent être assimilés aux déclarations des droits communes à de nombreux ordres constitutionnels continentaux.[82] La Petition of Right et le Bill of Rights visent plutôt à condamner certaines pratiques de la couronne et à rétablir l'autorité de la loi.[83] L'adoption du premier de ces instruments juridiques, le 7 juin 1628, s'est inscrite dans le contexte d'atteintes répétées aux droits des sujets de Charles Ier et de la violation de l'immunité parlementaire de députés de la Chambre des communes.[84]

Le Parlement, emmené par l'ancien juge en chef de la Cour du Banc du Roi, Edward Coke, a présenté au souverain ses griefs dans un document écrit, la

---

78 William Blackstone, *Commentaries on the Laws of England*, vol. 1 (Philadelphie: J.B. Lippincott Co., 1893), livre 1, p. 127; André Émond, *Constitution du Royaume-Uni – Des origines à nos jours* (Montréal: Wilson & Lafleur, 2009), 130; et Hersch Lauterpacht, *An International Bill of the Rights of Man* (Oxford: OUP, 2013), 56.

79 André Émond, *Constitution du Royaume-Uni – Des origines à nos jours* (Montréal: Wilson & Lafleur, 2009), 130; et Max Radin, «The Myth of Magna Carta», *Harvard Law Review*, no. 60 (1947): 1060, aux p. 1071–72.

80 André Émond, *Constitution du Royaume-Uni – Des origines à nos jours* (Montréal: Wilson & Lafleur, 2009), 154; Max Radin, «The Myth of Magna Carta», *Harvard Law Review*, no. 60 (1947): 1063; et Brian Z. Tamanaha, *On the Rule of Law: History, Politics, Theory* (Cambridge: CUP, 2004), 25.

81 Le texte de la Magna Carta en vigueur est celui de 1225 (Magna Carta, (1225) 9 Hen. III), reproduit dans les *Statutes of the Realm* de l'année 1297 (Magna Carta, (1297) 25 Éd. I).

82 A. V. Dicey, *Introduction to the Study of the Law of the Constitution* (Londres: Macmillan and Co., 1927), 195, note 1.

83 A. V. Dicey, *Introduction to the Study of the Law of the Constitution* (Londres: Macmillan and Co., 1927), 195, note 1; et L. J. Reeve, «The Legal Status of the Petition of Right», *Historical Journal* 29 (1986): 257, à la p. 276.

84 André Émond, *Constitution du Royaume-Uni – Des origines à nos jours* (Montréal: Wilson & Lafleur, 2009), 318–21; J. A. Guy, «The Origins of the Petition of Right Reconsidered,» *Historical Journal* 25 (1982): 289; et Bruce Smith, *Liberty and Liberalism – A Protest Against the Growing Tendency Toward Undue Interference by the State, with Individual*

Petition of Right.[85] Les députés y réclamaient le respect par le pouvoir royal des droits individuels garantis par la common law et par la Magna Carta. Après avoir d'abord refusé de s'y soumettre, Charles I s'est présenté devant les deux assemblées parlementaires réunies et il a déclaré en français « soit droit fait comme il est désiré ».[86] La Petition of Right rétablissait ainsi l'équilibre entre les prérogatives du roi et les pouvoirs du Parlement. Le Bill of Rights comporte, quant à lui, trois parties distinctes[87] La première énonce une liste de doléances adressées à Jacques II, le souverain en fuite, par la Chambre des communes et la Chambre des lords. La deuxième partie confirme l'accession au trône de Guillaume III et de Marie II, à la suite de la Glorieuse Révolution, et les règles organisant leur succession. Enfin, la troisième partie comprend treize articles qui définissent autant de limites aux pouvoirs de la couronne qui est dorénavant pleinement soumise à la loi. Le Bill of Rights et les textes constitutionnels évoqués précédemment reconnaissent aux individus des droits et des libertés, mais n'évoquent que rarement les limites qu'il convient de leur apporter.

Les limites imposées aux droits et aux libertés individuels

«Ma liberté personnelle ainsi confirmée par la liberté de tout le monde s'étend à l'infini»,[88] affirmait l'anarchiste russe Michel Bakounine. Si l'existence de la liberté est conditionnée par la vie en société, ajoutait-il, elle ne peut être

---

Liberty, Private Enterprise and the Rights of Property (Londres: Longmans, Green, and Co., 1887), 95–102.

85 Petition of Right, (1628) 3 Ch. I, c. 1.

86 André Émond, *Constitution du Royaume-Uni – Des origines à nos jours* (Montréal: Wilson & Lafleur, 2009), 321–22; L. J. Reeve, «The Legal Status of the Petition of Right», *Historical Journal* 29 (1986): 259–60; et Bruce Smith, *Liberty and Liberalism – A Protest Against the Growing Tendency Toward Undue Interference by the State, with Individual Liberty, Private Enterprise and the Rights of Property* (Londres: Longmans, Green, and Co., 1887), 103.

87 Bill of Rights, (1689) 1 Will. & Mary, sess. 2, c. 2. Cf. Geoffrey Lock, «The 1689 Bill of Rights», *Political Studies* 37 (1989): 540, à la p. 541.

88 Michel Bakounine, *Dieu et l'État*, in Œuvres, t. 1, 5e éd. (Paris: P.-V. Stock, 1895), 261, à la p. 281.

limitée par celle-ci. Cette approche traduit une conception absolue de la liberté, une liberté qui ne connaîtrait aucune limite.[89]

Elle ne correspond pas à l'appréhension britannique de la théorie générale des droits et libertés. Celle-ci s'accorde plutôt avec la conception relative de la liberté défendue par John Stuart Mill. La liberté, selon lui, signifie qu'un individu doit pouvoir poursuivre ses propres intérêts sans chercher à nuire aux intérêts d'autrui.[90] Si l'individu porte atteinte aux intérêts d'autrui, une contrainte peut alors s"exercer sur lui.[91] Les libertés individuelles connaissent dès lors des limites, celles-ci découlant soit de leur nature, soit de l'exercice du pouvoir par la puissance publique.[92]

Les limites inhérentes à la nature des droits et libertés

Les limites inhérentes à la formulation et à la nature des droits et libertés ont traditionnellement été appréhendées, au Royaume-Uni, à l'aide du modèle blackstonien. Il convient d'abord de présenter le modèle proposé par William Blackstone, avant de s"attarder à sa remise en question par la division de la Cour du Banc de la Reine de la Haute Cour de justice et son actualisation par la Chambre des lords.

Le modèle blackstonien de protection des droits et libertés

Avant l'incorporation en droit britannique de la Convention européenne des droits de l'homme, la common law appréhendait les libertés individuelles d'une manière négative. Sir Megarry a ainsi pu affirmer que l'Angleterre «

---

89 P. Wachsmann, *Libertés publiques*, op. cit., par. 73.

90 John Stuart Mill, *On Liberty*, 2e éd. (Boston: Ticknor & Fields, 1863), 28–29. Hobbes avait défendu, dès le XVIIe siècle, une conception semblable de la liberté: Thomas Hobbes, *Leviathan or The Matter, Form and Power of a Commonwealth, Ecclesiastical and Civil*, 2e éd. (Londres: George Routledge and Sons, 1886), 100–01.

91 John Stuart Mill, *On Liberty*, 2e éd. (Boston: Ticknor & Fields, 1863), 15, 23, 108 et 144–46.

92 William R. Lederman, «The Nature and Problems of a Bill of Rights», *Revue du Barreau canadien*, no. 37 (1959): 8.

n'est pas un pays où tout est interdit, sauf ce qui est expressément autorisé: c'est un pays où tout est permis, sauf ce qui est expressément interdit».[93]

L'approche traditionnelle des droits et libertés par la common law repose ainsi sur le concept de «liberté résiduelle».[94] Il implique d'abord qu'un individu est libre de faire tout ce qui n'est pas interdit par la loi.[95] Il suppose ensuite que l'État ne peut interférer avec les libertés individuelles sans l'autorisation explicite de la common law – et donc du juge – ou de la loi.[96] Cette conception est d'abord apparue dans les écrits d'Henry Care, à la fin du XVII siècle. L'auteur considère qu'un individu tient de sa naissance un «droit fondamental'à la liberté de sa personne et à la propriété de ses biens, un droit dont il ne peut être privé qu'à la suite d'un crime pour lequel la loi lui impose une peine privative de liberté ou la confiscation de ses biens.[97] Blackstone a reformulé et enrichi cette proposition dans ses commentaires sur le droit anglais.

Le juriste anglais distingue les «droits absolus», qui appartiennent aux hommes en tant qu'individus,[98] et les «droits relatifs», qui s"attachent aux individus en tant que membres de la société.[99] Les premiers leur sont conférés

---

93 *Malone c. Metropolitan Police Commissioner*, [1979] Ch. 344 (Ch. D.), à la p. 357.

94 Anthony Lester, «Human Rights and the British Constitution», in *The Changing Constitution*, dir. Jeffrey Jowell et Dawn Oliver (New York: OUP, 2011), 70, à la p. 71; Ian Loveland, *Constitutional Law, Administrative Law, and Human Rights – A Critical Introduction*, 9e éd. (Oxford: OUP, 2021), 450; et Adam Tomkins et Colin Turpin, *British Government and the Constitution – Text and Materials*, 6e éd. (Cambridge: CUP, 2010), 728.

95 Anthony Lester, «Human Rights and the British Constitution», in *The Changing Constitution*, dir. Jeffrey Jowell et Dawn Oliver (New York: OUP, 2011), 72; Ian Loveland, *Constitutional Law, Administrative Law, and Human Rights – A Critical Introduction*, 9e éd. (Oxford: OUP, 2021), 450; et Adam Tomkins et Colin Turpin, *British Government and the Constitution – Text and Materials*, 6e éd. (Cambridge: CUP, 2010), 728.

96 Anthony Lester, «Human Rights and the British Constitution», in *The Changing Constitution*, dir. Jeffrey Jowell et Dawn Oliver (New York: OUP, 2011), 72; Ian Loveland, *Constitutional Law, Administrative Law, and Human Rights – A Critical Introduction*, 9e éd. (Oxford: OUP, 2021), 450.

97 Henry Care, *British Liberties, or the Free-born Subject's Inheritance*, 5e éd. (Boston: F. Franklin, 1721), 2.

98 William Blackstone, *Commentaries on the Laws of England*, vol. 1 (Philadelphie: J.B. Lippincott Co., 1893), livre 1, 123–24.

99 ibid., 123. Blackstone les identifie aussi comme des «droits sociaux» (ibid., 124).

par « les lois immuables de la nature»,[100] tandis que les seconds résultent de la formation des États et leur sont donc postérieurs.[101]

Les droits relatifs n'existent que dans la relation de l'homme aux autres[102] et servent à assurer la jouissance effective des droits absolus.[103] Il s'agit des droits du Parlement, des limites à la prérogative royale, du droit d'accès à la justice, du droit de pétition et du droit de porter une arme pour se défendre.[104] Ils constituent des «droits subordonnés auxiliaires» qui complètent les droits absolus.[105] Ces derniers comprennent les droits à la sécurité personnelle, à la liberté individuelle et à la propriété privée.[106] Tout homme devrait pouvoir en jouir, qu'ils vivent ou non en société.[107] Il appartient en conséquence à la loi «de maintenir et de réglementer ces droits».[108] La protection des «individus dans la jouissance de ces droits absolus» constitue même «l'objectif principal de la société».[109]

Blackstone, lorsqu'il emploie l'expression «droits absolus», ne se réfère cependant pas à des droits qui ne connaîtraient aucune limite.[110] Au contraire, l'approche blackstonienne des droits et libertés consiste précisément à les considérer dans leur acception relative. Les droits ne sont absolus qu'à l'état de nature,[111] écrit-il. Une fois que l'homme quitte la nature et entre en société, il abandonne une partie de sa liberté et s'oblige à se conformer aux lois dont cette société s'est dotée.[112] La loi restreint ainsi sa liberté tant qu'il

---

100 ibid., 124 (notre traduction).
101 ibid., 124.
102 ibid., 124.
103 ibid., 140-41.
104 ibid., 140-44.
105 ibid., 140-41 (notre traduction).
106 ibid., 129-40.
107 ibid., 123.
108 ibid., 124 (notre traduction).
109 ibid. (notre traduction).
110 Albert W. Alschuler, «Rediscovering Blackstone», *University of Pennsylvania Law Review* 145 (1996): 1, aux p. 28 et 36.
111 Blackstone regroupe les droits absolus qui existent à l'état de nature sous l'appellation générale de «liberté naturelle»: William Blackstone, *Commentaries on the Laws of England*, vol. 1 (Philadelphie: J.B. Lippincott Co., 1893), livre 1, 125. Cette liberté, acquise à la naissance, permet à l'homme d'agir comme bon lui semble, sans contrainte, sauf celles des lois de la nature.
112 ibid., 125.

est «nécessaire et opportun» de le faire «à l'avantage général du public».[113] Une loi qui empêche un homme de nuire à autrui diminue certes sa liberté, mais augmente celle de la société dans son ensemble.[114] La loi ne se présente alors pas comme une limite à la liberté individuelle, selon les explications de Locke que Blackstone cite avec approbation, son but étant au contraire de la préserver et de l'étendre.[115] Elle permet à l'homme d'être libre de toute contrainte imposée par les autres membres de la société.[116] L'individu demeure en conséquence maître de sa propre conduite, le bien public constituant sa seule limite,[117] conclut Blackstone. Ce modèle, bien que parfois remis en cause, continue d'être le cadre de référence de compréhension des droits et libertés au Royaume-Uni.

La remise en question du modèle proposé par Blackstone

Au cours des dernières années, un courant jurisprudentiel a émergé de la division de la Cour du Banc de la Reine de la Haute Cour de justice et s'est éloigné de la conception blackstonienne des droits et libertés. Lord Steyn a soutenu, en 1994, que l'accès à la justice doit être classifié comme un «droit constitutionnel», bien que la constitution britannique ne repose pas sur un document écrit.[118] Le juge Laws a acquiescé à sa suite, en 1998, que la common law n'envisage généralement pas les «droits constitutionnels» en l'absence d'une constitution écrite.[119] Il a néanmoins reconnu l'existence du concept de droit constitutionnel, un droit qui «ne peut être abrogé par l'État, sauf par une disposition spécifique dans une loi du Parlement».[120]

---

113 ibid., 125 (notre traduction).

114 ibid., 125-26.

115 John Locke, *Two Treatises of Government*, nouv. éd., livre 2 (Londres: Whitmore and Fenn, 1821), par. 57.

116 ibid., 57.

117 William Blackstone, *Commentaries on the Laws of England*, vol. 1 (Philadelphie: J.B. Lippincott Co., 1893), livre 1, 126.

118 *R. c. Secretary of State for the Home Department, ex parte Leech (No. 2)*, [1994] QB 198, à la p. 210.

119 *R. c. Lord Chancellor, ex parte Witham*, [1998] QB 575, par. 12.

120 *R. c. Lord Chancellor, ex parte Witham*, [1998] QB 575, par. 13 (notre traduction).

Lord Sedley a expliqué, deux ans plus tard, la distinction qu'il convient d'opérer entre une approche fondée sur les « libertés », qui s"apparente au modèle blackstonien, d'une autre basée sur les «droits», C'est-à-dire sur des droits reconnus au plan constitutionnel. La liberté n'a d'existence réelle, explique le juge d'appel, que dans la mesure où elle n'est ni niée ni limitée par la loi ou une législation déléguée.[121] Un droit, en revanche, peut être affirmé face à de telles restrictions et doit être respecté par les tribunaux.[122] La Chambre des lords a d'ailleurs reconnu qu'un «droit fondamental» était en jeu et que le principe de légalité devait opérer comme un «principe constitutionnel» pour interpréter la loi à la base du recours.[123] Lord Hoffmann a estimé que les cours britanniques, lorsqu'elles interprètent une loi, «appliquent des principes de constitutionnalité»[124] semblables à ceux des systèmes juridiques qui reposent sur une stricte hiérarchie des normes.

La consécration de cette approche est intervenue sous la plume de lord Laws. Il a estimé sur la base que la common law actuelle reconnaît «qu'il existe des droits qui devraient normalement être classifiés comme constitutionnels ou fondamentaux».[125] Lord Brooke s'est appuyé sur un raisonnement semblable dans une autre affaire pour donner raison au demandeur,[126] mais la Chambre des lords a formellement rejeté cette appréhension des droits et libertés lorsqu'elle a entendu l'affaire en appel.[127]

Lord Rodger of Earlsferry a refusé de s'attacher à la terminologie employée par ses prédécesseurs. Il s'est plutôt attardé à la «substance de la règle» juridique qu'ils ont invoquée, une règle «perçue comme si importante» que le Parlement ne peut y porter atteinte sans une volonté clairement exprimée à cet effet.[128] Le juge a souligné que le terme droit constitutionnel «n'est pas suffisamment précis» pour fonder un recours « en responsabilité délictuelle sans preuve de dommage».[129] Il a appuyé son refus de reconnaître des «droits

---

121 *Redmond-Bate* c. *Director of Public Prosecutions*, [2000] HRLR 249 (QB), à la p. 257.

122 ibid., 257.

123 *R.* c. *Secretary of State for the Home Department, ex parte Simms*, [2000] 2 AC 115 (HL), 130-131 (LJ Steyn).

124 ibid., 130-31.

125 *Thoburn* c. *Sunderland City Council*, [2003] QB 151, par. 62 (notre traduction).

126 *Watkins* c. *Secretary of State for Home Department & Ors*, [2005] QB 883, par. 48-52.

127 *Watkins* c. *Home Office*, [2006] 2 AC 395 (HL).

128 ibid., par. 61 (notre traduction).

129 ibid., par. 62 (notre traduction).

constitutionnels» ou des «droits fondamentaux» notamment sur la difficulté de les identifier.[130] Il a estimé que les juges des instances inférieures, en utilisant ces expressions, ont cherché à incorporer les droits de la convention du Conseil de l'Europe «avant la lettre»,[131] C'est-à-dire avant l'entrée en vigueur du Human Rights Act. Cette loi marque en effet le passage en partie d'un système de libertés individuelles vers la reconnaissance de droits positifs.[132]

Les limites liées à l'exercice du pouvoir par la puissance publique

Au Royaume-Uni, le principe de la souveraineté parlementaire constitue une limite extrinsèque aux libertés individuelles,[133] C'est-à-dire une limite indépendante de la formulation et de la nature du droit ou de la liberté protégés. La compréhension de la souveraineté parlementaire comme limite aux droits et libertés passe par l'exposé de la contradiction initiale que recèle le modèle proposé par Dicey[134]. Elle a été en partie dépassée, en 1998, par l'adoption du Human Rights Act.

La souveraineté parlementaire et la contradiction initiale du modèle dicéen

Une appréhension dicéenne du système juridique anglais révèle une contradiction apparemment indépassable entre les garanties offertes par la rule of law et la souveraineté du Parlement.[135] Si le Parlement possède pleinement

130 ibid., par. 58-64.

131 ibid., par. 64 (en français dans le texte).

132 ibid., par. 64.

133 Tony Prosser, «Understanding the British Constitution», *Political Studies*, no. 44 (1996): 481.

134 Le modèle proposé par Dicey serait dépassé dans le Royaume-Uni d'aujourd'hui: *Jackson c. Attorney General*, [2006] 1 AC 262 (HL), par. 102 (LJ Steyn). Cf. Pavlos Eleftheriadis, «Parliamentary Sovereignty and the Constitution», *Canadian Journal of Law & Jurisprudence* 22 (2009): 267, aux p. 268–77.

135 T. Bingham, «The Rule of Law and the Sovereignty of Parliament», *Cambridge Law Journal*, no. 66 (2007): 224–25; Jeffrey Goldsworthy, «Legislative Sovereignty and the Rule of Law», in *Sceptical Essays on Human Rights*, dir. Tom Campbell, Keith D. Ewing et Adam Tomkins (New York: OUP, 2001), 61, à la p. 61; Jeffrey Goldsworthy,

la souveraineté, il ne peut être lié par le principe de la primauté du droit.[136] À l'inverse, la rule of law devrait s'imposer comme une limite juridique aux actes du Parlement si elle constitue le fondement des institutions anglaises.[137]

Dicey avait conscience de cette contradiction. Il estimait toutefois que l'exercice d'une souveraineté théoriquement absolue est borné par des limites internes et externes.[138] D'une part, l'exercice d'une telle souveraineté par le Parlement serait incompatible avec l'institution elle-même.[139] D'autre part, le Parlement rencontrerait une «résistance généralisée»[140] de la part de la population si d'aventure il tentait d'exercer une souveraineté sans limites.

Une telle conception du système juridique anglais, malgré la tentative de réconciliation opérée par Dicey entre les deux principes constitutionnels contradictoires, implique que les droits individuels peuvent théoriquement être limités par le Parlement.[141] Lord Hoffmann a clairement confirmé cette hypothèse: « La souveraineté parlementaire signifie que le Parlement peut, s"il le souhaite, légiférer à l'encontre des principes fondamentaux des droits de l'homme».[142] Le Parlement peut ainsi à tout moment modifier, limiter ou supprimer les droits garantis par la rule of law[143] ou par les textes

---

Parliamentary Sovereignty: Contemporary Debates (Cambridge: CUP, 2010), 57–78; et Emilio Santoro, «The Rule of Law and the "Liberties of the English», in *The Rule of Law – History: Theory and Criticism*, dir. Pietro Costa et Danilo Zolo (Dordrecht: Springer, 2007), 169–70.

136 Jan-Erik Lane, *Constitutions and Political Theory* (Manchester: Manchester University Press), 1996), 44.

137 ibid., 44.

138 A. V. Dicey, *Introduction to the Study of the Law of the Constitution* (Londres: Macmillan and Co., 1927), 76–78.

139 ibid., 77.

140 ibid. (notre traduction).

141 Hersch Lauterpacht, *An International Bill of the Rights of Man* (Oxford: OUP, 2013), 54; Ian Loveland, *Constitutional Law, Administrative Law, and Human Rights – A Critical Introduction*, 9e éd. (Oxford: OUP, 2021), 450; et A. W. B. Simpson, «Human Rights, Fundamental Freedoms, and the World of the Common Law», in *Human Rights and the End of Empire: Britain and the Genesis of the European Convention*, dir. A. W. B. Simpson (Oxford: OUP, 2004), 28 et 35.

142 *R.* c. *Secretary of State for the Home Department, ex parte Simms*, *op. cit.*, 131 (notre traduction).

143 Élisabeth Zoller, *Introduction au droit public*, 2e éd. (Paris: Dalloz, 2013), par. 103–04.

historiques évoqués précédemment.[144] Ces derniers protègent les individus contre l'arbitraire du souverain ou du gouvernement, mais pas contre celui du législateur.[145] Seule une intervention législative du Parlement lui-même pouvait encadrer le rapport entre la primauté du droit et la souveraineté de l'institution,[146] ce qu'il a fait en adoptant le Human Rights Act.

Le Human Rights Act: Une subtile limite à la souveraineté parlementaire

Le Human Rights Act 1998 constitue une réponse parlementaire au dilemme dicéen.[147] Elle complète ainsi les droits et libertés existants en incorporant les dispositions de la Convention européenne des droits de l'homme en droit britannique.[148] Une cour ou un tribunal appelé à trancher un litige relatif à un droit garanti par la convention doit dorénavant tenir compte, entre autres, de la jurisprudence de la Cour européenne des droits de l'homme et des décisions du Comité des Ministres du Conseil de l'Europe.[149]

Au terme de l'article 3 du Human Rights Act, le juge doit interpréter et appliquer les dispositions d'une loi ou d'une législation déléguée «d'une manière qui soit compatible» avec la convention et «dans la mesure où il est possible de le faire».[150] Le juge doit donner effet aux dispositions de la convention, bien qu'il serait arrivé à une conclusion différente en vertu des

---

144 W. Glen How, «The Case for a Canadian Bill of Rights», *Revue du Barreau canadien*, no. 26 (1948): 759, aux p. 763–71; et Edward McWhinney, «The Supreme Court and the Bill of Rights – The Lessons of Comparative Jurisprudence», *Revue du Barreau canadien* 37 (1959): 16, à la p. 18.

145 Frank R. Scott, «Dominion Jurisdiction over Human Rights and Fundamental Freedoms», *Revue du Barreau canadien*, no. 27 (1949): 497, à la p. 501.

146 *Jackson c. Attorney General*, [2006] 1 AC 262 (HL), par. 9.

147 Alison L. Young, *Parliamentary Sovereignty and the Human Rights Act* (Oxford: Hart, 2009), 3–5.

148 Human Rights Act 1998, c. 42, art. 1er. Cf. House of Commons, Parliamentary Debates, vol. 306 (16 février 1998), col. 767.

149 Human Rights Act 1998, c. 42, art. 2.

150 Human Rights Act 1998, c. 42, art. 3(1) (notre traduction). Il renvoie à un principe d'interprétation bien établi voulant que les termes d'une législation adoptée après la signature d'un accord international «doivent être interprétés, s'ils sont raisonnablement susceptibles d'avoir un tel sens, comme permettant d'exécuter l'obligation [internationale du Royaume-Uni] et non pas comme étant incompatibles avec celle-ci»:

règles d'interprétation classiques du droit anglais sans l'obligation découlant de cet article,[151] La Chambre des lords a souligné l'ambiguïté des termes « dans la mesure où il est possible de le faire».[152]

L'emploi du mot «possible» indique que le Parlement avait envisagé la possibilité bien réelle qu'une loi puisse ne pas être interprétée conformément à la convention. Tel que formulé, l'article 3 pourrait contraindre les tribunaux à s'écarter du sens non équivoque d'une disposition et de l'intention du législateur lorsqu'ils interprètent une loi pour en donner une lecture compatible avec la convention.[153] La plus haute juridiction britannique a ainsi estimé que le Parlement, en adoptant l'article 3, a octroyé au tribunal la capacité de modifier le «sens» et l'«effet» d'une législation,[154] mais qu'il n'a pas eu l'intention de lui permettre d'adopter «un sens incompatible avec une caractéristique fondamentale de la législation».[155]

L'obligation faite aux cours et aux tribunaux d'interpréter et d'appliquer les dispositions d'une loi en conformité avec la Convention européenne des droits de l'homme pose la question de l'étendue du pouvoir conféré aux juges par le Human Rights Act. La Chambre des lords a eu, par exemple, à décider si la loi sur le mariage[156] devait être interprétée comme incluant le mariage entre deux personnes du même sexe lorsque l'un des partenaires a subi un changement de sexe. Elle a estimé que la question soulevait des problèmes généraux qui devaient faire l'objet d'un débat plus large, un débat qui appartenait au Parlement et non aux tribunaux.[157] Elle a donc émis une déclaration d'incompatibilité en vertu de l'article 4 du Human Rights Act.[158]

La formulation de l'article 3 interroge également sur les limites du pouvoir d'interprétation du juge. Ce pouvoir s"applique même en l'absence

---

Garland c. British Rail Engineering Ltd. (No. 2), [1983] 2 AC 751 (HL), à la p. 771 (LJ Diplock, notre traduction).

151 Mary Arden, *Human Rights and European Law – Building New Legal Orders* (Oxford: OUP, 2015), 98.

152 ibid., par. 30 (LJ Nicholls of Birkenhead); *Jackson c. Attorney General*, [2006] 1 AC 262 (HL), par. 105 (LJ Hope of Craighead).

153 ibid., par. 32.

154 ibid., par. 33.

155 Matrimonial Causes Act 1973, c. 18.

156 Matrimonial Causes Act 1973, c. 18.

157 *Bellinger* c. *Bellinger*, [2003] 2 AC 467 (HL), par. 43-49.

158 ibid., par. 55.

d'ambiguité de la loi.[159] Il va bien au-delà de la règle qui permettait aux tribunaux de prendre en compte un accord international pour lever toute ambiguïté sur la portée d'une disposition législative.[160] Il convient de se demander à quel moment le juge empiète sur les pouvoirs du Parlement et sort du rôle qui est le sien en vertu des principes d'interprétation des lois (statutory interpretation). Après quelques hésitations, la Chambre des lords a posé de claires limites au pouvoir du juge en vertu de l'article 3. Elle rappelle que le juge doit veiller à ne pas s'écarter «par inadvertance de sa compétence en matière d'interprétation».[161] Elle souligne à cet effet qu'un juge qui s"éloignerait sensiblement des fondements du texte qu'il est appelé à interpréter pourrait franchir la «frontière entre interprétation et amendement»[162] de la loi.

Si le juge estime qu'une disposition de la loi est incompatible avec la convention, il lui est permis d'avoir recours à une autre disposition du Human Rights Act. Il «peut» faire une déclaration de cette incompatibilité[163] en vertu de l'article 4. Cette possibilité est sa «seule alternative»[164] s"il ne parvient pas à interpréter la loi conformément à la convention. Le juge ne peut en effet prononcer la nullité de la loi, car il ne conserve qu'un pouvoir d'interprétation.[165] De plus, la déclaration d'incompatibilité n'affecte pas la validité de la législation visée[166] ni l'issue de l'affaire portée devant le juge.[167] Elle n'est qu'un moyen pour le juge de porter à la connaissance du Parlement l'opinion de la cour.[168] Le Parlement demeure souverain et le seul à pouvoir modifier,

---

159 *R.* c. *A (No. 2)*, [2002] 1 AC 45 (HL), par. 44 (LJ Steyn).

160 *R. c. Director of Public Prosecutions, ex parte Kebeline*, [2000] 2 AC 326 (HL), à la p. 373 (LJ Cooke of Thorndon); et Secretary of State for the Home Department, *Rights Brought Home: The Human Rights Bill* (1997), par. 2.7.

161 *Re S (Minors) (Care Order: Implementation of Care Plan)*, [2002] 2 AC 291 (HL), par. 41 (LJ Nicholls of Birkenhead, notre traduction).

162 ibid., par. 40 (notre traduction).

163 Human Rights Act 1998, c. 42, art. 4(2) et (4).

164 *Ghaidan* c. *Godin-Mendoza*, *op. cit.*, par. 49 (LJ Steyn). *Cf. R.* c. *Secretary of State for the Home Department, ex parte Anderson*, [2003] 1 AC 837 (HL).

165 Mary Arden, *Human Rights and European Law – Building new legal orders*, Oxford, OUP, 2015, p. 96.

166 Human Rights Act 1998, c. 42, art. 4(6).

167 Mary Arden, *Human Rights and European Law – Building New Legal Orders* (Oxford: OUP, 2015), 100.

168 ibid., 100.

supprimer ou conserver intacte une loi déclarée incompatible.[169] Il peut décider de maintenir en vigueur une loi nonobstant le fait qu'elle viole l'une des dispositions de la Convention européenne des droits de l'homme.[170] Il lui appartient ainsi de déterminer la réponse à donner à une déclaration d'incompatibilité,[171] la contrainte qu'impose le Human Rights Act sur le Parlement étant de nature «politique et non juridique».[172] Le recours à l'article 3 plutôt qu'à l'article 4 a été controversé un temps et la jurisprudence a été hésitante sur la question.[173] Lord Steyn voyait dans la déclaration d'incompatibilité une «mesure de dernier recours».[174]

Le législateur s'attendait d'ailleurs à ce que « dans presque tous les cas» les tribunaux soient en mesure d'interpréter la loi de manière compatible avec la convention.[175] Le chancelier a même estimé devant la Chambre des lords au cours des débats parlementaires qu'une déclaration d'incompatibilité serait inutile « dans 99 pour cent des cas qui se présenteront».[176] Les cours et les tribunaux britanniques ont pourtant choisi cette voie quarante-sept fois

---

169 Anthony Lester, «Human Rights and the British Constitution», in *The Changing Constitution*, dir. Jeffrey Jowell et Dawn Oliver (New York: OUP, 2011), 85–88; Andrew Le Sueur, Jo Eric K. Murkens et Maurice Sunkin, *Public Law – Text, Cases, and Materials*, 2e éd. (Oxford: OUP, 2013), 189; et Adam Tomkins et Colin Turpin, *British Government and the Constitution – Text and Materials*, 6e éd. (Cambridge: CUP, 2010), 63.

170 *Ghaidan c. Godin-Mendoza*, [2004] 2 AC 557 (HL), par. 43 (LJ Steyn).

171 Un ministre de la couronne «peut» prendre une «mesure corrective» («remedial action») en vue d'«éliminer l'incompatibilité»: Human Rights Act 1998, c. 42, art. 10(2) et (3) (notre traduction). S'il prend une telle mesure, il doit le faire par une «ordonnance corrective» («remedial order») soumise préalablement aux deux chambres du Parlement: ibid., ann. 2 (notre traduction)..

172 *R.* c. *Secretary of State for the Home Department, ex parte Simms*, *op. cit.*, p. 131 (notre traduction).

173 *Secretary of State for the Home Department c. JJ*, [2008] 1 AC 385 (HL); *Secretary of State for the Home Department c. MB*, [2008] 1 AC 440 (HL); *Secretary of State for the Home Department c. AF*, [2010] 2 AC 269 (SC); et *Secretary of State for the Home Department c. AP*, [2011] 2 AC 1 (SC).

174 *R. c. A (No. 2)*, [2002] 1 AC 45 (HL), par. 44.

175 House of Commons, Parliamentary Debates, vol. 306 (16 février 1998), col. 778 (Jack Straw, notre traduction).

176 House of Lords, Parliamentary Debates, vol. 585 (5 février 1998), col. 778 (notre traduction).

depuis l'entrée en vigueur du Human Rights Act,[177] circonscrivant eux-mêmes l'étendue de leur pouvoir en vertu cette loi.

Conclusion

La Chambre des lords avait souligné en obiter dictum, avant l'entrée en vigueur de la loi, que le Human Rights Act préserve la souveraineté parlementaire.[178] Le Parlement a d'ailleurs critiqué le recours à l'article 3 plutôt qu'à la déclaration d'incompatibilité de l'article 4,[179] notamment dans une décision de la Chambre des lords relative à des dispositions adoptées dans le cadre de la lutte contre le terrorisme:[180] «Le régime du Human Rights Act octroie délibérément au Parlement un rôle central pour décider de la meilleure façon de protéger les droits garantis par la CEDH».[181] Les craintes liées à l'étendue du pouvoir du juge sous l'article 3 du Human Rights Act ont d'ailleurs poussé le législateur à exclure l'Illegal Migration Act 2023 de la portée de ladite disposition[182]

Si le droit constitutionnel anglais est «dominé» par le principe de la souveraineté parlementaire,[183] celle-ci «n'est plus […] absolue»,[184] a affirmé Lord Hope of Craighead en obiter dictum dans une décision de la Chambre des lords.[185] Il rappelle que le Parlement a lui-même décidé de limiter ses propres

177 Soit entre le 2 octobre 2000 et la fin juillet 2023: Parliament, Joint Committee on Human Rights, *Responding to Human Rights Judgments – Report to the Joint Committee on Human Rights on the Government's Response to Human Rights Judgments 2022–2023* (2023), 43.

178 *R. c. Director of Public Prosecutions, ex parte Kebeline*, [2000] 2 AC 326 (HL), 333 (LJ Steyn, notre traduction).

179 Parliament, Joint Committee on Human Rights, *Counter-Terrorism Policy and Human Rights (Eighth Report): Counter-Terrorism Bill – Ninth Report of Session 2007–08*, doc. HC 199/HL Paper 50 (2008), par. 47 (notre traduction).

180 *Secretary of State for the Home Department c. MB*, [2008] 1 AC 440 (HL).

181 Parliament, Joint Committee on Human Rights, *Counter-Terrorism Policy and Human Rights (Eighth Report): Counter-Terrorism Bill – Ninth Report of Session 2007–08*, doc. HC 199/HL Paper 50 (2008), par. 47 (notre traduction).

182 Illegal Migration Act 2023, c. 37, art. 1(5).

183 *Jackson* c. *Attorney General*, *op. cit.*, par. 9 (LJ Bingham of Cornhill, notre traduction).

184 *Jackson c. Attorney General*, [2006] 1 AC 262 (HL), par. 104 (LJ Hope of Craighead).

185 Cf. Tom Mullen, «Reflections on Jackson v. Attorney General: Questioning Sovereignty», *Legal Studies* 27 (2007): 1.

pouvoirs[186] en adoptant le Human Rights Act et l'European Communities Act.[187] Lord Steyn a avancé dans la même affaire que l'adoption du Human Rights Act «a créé un nouvel ordre juridique»,[188] remettant en cause le modèle classique proposé par Dicey. Les tribunaux britanniques pourraient ainsi avoir le pouvoir d'annuler une loi du Parlement si elle violait les principes constitutionnels fondamentaux.[189] L'adoption du Human Rights Act a incontestablement réduit le périmètre de la souveraineté du Parlement, mais elle (la souveraineté) demeure une limite bien réelle à la protection des droits et libertés individuels.[190]

---

186 *Jackson c. Attorney General*, [2006] 1 AC 262 (HL), par. 105. Cf. N. W. Barber, «The Afterlife of Parliamentary Sovereignty», *International Journal of Constitutional Law* 9 (2011): 144, aux p. 149–51.

187 European Communities Act 1972, c. 68.

188 Jackson c. Attorney General, [2006] 1 AC 262 (HL), par. 102.

189 La position de Lord Steyn et de Lord Hope of Craighead semble avoir été implicitement rejetée par Lord Bingham of Cornhill et Lord Carswell: Jackson c. Attorney General, [2006] 1 AC 262 (HL), par. 9 et 168.

190 «Néanmoins, la souveraineté du Parlement demeure un principe général de notre constitution», concède Lord Steyn dans ses motifs (Jackson c. Attorney General, [2006] 1 AC 262 (HL), par. 102, notre traduction, souligné dans le texte).

Emergence of Constitutional controle in Kazakhstan

Yesbol Omirzhanov[1]
Al-Farabi Kazakh National University

The article is an analysis of the evolution of constitutional controle in the Republic of Kazakhstan after the country become independent. The frame of analysys is chronological and start in part with an analysis of the first Constitutional Court of Kazakhstan (active between 1992 and 1995). Analyzing its competence, structure and activities this part ends with a case illustrating the answer of this first Constititutional Court of Kazakhstan to a constitutional crisis opposing the Executive and Legislative powers. The second part of the article examines the Second Constitutional Court of Kazakhstan: the Constitutional Council (active between 1996 and 2022). Evaluating its competence, structure and activities, this part also illustrates a significant case solved by the Constitutional Council. The third part of the paper deals with the initial period of the activity of the third Constitutional Court of Kazakhstan, established in January 2023. After analyzing its expanded competences, its structure, and activities, this part also offers an illustrative case solved by the third Constitutional Court.

The First Constitutional Court of Kazakhstan (1992–1995)

After gaining independence, Kazakhstan abandoned the planned economy and switched to a market economy. The problem of interpretation of individual laws and the Constitution itself acquired an urgent significance as an essential condition in law enforcement activities of all government bodies and subjects.[2] The corresponding institution was established by the Constitutional

---

1 The author acknowledges help from Ms. Binur Bertayeva, assistant professor of the Medical Law Chair at Asfendiyarov Kazakh National Medical University, who studies human rights protection, theory, and history of the state and law. For the present chapter, she helped in collecting data about the Constitutional Council of the Republic of Kazakhstan and in providing support for the analysis of the collected data.

2 A. Dosaeva, «Problems and Prospects for Improving the Activities of the Body of Constitutional Control on Appeals from Courts in the Republic of Kazakhstan»

Law of Kazakhstan of December 16, 1991, "On State Independence of the Republic of Kazakhstan," Article 10 of which stated that "The highest body of judicial protection of the Constitution is the Constitutional Court of the Republic."

The Constitutional Court began operating in 1992, when the laws "On the Constitutional Court of the Republic of Kazakhstan" and "On Constitutional Court Procedure" were adopted. It consisted of eleven persons,[3] including a Chairman and ten judges, and it operated from 1992 to 1995. It was the highest judicial body for the protection of Constitution, was independent of state and other bodies, officials, and public associations, and was subject only to the Constitution. It resolved cases but refrained from establishing and examining factual circumstances when they fell within the competence of other courts or bodies. Its competence consisted of control over the compliance of the normative legal acts[4] with the Constitution.[5]

(research thesis, Al-Farabi Kazakh National University, n.d.), 39,<https://www.kaznu.kz/content/files/pages/folder17928/pdf>

3 Parliament elected all the members on the proposal of the head of state through open voting for a ten-year term. At meetings of the Supreme Council committees, candidates for the posts of judges of the Constitutional Court were discussed. A candidate for the post of judge of the Constitutional Court of the Republic of Kazakhstan had to obtain the consent of the Presidium of the Supreme Council of the Republic of Kazakhstan individually. The candidate who received the majority of votes from the total number of people's deputies of the Supreme Council of Kazakhstan became the elected judge. Only a citizen of the Republic of Kazakhstan who is no younger than 35 and no older than 60 years of age, resides within the country, has a higher legal education, and has at least ten years of professional experience could become a judge of the Constitutional Court of the Republic of Kazakhstan.

4 Such normative acts are: 1) laws and other acts adopted by the Supreme Council; 2) decrees and other acts of the President; 3) resolutions of the Cabinet of Ministers; 4) regulations of ministries, state committees, and departments; 5) regulations of the Prosecutor General of the Republic of Kazakhstan, guiding clarifications of the Supreme and Higher Arbitration Courts of the Republic of Kazakhstan; 6) international treaties and other obligations of the Republic of Kazakhstan that have not entered into force. Cf. Constitutional Law of the Republic of Kazakhstan «On the Constitutional Court of the Republic of Kazakhstan», June 5, 1992, <https://online.zakon.kz/Document/?doc_id=1001172&pos=17;-40#pos=17;-40>

5 The Constitutional Court of the Republic of Kazakhstan, on the recommendation of the Supreme Council of the Republic, gave opinions on compliance by the President, Vice-President, members of the Cabinet of Ministers, the Chairman of the Supreme Court, the Chairman of the Supreme Arbitration Court, the Prosecutor General

Internal and external circumstances required drafting a new Constitution, which the Supreme Council of Kazakhstan adopted on January 28, 1993. The Constitutional Court took[6] into account almost all acts of the current legislation of that time.

From July 1992 to August 1995, the Constitutional Court considered fifteen applications on the merits concerning the protection of property rights, labor rights, the principle of the separation of powers, the activities of the Supreme Council and local councils of people's deputies, constitutional procedures for the adoption of laws, the independence of the courts, and electoral legislation.[7] The most significant and last case of the Constitutional Court was the so-called "Kvyatkovskaya Case," which initiated and implemented a mechanism of change in the country's political system. One of the candidates for deputies of the Supreme Council in the March 1994 elections, Tatyana Kvyatkovskaya, filed a lawsuit against the Central Election Commission with the Constitutional Court of Kazakhstan for violating the Election Code in

---

of the Republic, as well as diplomatic and other representatives of the Republic of Kazakhstan with the Constitution and laws of the Republic of Kazakhstan in case of raising the issue of early termination of their powers. Also, the Constitutional Court of the Republic of Kazakhstan considered cases on the constitutionality of law enforcement practices affecting citizens' constitutional rights.

6 Following the 1993 Constitution, the Constitutional Court considered the constitutionality of the laws and regulations of the Supreme Council; the normative acts of the President, the Government, ministries, state bodies, and departments; the guiding explanations of the Supreme Court, Supreme Court of Arbitration; regulations of the Attorney General. The Constitutional Court also reviewed the constitutionality of international treaties and other obligations of the Republic that had not entered into force. The Constitutional Court could be addressed by officials specified in the law and citizens entitled to initiate proceedings on matters directly affecting their constitutional rights if they were not under the jurisdiction of other courts. Also, when other courts did not apply the rules of constitutional law to be applied, when they applied the provisions of the Constitution of the Republic of Kazakhstan that were not applicable in the given case or misinterpreted the norms of constitutional law. The Constitutional Court could initiate proceedings on its initiative on the conformity to the Constitution of the Republic of laws and normative legal acts, as well as on the constitutionality of law enforcement practice affecting the constitutional rights of citizens of the Republic of Kazakhstan.

7 I. Rogov, «Constitutional Control: Affirmation of Supremacy and Direct Application of the Constitution,» in Establishment and Development of Modern Kazakh Statehood (First-Hand) (Astana: AIFC, n.d.), 229–305, <https://aifc.kz/uploads/%D0%A1%.pdf>

the Abylaikhan electoral district. Journalist T. Kvyatkovskaya, who ran in the Abylaikhan constituency of Almaty, lost by a minimal margin to the deputy head of the capital's administration. In April, she filed a claim with the Constitutional Court to invalidate the elections in her constituency. In the first stage, the claim was private and concerned violations of the electoral system exclusively in the Abylaikhan district. Many candidates for deputy declared violations, but only Kvyatkovskaya's claim was drawn up as legally correct and accepted for consideration.

The hearings began in July and lasted intermittently until February 15, 1995. During the procedure, issues related to violations in the Abylaikhan district were disjointed into a separate case and sent to a civil court. On February 15, Kvyatkovskaya demanded that the entire method of counting votes established by the Central Election Commission in its February 1, 1994 resolution be declared unconstitutional. Late in the evening of March 6, 1995, the Constitutional Court satisfied Kvyatkovskaya's claim,[8] and issues a resolution about the decision of the Central Election Commission about methods for counting votes in elections, recognizing them as inconsistent with Article 60 of the Constitution. Thus, the results of the elections of deputies to the Supreme Council and, consequently, the legitimacy of the Supreme Council itself were nullified. The official disagreements between the Head of State (the President) and the Chairman of Parliament (Supreme Council) on the matter were overcome by the required majority vote of the constitutional judges.

The Court, at the request of the President,[9] gave an explanation indicating that the recognized violations of the Constitution took place on the territory of the Republic and equally affected the constitutional rights of all citizens constituting the electorate. More importantly, the Court gave comprehensive instructions for the future. The resolution of the Court expresses the infringement of the Constitution by the last elections to the Supreme Council and, accordingly, by the powers of the elected deputies, and also

8 T. Burchilina, «History of Tatyana Kvyatkovskaya's Claim», Kommersant, March 15, 1995, <https://www.kommersant.ru/doc/104286>

9 Additional ruling of the Constitutional Court of the Republic of Kazakhstan dated March 11, 1995; S. G. Sheretov, Contemporary History of Kazakhstan (1985–2002) (Almaty: n.p., 2003), 45.

expresses that the President has the right to adopt regulatory decisions in connection with this situation.

In this case, the Constitutional Court's resolution enabled the President to act in favor of strengthening the presidential power. On March 6, 1995, the Constitutional Court of Kazakhstan declared the Supreme Council, elected on March 7, 1994, that took power on March 6, 1995, as illegitimate. On March 11, 1995, the President immediately issued a decree on the measures arising from the resolution of the Constitutional Court, that is, the dissolution of the Supreme Council.[10] After the dissolution of the Supreme Council, the successive resignations of the Cabinet of Ministers and the Central Election Commission were not long in coming. In essence, with this decision, the Constitutional Court also stopped its activities.

The Second Constitutional Court of Kazakhstan: The Constitutional Council (1996–2022)

A new Constitution was adopted on August 30, 1995, establishing another stage in the history of Constitutional interpretation, which lasted from February 1996 to June 2022. According to Article 1 of the Constitutional Law of the Republic,[11] the Constitutional Council becomes the State body responsible for ensuring the supremacy of the Constitution throughout the country.[12] By Article 4 of the Constitution, the current law of the Republic includes the Constitution, relevant laws, other normative legal acts, international

---

10 M. Suleimenov, «Constitution of the Republic of Kazakhstan: Historical Path of Development and Change», <https://online.zakon.kz/Document/?doc_id=33590347&pos=6;-106#pos=6;-106>

11 Constitutional Law of the Republic of Kazakhstan of December 29, 1995, «On the Constitutional Council of the Republic of Kazakhstan», <https://online.zakon.kz/Document/?doc_id=1004022&pos=2;-106#pos=2;-106>

12 1) In the exercise of its powers, it is independent and self-sufficient from state bodies, organizations, officials, and citizens; it is subject only to the Constitution of the Republic and cannot be based on political or other motives; 2) Exercise its powers by the Constitution of the Republic and the Constitutional Law, refraining from establishing and investigating other issues whenever this is within the competence of the courts or other state bodies. 2) Exercise its powers by the Constitution of the Republic and the Constitutional Law, refraining from establishing and investigating other issues whenever this is within the competence of the courts or other State bodies.

treaties, and other obligations of the Republic of Kazakhstan, as well as normative decisions of the Constitutional Council and the Supreme Court. The Resolution of the Constitutional Council of the Republic of Kazakhstan of October 28, 1996, No. 6, interpreted Article 4 content[13] and confirmed that normative interpretative decisions of the Constitutional Council and the Supreme Court were part of the current law.

The Constitutional Council of the Republic of Kazakhstan was an autonomous state organ that was not part of the judicial system. It has monitored the compliance of the existing law with the Constitution by exercising preliminary and subsequent constitutional control. Constitutional proceedings could be instituted only upon the request of a limited number of subjects: the President, the Prime Minister, the Chairmen of the Chambers of Parliament, and at least one-fifth of the total number of deputies to Parliament and courts.

The Constitutional Council exercised its powers with independence, autonomy, objectivity, irremovability, collegiality and submission only to the Constitution. In the creation of the Constitutional Council, in determining its legal status and competence, there was an orientation towards the experience of France, where a similar institution has been functioning since 1958. However, there are significant differences between them, particularly regarding the formation of these bodies. Thus, the term of office of the members of the Constitutional Council of France is longer than that of their colleagues in Kazakhstan, and it is nine years, with one-third of its composition being

---

[13] The Resolution of the Constitutional Council of the Republic of Kazakhstan of October 28, 1996, No. 6 states that the current law of the Republic of Kazakhstan is considered the system of norms contained in normative legal acts adopted by authorized bodies in the prescribed manner: the Constitution and the laws of the Republic corresponding to it, Presidential decrees, resolutions of the Parliament, its chambers and the Government of the Republic, other normative legal acts, international treaties ratified by the Republic of Kazakhstan, normative resolutions of the Constitutional Council and the Supreme Court of the country. Collection of Normative Decisions of the Constitutional Council of the Republic of Kazakhstan, 4th ed., ed. K. Mami (Nur-Sultan: n.p., 2019), 518, <https://www.gov.kz/uploads/2021/7/15/18ac3c37bd4f6e966367d494079a7355_original.4739382.pdf>

renewed every three years. The number of members of the French Council is much more significant: not six councilors as in Kazakhstan, but nine.[14]

According to article 72 of the Constitution of the Republic of Kazakhstan, the Constitutional Council on the application of the President of the Republic of Kazakhstan, the Chairman of the Senate, the Chairman of the Majilis, at least one-fifth of the total number of deputies of the Parliament and the Prime Minister have specific constitutional competences.[15] If a judiciary Court finds that a law or other normative legal act to be applied infringes[16] the human and civil rights and freedoms enshrined in the Constitution, it is obliged to suspend proceedings in the case and to apply to the Constitutional Council for a declaration of unconstitutionality.[17] Decisions of the Constitutional

14 In France, three councilors are appointed by the President of the Republic (he appoints the President of the Constitutional Council from among its members), three by the President of the National Assembly, and three by the President of the Senate. Cf. J. Ostapovich, «Formation of the Constitutional Council of the Republic of Kazakhstan, Its Constitutional and Legal Foundations», Bulletin of Tomsk State University 341 (2010): 123.

15 It is competent to: 1) Resolve the issue of whether the election of the President of the Republic, deputies of the Parliament, and the conduct of the republican referendum were correct in case of dispute; 2) Review laws passed by Parliament to ensure compliance with the Constitution of the Republic before signing them by the President; 2-1) Consider the conformity of the Constitution of the Republic with the resolutions adopted by Parliament and its chambers; 3) The international treaties of the Republic were considered to be following the Constitution before ratification; 4) Officially interpret the Constitution; 5) In case of early dismissal of the President in case of persistent inability to perform his duties due to illness, the Constitutional Council could give an opinion on the observance of established constitutional procedures. Furthermore, the Constitutional Council provided its opinion regarding the adherence to established constitutional procedures in the case of a charge of high treason against the President. The Constitutional Council considered appeals from the President of the Republic in cases where the President submits an application to the Constitutional Council for consideration of a law or other legal act that has entered into force for conformity with the Constitution of the Republic.

16 According to Article 78 of the Constitution of the Republic of Kazakhstan, the Court is obliged to apply to the Constitutional Council with representation if it finds that a law or other regulatory legal act to be applied infringes on the rights and freedoms of people and citizens enshrined in the Constitution.

17 The Constitution of the Republic of Kazakhstan (adopted by Republican Referendum on August 30, 1995) (with amendments and additions as of March 10, 2017), https://online.zakon.kz/Document/?doc_id=39732256&pos=6;-106#pos=6;-106.

Council took effect on the day of their adoption, were generally binding throughout the territory of the Republic, final, and not subject to appeal.

Only the President of the Republic has the right to object to the decision of the Constitutional Council. This right was derived from his legal status as a symbol and guarantor of the Constitution's inviolability, human and civil rights, and freedoms. The objection did not mean the annulment of the decision of the Constitutional Council but was only an occasion for reconsidering the issue. The Council's decision remains valid if two-thirds of the total number of members of the Constitutional Council overcome the President's objections. If this quorum did not meet the President's objection, the decision of the Constitutional Council was considered rejected. Over the years, the President has submitted three objections to the decisions of the Constitutional Council, and only one decision has partially overcome his objections.

One of the tasks of the Constitutional Council was to prepare annual messages on the state of constitutional legality in the Republic. In this document, based on the complaints examined, the Constitutional Council analyzed existing legislation and its implementation in terms of its conformity with the Constitution. According to the Constitution, such messages were heard at a joint session of the Chambers of Parliament so that their "addressee" was primarily the highest representative body of the Republic, the Parliament. The text of the message was also submitted to the President of the Republic.[18]

The legal positions of the normative decisions of the Constitutional Council were determined based on a systematic and deep doctrinal legal analysis of the constitutional norms in their relation to the general provisions and principles of the Constitution. Authorized state bodies and officials considered recommendations for improvement of legislation contained in decisions of the Constitutional Council with mandatory notification of the Constitutional Council on the adopted decision. Specific authors offer the following classification of decisions of the Constitutional Council:

---

18 In addition, the Constitutional Law «On the Constitutional Council of the Republic of Kazakhstan» established that the Chairman of the Constitutional Council shall, at the request of the President of the Republic, provide him with information on the state of constitutional legality in the country. See Abstracts of the speech of the Chairman of the Constitutional Council of the Republic of Kazakhstan by I. Rogov at the II World Conference on Constitutional Justice «Separation of Powers and Independence of Constitutional Courts and Equivalent Bodies», Brazil, 16–18 January 2011, <https://www.venice.coe.int/WCCJ/Rio/Papers/KAZ_Rogov_RUS.pdf>

- Decisions on building a democratic, secular, legal, social, sovereign and unitary state with a presidential form of government.
- Decisions on strengthening the mechanism for ensuring, guaranteeing, and protecting human and civil rights and freedoms.
- Decisions on the development of the economic base of the Republic of Kazakhstan.
- Decisions on strengthening the status of the state language.
- Decisions on strengthening the status of state symbols of the Republic.[19]

Since February 1996, the Constitutional Council has received more than 200 appeals: from the President – 27, from the Chairmen of the Chambers of Parliament and its deputies – 77, from the Prime Minister – 27, and from Courts – 71. The Constitutional Council also adopted more than 140 normative resolutions.[20] The Constitutional Council gave formal interpretations of the Constitution, opinions on draft amendments and additions to the Constitution and considerations of laws and international treaties for conformity with the Constitution. All its binding decisions developed a progressive constitutional and legal doctrine and a creative understanding of the legal institutions. However, there are some critical opinions regarding the Constitutional Council's nature. According to some authors, the Kazakhstani Constitutional Council resembles an office of Presidential Administration, while its Tajikistani and Uzbekistani counterparts work more like redundant part-time interpreters of statutes and occasional enforcers of authoritarian rule by law.[21] This opinion about the Constitutional Council was formed because it (the Council) supported the idea of extending President Nursultan

19 D. Baymakhanova and others, «Specifics of Decisions of the Constitutional Council of the Republic of Kazakhstan That Affect the Foundations of the Constitutional System,» *Journal of Actual Problems of Jurisprudence* 93, no. 1 (2020): 60–68, <https://doi.org/10.26577/JAPJ.2020.v93.i1.06>

20 The Message of the Constitutional Council of the Republic of Kazakhstan «About the State of Constitutional Legality in the Republic of Kazakhstan» (Nur-Sultan, June 20, 2022), <https://online.zakon.kz/Document/?doc_id=39370279&pos=3;-88#pos=3;-88>

21 A. Trochev and A. Juzgenbayev, «Instrumentalization of Constitutional Law in Central Asia», in *Research Handbook on Central Asian Law*, ed. R. Abazov et al. (Cheltenham: Edward Elgar Publishing, 2023), 159–78, <https://doi.org/10.4337/9781800378346.00014>

Nazarbayev's powers and recognized the President's exclusive right to call early presidential elections individually.

Although the Constitutional Council has never been critical of the decisions of the contemporary state powers, adequate decisions have been made on specific requests. In matters related to the protection of human rights, the Constitutional Council adopted many viable Resolutions.

For example, on September 14, 1998, the Constitutional Council received a submission from the Zhambyl Regional Court to recognize the Regulations on the procedure for compensation for damage caused to a citizen by illegal actions of the bodies of inquiry, preliminary investigation, prosecutor's office and court, approved by the Decree of the Presidium of the Supreme Council of the USSR from May 18, 1981 (hereinafter Regulations), not in compliance with the Constitution of the Republic of Kazakhstan and not valid on the territory of Kazakhstan.

Having studied the available materials on the appeal, the Constitutional Council found that the submission of the Zhambyl Regional Court could not be satisfied. The Zhambyl Regional Court motivates its submission by the fact that the Regulation, in contrast to Article 9 of the Civil Code and Articles 41-44 of the Criminal Procedure Code of the Republic of Kazakhstan, does not provide for the possibility of compensation for moral damage to persons who suffered from the illegal actions of the mentioned bodies. Indeed, the Regulations do not contain a rule that would provide for compensation for moral damage. But this does not deprive a citizen of the right to demand compensation for this type of harm, since such a right is recognized for him by Article 14 of the Civil Code of the Republic of Kazakhstan (General Part), entered into force on March 1, 1995, and Articles 41-44 of the Criminal Procedure Code of the Republic, entered in force from January 1, 1998. Which of the named acts should be applied cannot arise imediately: according to paragraph two of the Resolution of the Supreme Council of the Republic of Kazakhstan dated December 16, 1991, "On the procedure for enacting the constitutional law of the Republic of Kazakhstan On State Independence of the Republic of Kazakhstan," the norms of USSR legislation can be applied on the territory of the Republic of Kazakhstan, since they do not contradict this constitutional law, other legislative and regulatory acts of the Republic of Kazakhstan.

Thus, the assertion of the Zhambyl Regional Court that the Regulations from May 18, 1981 infringes on the rights and freedoms of individuals and citizen enshrined in the Constitution, in particular, deprives him of the right to judicial protection provided for in Article 13 of the Constitution of the Republic of Kazakhstan, is untenable. Any person who has suffered moral damage, including by illegal actions of the bodies of inquiry, preliminary investigation, prosecutor's office and court, is entitled to file a claim to court for compensation for such damage on the basis of the relevant norms of of the Civil Code (General part) and the Criminal Procedure Code of the Republic of Kazakhstan, as well as the norms of the Fundamentals of Civil Legislation of the USSR and Soviet Republics dated May 31, 1991, which, in accordance with the resolution of the Supreme Council of the Republic of Kazakhstan dated January 30, 1993 are applied temporarily, until the adoption of a special part Civil Code of the Republic of Kazakhstan.

The absence in the Regulations of norms providing for compensation for moral damage, is not an obstacle to filing such claims in court, since priority in application, according to the resolution of the Supreme Council of the Republic of Kazakhstan dated December 16, 1991, "On the procedure for enacting the constitutional law of the Republic of Kazakhstan on state independence of the Republic of Kazakhstan," belongs to the above-mentioned codes of the Republic of Kazakhstan, as well as the Fundamentals of civil legislation of the USSR and Soviet Republics in view of the authorization of the temporary application of the law of the former USSR by the resolution of the Supreme Council of the Republic of Kazakhstan dated January 30, 1993 "On the regulation of civil legal relations during the period of economic reform."

Under the above circumstances, there is no reason to assert that the Regulation infringes on the rights and freedoms of individuals and citizen enshrined in the Constitution, in particular, it deprives them of the constitutional right to judicial protection. In terms of compensation for moral damage, the Regulation challenged in the submission of the Zhambyl Regional Court for the reasons stated above is not subject to application. The submission of the Zhambyl Regional Court to recognize the Regulations as inconsistent with the Constitution of the Republic cannot be satisfied for the following reasons.

The Zhambyl Regional Court sees the inconsistency of the Regulations with the Constitution of the Republic of Kazakhstan in the fact that this Regulation does not provide for the possibility of compensation for moral damage. But in this normative act there is no specific legal norm that would directly prohibit compensation for moral damage, and which could be recognized as infringing on the right of a citizen to demand compensation for moral damage.

There is also no reason to recognize the Regulation as a whole as unconstitutional. In the submission of the Zhambyl Regional Court, no other arguments are given about the unconstitutionality of the said Regulation, except for the absence of a norm in it on compensation for moral damage. In the final part of its submission, the Zhambyl Regional Court asks to recognize the Regulations as inconsistent with the Constitution and ineffective on the territory of Kazakhstan in connection with the adoption of the new Criminal Procedure Code of the Republic of Kazakhstan.

The Constitutional Council finds this requirement of the regional court to be unfounded: recognition of the act as invalid ("ineffective") in connection with the adoption of a new normative legal act is not within the competence of the Constitutional Council and is carried out in the manner established by the Law of the Republic of Kazakhstan "On normative legal acts." The General Prosecutor's Office of the Republic of Kazakhstan, considers, with reference to the Decree of the Government of the Republic of Kazakhstan dated January 14, 1997 No. 64 "On work to further improve acts," that the Regulations dated May 18, 1981 have lost legal force.

The Supreme Court of the Republic, on the contrary, proceeds from the fact that this Regulation retains legal force and can be used in judicial practice. If courts and other government bodies, due to the absence of a normative act of similar content in the Republic of Kazakhstan, temporarily apply the act in question in compliance with the requirements set out in paragraph 2 of the Resolution of the Supreme Council of the Republic of Kazakhstan dated December 16, 1991, "On the procedure for enacting the constitutional law of the Republic of Kazakhstan On State independence of the Republic of Kazakhstan," then the issue of recognizing it as invalid (lost in force on the territory of the Republic of Kazakhstan) can be resolved only after Kazakhstan has adopted its own act of this kind and purpose. If the normative act in question has truly lost force, then the courts should not apply it. The current legislation of the Republic of Kazakhstan does not include within the competence of the Constitutional Council the verification of the constitutionality of acts that have lost legal force. Thus, the Constitutional Council has shown that it is always acting to protect human rights.

The third Constitutional Court of Kazakhstan (after 2023)

A new stage in the history of the interpretation of law in Kazakhstan begins in June 2022. A new package of reforms was presented by the President of the Republic, K.K. Tokayev, on March 16, 2022, in his Address to the Nation, «New Kazakhstan: A Way of Renewal and Modernization», and concretized in the National Plan of Measures for its Implementation. The goals set in the Address and the determined political and legal resources of systemic reforms are aimed at further strengthening constitutionalism, a new model of formation and interaction of power institutions, and the creation of a new political culture.[22]

After the amendments to the Constitution adopted at the Republican referendum on May 6, 2022, the Constitutional Council was abolished, and a new Constitutional Court was created instead.

According to paragraph 4, Article 72 of the Constitution, the Constitutional Court gives an official interpretation of the norms of the Constitution at the request of the President of the Republic of Kazakhstan, the Chairman of the Senate, the Chairman of the Mazhilis, at least one-fifth of the total number of deputies of the Parliament, and the Prime Minister.

On January 1, 2023, the Constitutional Court of the Republic of Kazakhstan began to function. The Law "On the Constitutional Court of the Republic of Kazakhstan" was adopted in this respect. The Law regulates the formation and organization of activity of the Constitutional Court, the competence of the Constitutional Court,[23] and the procedure of constitutional proceedings,

22 Address of the Head of State Kassym-Zhomart Tokayev to the Nation of Kazakhstan, March 16, 2022, <https://www.akorda.kz/ru/poslanie-glavy-gosudarstva-kasym-zhomarta-tokaeva-narodu-kazahstana-1623953>

23 According to Constitutional Law on Constitutional Court, in case of a dispute, the issue of the correctness of holding elections of the President of the Republic, deputies of the Parliament, and holding a republican referendum shall decide on the propriety of conducting: 1) Elections of the President of the Republic of Kazakhstan; 2) Elections

including consideration of citizens' appeals. The Constitutional Court[24] received all the powers of the former Constitutional Council. As before, the Constitutional Court is not part of the judicial system and does not belong to the courts of general jurisdiction.[25] The Constitutional Court comprises eleven judges, including the Chairman and his deputy.[26] According to Article

of deputies of the Parliament of the Republic of Kazakhstan; 3) Republican referendum. The Constitutional Court shall consider compliance with the Constitution of the Republic of Kazakhstan: 1) Prior to signing by the President of the Republic of Kazakhstan, the laws adopted by the Parliament of the Republic of Kazakhstan; 2) Resolutions adopted by the Parliament of the Republic of Kazakhstan and its Chambers; 3) International treaties of the Republic of Kazakhstan before their ratification. The Constitutional Court shall provide the following: 1) Official interpretation of the rules of the Constitution of the Republic of Kazakhstan; 2) Before adoption by the Parliament of the Republic of Kazakhstan, respectively, the decision on early dismissal of the President of the Republic of Kazakhstan, the final decision on dismissal of the President of the Republic of Kazakhstan – a conclusion on compliance with the established constitutional procedures.

24 The Constitutional Court: 1) Based on the results of the generalization of the constitutional proceedings practice, annually shall direct a message to the Parliament of the Republic of Kazakhstan on the state of constitutional legality in the Republic of Kazakhstan; 2) Shall consider requests of the President of the Republic of Kazakhstan, as well as requests of courts; 3) At the request of citizens, shall consider for compliance with the Constitution of the Republic of Kazakhstan the regulatory legal acts of the Republic of Kazakhstan that directly affect their rights and freedoms enshrined in the Constitution of the Republic of Kazakhstan; 4) Shall consider requests of the Prosecutor General of the Republic of Kazakhstan; 5) Should applications for the Commissioner for Human Rights in the Republic of Kazakhstan; 6) Shall decide exclusively on issues of law and shall not assess the actual circumstances that gave rise to the application; 7) Also, the Constitutional Court has the right to require and receive documents, materials, and other information from all state bodies and organizations and also to involve, by the established procedure, experts (specialists) for expert and research advisory work (on such requests, the necessary documents and other information must be provided within fifteen working days, unless otherwise specified by the Constitutional Court); 8) Shall exercise other powers established by this Constitutional Law.

25 Main Questions Regarding the Activities of the Constitutional Court (B. Nurmukhanov, Deputy Chairman of the Constitutional Court), <https://online.zakon.kz/Document/?doc_id=39777476>

26 The Chairman of the Constitutional Court shall be appointed by the President of the Republic of Kazakhstan with the consent of the Senate of the Parliament of the Republic of Kazakhstan. The deputy chairman of the Constitutional Court shall be appointed by the President of the Republic of Kazakhstan on the proposal of the

58 of Constitutional Law on Constitutional Court, the Constitutional Court shall make decisions collegially.[27]

The main difference between the Constitutional Court and the Constitutional Council is that citizens have direct access to the Constitutional Court. In other words, for the Constitutional Council, which has been in operation for almost 27 years, citizens could not directly address this body and challenge the constitutionality of laws and other regulations that affect their rights and freedoms as enshrined in the Constitution. Now, they have this opportunity. Citizens can appeal to the Constitutional Court after exhausting all other legal remedies. It is an additional tool for protecting their rights when they have failed to protect them in other ways.

Article 45 of the Constitutional Law establishes the procedure and conditions for citizens' appeals to the Constitutional Court. Citizens may challenge laws and other normative legal acts directly affecting their rights and freedoms before the Constitutional Court. In order to apply to the Constitutional Court, they must meet the following conditions: Firstly, this normative legal act must affect the rights of the person in a particular life situation. With the

---

Chairman of the Constitutional Court from among the judges of the Constitutional Court. Four judges of the Constitutional Court shall be appointed by the President of the Republic of Kazakhstan, three judges of the Constitutional Court shall be appointed by the Senate and the Mazhilis of the Parliament of the Republic of Kazakhstan on the proposal of the Chairmen of the Chambers of the Parliament of the Republic of Kazakhstan.

27 The Constitutional Court shall adopt a decision by a majority of votes of the judges participating in the session by open voting, except in the case provided for in paragraph 3 of Article 25 of this Constitutional Law. In the event of a tie in the Constitutional Court judges' votes at decision-making, the vote of the Constitutional Court Chairman, who in all cases is the last to cast his vote, shall be decisive. If the corresponding Constitutional Court judge replaces the Constitutional Court Chairman in his authority, this rule shall not apply. In this event, a second vote shall be held with the participation of the Chairman or the Constitutional Court judge who did not participate in the first vote. During the Constitutional Court session, none of its judges participating in the session shall be entitled to abstention from or non-participation in the vote. Decisions adopted by the Constitutional Court before the Chairman signs them shall be first signed by the judges who took part in the voting. The judge of the Constitutional Court who disagrees with its final decision shall be entitled to state his opinion in writing, which shall be attached to the constitutional proceedings materials. The Constitutional Court judge shall not be entitled to publish his dissenting opinion or publicly refer to it.

application of the act, a court decision must be rendered and has become enforceable. The following condition is that the application must be filed within one year of the court decision in the case. The Constitutional Law establishes such a time limit. There are exceptions to these general conditions. If the rule of law is categorical, it does not allow for different interpretations of the law, expressly prescribes specific actions by the citizen, then the citizen may apply to the Constitutional Court without prior recourse to the judicial authorities.[28]

Many citizens applied to the new Constitutional Court, and in just six months, eighteen cases had been considered with a final decision. Of these, fourteen have been petitioned by citizens, two by the President, one by deputies, and one by the Deputy Prime Minister for interpretation of the previously issued decision of the Constitutional Council. The most frequently contested rules were the Code of Criminal Procedure (three applications) and the Code of Administrative Offences (two applications). According to the Constitutional Court, 44% of the legal provisions considered were constitutional, 19 percent were unconstitutional, and 37% were found by the Court to be constitutional but interpreted by the Constitutional Court.[29] That shows the Constitutional Court's effectiveness and citizens' trust in this institution.

The new Constitutional Court's activities provide one more example. The Court considered A. Auganbaev's appeal in an open session about compliance with the Constitution of the Republic of Kazakhstan, part two of Article 80 of the Criminal Procedure Code of July 4, 2014. From the appeal and the materials presented, it follows that during the criminal prosecution, the prosecution used the opinion of specialists, including current employees of the prosecutor's office, as evidence. The Court of First Instance recognized the expert opinion as unacceptable evidence and issued an acquittal. Subsequently, the appellate Court overturned the acquittal and found the subject of the appeal guilty of committing the crime charged against him. According to A. Auganbaev, part two of Article 80 of the Code of Criminal Procedure, which allows for the involvement of an employee of an authorized

28 Main Questions Regarding the Activities of the Constitutional Court (B. Nurmukhanov, Deputy Chairman of the Constitutional Court), <https://online.zakon.kz/Document/?doc_id=39777476>

29 O. Bassarova, «Three Thousand Kazakhstanis Appealed to the Constitutional Court», Kursiv, July 11, 2023, <https://kz.kursiv.media/2023-07-11/lsbs-ksobracdheniya/?>

unit of a law enforcement or particular government body of the Republic of Kazakhstan as a specialist to conduct research and give an opinion, does not comply with the Constitution.

The Constitutional Court of the Republic of Kazakhstan, after a complete study of the case and analysis of the current legislation, decided to recognize part two of Article 80 of the Criminal Procedure Code of the Republic of Kazakhstan by the Constitution of the Republic of Kazakhstan in the following interpretation:

The involvement as a specialist of an employee of an authorized unit of a law enforcement or particular government agency of the Republic of Kazakhstan is permissible if this employee is a person not interested in the case, has unique knowledge and special competence necessary to assist in the collection, research, and assessment of the evidence. The functional purpose of such a unit should be to conduct research based on employees' unique knowledge and special competence without exercising higher supervision over compliance with the rule of law on the territory of the Republic of Kazakhstan, pre-trial investigation, and maintaining state prosecution in Court.

Court and other law enforcement bodies' decisions based on a different interpretation of part two of Article 80 of the Criminal Procedure Code of the Republic of Kazakhstan and leading to the infringement of the rights and freedoms of man and citizen enshrined in the Constitution are not subject to execution. They must be reviewed in the prescribed manner.

The Government of the Republic of Kazakhstan, no later than six months after the publication of this regulatory resolution, must submit to the Mazhilis of the Parliament of the Republic of Kazakhstan a draft law aimed at improving the legal regulation of the procedure for attracting specialists in criminal proceedings, taking into account the legal positions of the Constitutional Court of the Republic of Kazakhstan set out in this regulatory resolution.

Such examples show the need for the Constitutional Court to protect citizens' constitutional rights and freedoms, ensure the balance of powers, and prevent violations of the legal order. Thus, Kazakhstan returned to a model of interpretation created during the independence period. During the Constitutional Council's functioning period, a good model of law interpretation was formed. The future use by the Constitutional Court of the experience previously gained by the Constitutional Council will contribute to an effective strengthening of constitutionalism and constitutional legality in Kazakhstan.

According to Rogov, former Chairman of the Constitutional Council of the Republic of Kazakhstan, the name of the body of constitutional control does not matter – the Court or the Council. It is essential to know the powers, independence and competence of staff. That is all that matters.[30] Therefore, we hope for the integrity of the members of the Constitutional Court in matters related to the protection of human rights and compliance with the principle of the legitimacy of state power.

In our opinion, the Constitutional Court will ensure the implementation of the principle of separation of powers, the continuity and irreversibility of the constitutional process and the responsibility of public authorities to society and the people. The Constitutional Court will also allow citizens, political parties and public associations to defend their violated rights by directly appealing to them.

---

30 T. Nurseitova, "Which Path Will the Constitutional Justice of Kazakhstan Take?" <https://online.zakon.kz/Document/?doc_id=33205159&pos=5;-108#pos=5;-108>

PART III

On the border between Legal Orders: National Judges Applying International aw

Les juges nationaux face à la Convention relative au contrat de transport international de Marchandises par Route (CMR)

Sandie Calme
Barreau de Paris

La Convention relative au contrat de transport international de marchandises par route (CMR) est une règlementation économique de l'espace économique paneuropéen en portant sur une activité commerciale séculaire. C'est une norme de droit transnational dont se saisissent les juges nationaux des Etats concernés en ayant à cœur leur propres conceptions du droit, dès lors qu'un litige relève de sa portée. Conceptuellement, la Convention CMR crée les conditions d'un foisonnement régulé de jurisprudences nationales, et en réponse, les juges nationaux, souvent eux-mêmes rompus à l'exercice du droit comparé, prompts à garantir la qualité de leurs décisions, participent à l'harmonisation du droit. A l'appel de ce texte d'actualité et d'avenir, les juges nationaux dessinent ensemble les contours d'une matière sans cesse renouvelée en y apportant chacun l'originalité de leur approche.

La CMR : Une base juridique qui appelle à l'interprétation des juges nationaux

Genèse et structure de la CMR

La Convention relative au contrat de transport international de marchandises par route est le fruit d'une réflexion commune[1] entre parties prenantes de plusieurs Etats, qui prend notamment sa source dans les travaux de la Commission économique pour l'Europe des Nations Unies. Parmi les nombreux acteurs qui ont contribué à l'avènement de cette convention de droit uniforme, on compte l'Institut international pour l'unification du droit privé

---

1 Voir Roland Loewe, «Note explicative sur la Convention au contrat de transport international de marchandises par route (CMR) du 19 mai 1956», in *Droit européen des transports* (1976): 407–501.

(Unidroit), la Chambre de commerce internationale, l'Union internationale des transports routiers, l'Office central des transports internationaux par chemins de fer (OCTI), l'Union internationale des chemins de fer (UIC), ou encore l'Union internationale d'assurance transports.

L'idée d'un droit commun à plusieurs Etats pour agencer l'organisation juridique d'une activité économique transnationale est également à la source de cette convention, qui aspire à un certain degré d'uniformité tout en demeurant sectorielle. C'est dans cet esprit qu'au lendemain de la seconde guerre mondiale, l'idée de cette convention internationale pacifiante dédiée au secteur des transports routiers internationaux a pu voir le jour.

Le préambule de la Convention CMR fait état de ce que les parties contractantes ont reconnu « l'utilité de régler d'une manière uniforme les conditions du contrat de transport international de marchandises par route, particulièrement en ce qui concerne les documents utilisés pour ce transport et la responsabilité du transporteur ». Ce sont donc ces aspects de l'activité de transport international routier de marchandises qui sont au cœur de cette convention sectorielle. Ouverte à la signature le 19 mai 1956 et signée ce même jour par l'Autriche, la France, le Luxembourg, les Pays-Bas, la Pologne, la République Fédérale d'Allemagne, la Suède, la Suisse et la Yougoslavie, la Convention CMR est entrée en vigueur, par le dépôt des instruments de ratification de cinq premiers Etats – l'Autriche, la France, l'Italie, les Pays-Bas et la Yougoslavie – en date du 2 juillet 1961, avec une célérité qui démontre son caractère consensuel.

La convention CMR est bâtie selon une structure classique. Après un court préambule, un chapitre I délimite son champ d'application en deux articles. Un chapitre II se compose d'un seul article 3 déterminant les personnes dont le transporteur routier international de marchandises doit répondre. Un chapitre III sur la conclusion et l'exécution du contrat de transport s'étend des articles 4 à 16. Le chapitre IV sur la responsabilité du transporteur s"étend des articles 17 à 29. Le chapitre V (articles 30 à 33) détaille certaines modalités des réclamations et actions. Les articles 34 à 40 (chapitre VI) portent sur les transports effectués par plusieurs transporteurs successifs. Un seul article 41 compose le chapitre VII délimitant la nullité des dispositions contraires à la convention CMR. Le chapitre VIII comporte des dispositions finales sur des questions classiques relatives aux relations entre Etats parties telles que l'entrée en vigueur, l'adhésion, la dénonciation, la révision, les différends entre Etats, les déclarations et réserves étatiques (articles 42 à 51).

Champ d'application

Champ d'application matériel

La Convention CMR est centrée sur aspects du transport international routier de marchandises, orientée sur les thèmes du contrat de transport, des documents de transport et de la responsabilité du transporteur. Son champ d'application matériel est ainsi relativement restreint. L'article 1er alinéa 1er de la Convention CMR prévoit qu'elle «s'applique à tout contrat de transport de marchandises par route à titre onéreux au moyen de véhicules, lorsque le lieu de la prise en charge de la marchandise et le lieu prévu pour la livraison, tels qu'ils sont indiqués au contrat, sont situés dans deux pays différents dont l'un au moins est un pays contractant», «quels que soient le domicile et la nationalité des parties». Il est prévu qu'elle «s'applique même si les transports rentrant dans son champ d'application sont effectués par des États ou par des institutions ou organisations gouvernementales» (article 1er alinéa 3).

L'alinéa 2 de l'article 1er, pour définir le terme de véhicules au sens de la Convention CMR, fait expressément référence à l'article 4 de la Convention sur la circulation routière du 19 septembre 1949, les automobiles, véhicules articulés, remorques et semi-remorques définis par cet article 4 étant des véhicules au sens de la Convention CMR.[2] Force est de constater que certains termes de la définition du champ d'application matériel de la Convention

2 La Convention sur la circulation routière du 19 septembre 1949 définit les automobiles comme des «véhicules pourvus d'un dispositif mécanique de propulsion circulant sur la route par leurs moyens propres, autres que ceux qui se déplacent sur rails ou sont reliés à un conducteur électrique, et servant normalement au transport de personnes ou de marchandises», sous réserve de l'annexe 1, les véhicules articulés étant des automobiles suivies «d'une remorque sans essieu avant, accouplée de telle manière qu'une partie de la remorque repose sur le véhicule tracteur et qu'une partie appréciable du poids de cette remorque et de son chargement soit supportée par le tracteur, une telle remorque est dénommée 'semi-remorque',» les remorques étant des véhicules destinés «à être attelé à une automobile.»

CMR, tel que présenté en son article 1er alinéa 1er, ne font pas l'objet d'une définition au sein de cette convention.

Outre la définition de son champ d'application matériel général, la Convention CMR vient préciser, en son article 1er alinéa 4, les types de transports routiers internationaux de marchandises auxquels elle entend ne pas s"appliquer: les transports postaux régis par les conventions postales internationales, les transports funéraires et les transports de déménagement. Alors que l'article 1 alinéa 5 de la Convention CMR pose le principe de son application impérative dès lors que les conditions d'applications matérielles qu'elle fixe sont remplies, il autorise les Parties contractantes à déroger, par des accords bilatéraux ou multilatéraux, à son application, pour leur trafic frontalier ou pour permettre l'emploi de la lettre de voiture représentant la marchandise quant aux transports empruntant exclusivement le territoire de ces Parties contractantes.

En son article 2, la Convention CMR porte une attention particulière à la question de l'articulation entre plusieurs modes de transport. Ainsi, elle prévoit de s'appliquer si le véhicule de transport des marchandises fait l'objet d'un transport maritime, ferroviaire, fluvial ou aérien sur une partie du parcours sans rupture de charge, sauf le cas exceptionnel de dérogation prévu en son article 14 qui peut conduire à emprunter un autre mode de transport par nécessité, mais avec une dérogation restrictive.[3]

Il y a donc ici possibilité d'application par le juge d'un autre droit que celui de la Convention CMR pour la responsabilité du transporteur routier dans des cas limités mais pour lesquels le juge devra rechercher les dispositions impératives de la loi applicable. Il est précisé que s'il s'avère que de telles dispositions impératives sont inexistantes, on en revient à appliquer la Convention CMR. Ces dispositions quant à l'articulation des modes de

---

3 S'il «est prouvé qu'une perte, une avarie ou un retard à la livraison de la marchandise qui est survenu au cours du transport par l'un des modes de transport autre que la route n'a pas été causé par un acte ou une omission du transporteur routier et qu'il provient d'un fait qui n'a pu se produire qu'au cours et en raison du transport non routier, la responsabilité du transporteur routier est déterminée non par la présente Convention, mais de la façon dont la responsabilité du transporteur non routier eût été déterminée si un contrat de transport avait été conclu entre l'expéditeur et le transporteur non routier pour le seul transport de la marchandise conformément aux dispositions impératives de la loi concernant le transport de marchandises par le mode de transport autre que la route.»

transport sur la responsabilité du transporteur s'appliquent également si le transporteur routier est également le transporteur non routier, «comme si sa fonction de transporteur routier et sa fonction de transporteur non routier étaient exercées par deux personnes différentes» (article 2 alinéa 2).

Champ d'application géographique et réserves

La Convention CMR, signée par neuf Parties contractantes, en compte cinquante-huit, qui sont toutes des Etats, le dernier en date étant l'Afghanistan, qui y a adhéré le 7 octobre 2020. Du fait du caractère technique de l'activité de transport international routier de marchandises, la Convention CMR couvre une forme de réseau routier international pourvu d'une certaine cohésion qui concerne particulièrement le continent européen et s'étend au-delà des contours de l'Union européenne.

Si l'Union européenne[4] partage une compétence avec les Etats membres pour ce qui concerne le domaine des transports, qui fait l'objet de politique européenne des transports, alors que l'ensemble des Etats membres de l'Union européenne intègrent au sein de leurs droits des transports les dispositions de la Convention CMR, la teneur de cette convention internationale n'a pas amené l'Union européenne à choisir de s'y associer en tant que Partie contractante.[5]

Il n'en demeure pas moins que cette convention, issue de l'initiative de la Commission économique pour l'Europe des Nations Unies, relève d'un projet européen et transnational de régulation du secteur des transports routiers internationaux de marchandises.Dans les faits, on ne retrouve pas de jurisprudence particulière de la Cour Internationale de Justice concernant la Convention CMR. Les divergences se retrouvent dans le cadre d'autres décisions de justice émises par des autorités transnationales pour des différends interétatiques,

4 Traditionnellement, en qualité d'organisation régionale d'intégration économique, l'Union européenne adhère fréquemment aux conventions internationales présentant un intérêt pour l'Union européenne, comme par exemple la Convention de Montréal pour l'unification de certaines règles relatives au transport aérien international ou la Convention relative aux transports internationaux ferroviaires.

5 Alors que le texte même de cette convention ne prévoit pas expressément un projet d'adhésion pour organisations d'intégration économique régionale, ce qui est certainement dû à l'ancienneté du dispositif.

lorsque ces décisions révèlent des conceptions différentes du droit international entre des Etats qui chacun estiment procéder à une juste appréciation du droit international et peuvent se refuser à l'application de telles décisions[6]

Pour ce qui est de l'application territoriale de la Convention CMR, des reconfigurations de frontières étatiques et des bouleversements territoriaux au cours de l'histoire se sont adaptés tout en reprenant l'application de la Convention CMR en transport international routier de marchandises.[7] Les juges nationaux adaptent leur jurisprudence quand ils sont eux-mêmes confrontés à des mouvements de territoires. A cela s"ajoute que la Convention CMR est l'objet de protocoles additionnels, celui du 5 juillet 1978, entre 48 Etats parties, sur l'unité monétaire à utiliser pour le calcul des indemnités, celui du 20 février 2008, relatif à la lettre de voiture électronique, qui compte 33 Etats parties. Ces spécificités font du droit international des transports routiers internationaux de marchandises concerné une matière intrinsèquement à géométrie variable.

C'est également à la croisée des chemins entre des réalités techniques et juridiques que la question d'application territoriale de la Convention CMR est traitée, dans la mesure où seule la possibilité technique de transport international routier de marchandises entre «deux pays différents dont l'un au moins est un pays contractant», dans le champ d'application de la Convention CMR, mène à son application.

Substance et interstices dans les dispositions de la CMR

La Convention CMR a été élaborée conjointement par des juristes représentatifs d'ordres juridiques nationaux et locaux différents, de sorte que son appréhension est facilitée pour des conceptualisations juridiques diverses. Des notions juridiques clés telles que les termes de contrat, de responsabilité, de

6 voir par exemple, sur ce point, notamment, Calme, Sandie, Déclaration conjointe de la France, de l'Allemagne et du Royaume-Uni sur une situation en mer de Chine méridionale: des conceptualisations communes au-delà du cadre de l'Union Européenne, in *Revue d'Allemagne et des pays de langue allemande* (2020): 437–42.

7 C'est ainsi que l'Espagne et le Royaume-Uni ont procédé officiellement à des communications sur la consistance de leur différend au sujet de Gibraltar, le Royaume-Uni entendant étendre l'application territoriale de la Convention CMR à Gibraltar alors que l'Espagne se prévalait de l'article X du Traité d'Utrecht signé le 13 juillet 1713 n'accordant pas à Gibraltar de communications terrestres avec l'Espagne, pour s'opposer à cette communication du Royaume-Uni.

préposé, de transporteur notamment, récurrentes au sein de cette convention, sont perçues différemment au sein des ordres juridiques des Etats parties, ce qui amène le juge à percevoir différemment la convention elle-même, outre la question des divergences entre jurisprudences locales.

La Convention CMR se focalise prioritairement sur des questions propres à la responsabilité civile, adaptées au contexte du transport routier international de marchandises. Ce faisant, la Convention CMR fait du contrat de transport international routier de marchandises un contrat spécial soumis à un régime juridique détaillé. La caractéristique très apparente de la convention CMR consiste à prévoir des limitations de responsabilité, notamment quant à la responsabilité du transporteur routier international de marchandises, dès lors que le contexte autorise cette limitation. Ces cas de limitations[8] correspondent à un souci de préservation des réalités économiques de l'activité de transport routier international de marchandises, afin de ne pas compromettre

---

8 Selon l'article 17 de la convention CMR: «1. Le transporteur est responsable de la perte totale ou partielle, ou de l'avarie, qui se produit entre le moment de la prise en charge de la marchandise et celui de la livraison, ainsi que du retard à la livraison. 2. Le transporteur est déchargé de cette responsabilité si la perte, l'avarie ou le retard a eu pour cause une faute de l'ayant droit, un ordre de celui-ci ne résultant pas d'une faute du transporteur, un vice propre de la marchandise, ou des circonstances que le transporteur ne pouvait pas éviter et aux conséquences desquelles il ne pouvait pas obvier. 3. Le transporteur ne peut exciper, pour se décharger de sa responsabilité, ni des défectuosités du véhicule dont il se sert pour effectuer le transport, ni de fautes de la personne dont il aurait loué le véhicule ou des préposés de celle-ci. 4. Compte tenu de l'article 18, paragraphes 2 à 5, le transporteur est déchargé de sa responsabilité lorsque la perte ou l'avarie résulte des risques particuliers inhérents à l'un des faits suivants ou à plusieurs d'entre eux: a) Emploi de véhicules ouverts et non bâchés, lorsque cet emploi a été convenu d'une manière expresse et mentionné dans la lettre de voiture; b) Absence ou défectuosité de l'emballage pour les marchandises exposées par leur nature à des déchets ou avaries quand elles ne sont pas emballées ou sont mal emballées; c) Manutention, chargement, arrimage ou déchargement de la marchandise par l'expéditeur ou le destinataire ou des personnes agissant pour le compte de l'expéditeur ou du destinataire; d) Nature de certaines marchandises exposées, par des causes inhérentes à cette nature même, soit à perte totale ou partielle, soit à avarie, notamment par bris, rouille, détérioration interne et spontanée, dessiccation, coulage, déchet normal ou action de la vermine et des rongeurs; e) Insuffisance ou imperfection des marques ou des numéros de colis; f) Transport d'animaux vivants. 5. Si, en vertu du présent article, le transporteur ne répond pas de certains des facteurs qui ont causé le dommage, sa responsabilité n'est engagée que dans la proportion où les facteurs dont il répond en vertu du présent article ont contribué au dommage».

la pérennité de ce secteur commercial. La convention CMR amenage aussi un systeme corelatif de preuves.[9]

Pour endiguer les potentiels excès, la convention CMR enonce que ces limitations pouvent être levées dans des cas d'excès.[10] La lettre de voiture, les responsabilités et le régime juridique du contrat de transport font l'objet de prescriptions détaillées, de manière à conférer au transport international routier de marchandises un régime spécial dont les justiciables sont appelés à se prévaloir devant les juridictions nationales, en corrélation avec les dispositions juridiques locales. A titre d'exemple de ce caractère dérogatoire, se superposant au droit commun, le chapitre spécifique aux réclamations et actions de la Convention CMR traite jusque la question de la compétence juridictionnelle et la prescription de l'action en responsabilité.

---

9 Selon l'article 18 de la convention CMR, dont l'article 17 cite les paragraphes 2 à 5: «1. La preuve que la perte, l'avarie ou le retard a eu pour cause un des faits prévus à l'article 17, paragraphe 2, incombe au transporteur. 2. Lorsque le transporteur établit que, eu égard aux circonstances de fait, la perte ou l'avarie a pu résulter d'un ou de plusieurs des risques particuliers prévus à l'article 17, paragraphe 4, il y a présomption qu'elle en résulte. L'ayant droit peut toutefois faire la preuve que le dommage n'a pas eu l'un de ces risques pour cause totale ou partielle. 3. La présomption visée ci-dessus n'est pas applicable dans le cas prévu à l'article 17, paragraphe 4 a, s'il y a manquant d'une importance anormale ou perte de colis. 4. Si le transport est effectué au moyen d'un véhicule aménagé en vue de soustraire les marchandises à l'influence de la chaleur, du froid, des variations de température ou de l'humidité de l'air, le transporteur ne peut invoquer le bénéfice de l'article 17, paragraphe 4 d, que s'il fournit la preuve que toutes les mesures lui incombant, compte tenu des circonstances, ont été prises en ce qui concerne le choix, l'entretien et l'emploi de ces aménagements et qu'il s'est conformé aux instructions spéciales qui ont pu lui être données. 5. Le transporteur ne peut invoquer le bénéfice de l'article 17, paragraphe 4 f, que s'il fournit la preuve que toutes les mesures lui incombant normalement, compte tenu des circonstances, ont été prises et qu'il s'est conformé aux instructions spéciales qui ont pu lui être données».

10 L'article 29 de la convention CMR dispose comme suit: «1. Le transporteur n'a pas le droit de se prévaloir des dispositions du présent chapitre qui excluent ou limitent sa responsabilité ou qui renversent le fardeau de la preuve, si le dommage provient de son dol ou d'une faute qui lui est imputable et qui, d'après la loi de la juridiction saisie, est considérée comme équivalente au dol. 2. Il en est de même si le dol ou la faute est le fait des préposés du transporteur ou de toutes autres personnes aux services desquelles il recourt pour l'exécution du transport lorsque ces préposés ou ces autres personnes agissent dans l'exercice de leurs fonctions. Dans ce cas, ces préposés ou ces autres personnes n'ont pas davantage le droit de se prévaloir, en ce qui concerne leur responsabilité personnelle, des dispositions du présent chapitre visées au paragraphe 1».

Les termes juridiques employés au sein de la Convention CMR, qu'elle définit seulement en partie, peuvent faire l'objet de conceptualisations propres aux ordres juridiques nationaux et locaux des Etats parties, de manière à laisser entrevoir quelques interstices au sein de cette convention de droit uniforme, ce qui est amené à avoir une incidence sur les jurisprudences. En même temps, la Convention CMR laisse leur place aux conflits de lois.[11] Ici encore, la Convention CMR ne fait pas complètement obstacle à une possibilité d'interférence de droits nationaux ou locaux.

Concrétisations jurisprudentielles

Les juges nationaux sont à la hauteur des sollicitations de ce texte transnational. De manière concrète, bien que les méthodes diffèrent, on observe une jurisprudence homogène qui suscite des réflexions sur l'inflation normative et adopte une perspective singulière concernant la mise en œuvre du droit domestique. Néanmoins, cette jurisprudence démontre également l'apport constructif du droit de l'Union à l'échelle eurasienne.

Méthode du droit continental et méthode de common law

Les juges nationaux abordent les contentieux de droit des transports routiers internationaux de marchandises à partir de méthodes d'analyses distinctes, de droit continental et de common law.[12]

---

11 Notamment, à titre d'exemple, selon l'article 28 de la convention CMR: «1. Lorsque, d'après la loi applicable, la perte, l'avarie ou le retard survenu au cours d'un transport soumis à la présente Convention peut donner lieu à une réclamation extra-contractuelle, le transporteur peut se prévaloir des dispositions de la présente Convention qui excluent sa responsabilité ou qui déterminent ou limitent les indemnités dues. 2. Lorsque la responsabilité extra-contractuelle pour perte, avarie ou retard d'une des personnes dont le transporteur répond aux termes de l'article 3» (sur les personnes dont répond le transporteur) «est mise en cause, cette personne peut également se prévaloir des dispositions de la présente Convention qui excluent la responsabilité du transporteur ou qui déterminent ou limitent les indemnités dues».

12 Ainsi, Ainsi, la Fondation pour le droit continental vient délimiter le nouvel ordre juridique ainsi conceptualisé. Cet organisme associant le secteur public et le secteur privé se donne notamment pour objectif la promotion de la tradition continentale en matière

Force est de constater que le droit continental et le droit de common law semblent s"inscrire dans un rapport de concurrence, de competition.[13]

Justement, sur l'opposition entre «droit de common law» et «droit continental», dans le cadre de la journée annuelle de l'Association Française des Juristes d'Entreprise du 6 février 2018, le Professeur émérite Barthélémy Mercadal est revenu sur cette rivalité qui remonterait à un rapport Doing Business de la Banque mondiale de 2004, selon laquelle le droit de common law serait davantage orienté sur les faits de l'espèce par contraste avec une certaine rigidité juridique inadaptée qui serait reprochée au droit civil.[14]

A cette occasion meme, la Professeure Bénédicte Fauvarque-Cosson met en avant l'importance du droit continental, notamment de par le Code civil, qui connaît un rayonnement à l'échelle mondiale, au-delà des tendances de civilistes à associer codification et sécurité juridique et de l'association opérée par le droit de common law entre liberté contractuelle et sécurité du droit.[15] En effet, au sein des ordres juridiques dits de common law, des éléments de codification se rapprochant de la méthode civiliste sont amenés à surpasser la prise en compte

---

juridique et dans le domaine judiciaire. Pour ce faire, il mène des travaux tels que celui du Code européen des affaires, qui aspire à une rationalisation du droit européen des affaires à partir du droit continental, en tant que «droit romano-germanique». Il s'agit de se concerter entre experts du domaine juridique et de l'entrepreneuriat en vue de mettre au point des recommandations à destination des colégislateurs à l'échelle de l'Union européenne, avec l'appui de la Commission européenne, manifesté dans son Livre blanc sur l'avenir de l'Europe du 1er mars 2017 notamment. Par ce travail de codification, une harmonisation du droit des affaires de l'Union européenne est à l'étude. Cf. Laure Belanger, «Un code européen des affaires, le droit au cœur de la consolidation de l'Europe», *JCP édition générale*, no. 16, 17 avril 2017, 455

13 Arnaud Dumourier, «Droit continental versus common law: Des enjeux économiques, financiers et d'influence», *Le Monde du droit*, 23 février 2018, https://www.lemondedudroit.fr/decryptages/61449-droit-continental-versus-common-law-enjeux-economiques-financiers-influence.html.

14 Arnaud Dumourier, «Droit continental versus common law: Des enjeux économiques, financiers et d'influence», *Le Monde du droit*, 23 février 2018, https://www.lemondedudroit.fr/decryptages/61449-droit-continental-versus-common-law-enjeux-economiques-financiers-influence.html.

15 Arnaud Dumourier, «Droit continental versus common law: Des enjeux économiques, financiers et d'influence», *Le Monde du droit*, 23 février 2018, https://www.lemondedudroit.fr/decryptages/61449-droit-continental-versus-common-law-enjeux-economiques-financiers-influence.html.

d'éléments factuels dans le traitement des contentieux selon la méthode du rapprochement des faits de l'espèce avec des précédents jurisprudentiels.

Dans le cadre d'un litige récent en droit des transports routiers internationaux de marchandises[16] où un convoi avait été endommagé, il a été établi par le juge anglais, au sein d'un jugement citant de très nombreux éléments factuels tels que des témoignages, que le droit anglais des transports routiers internationaux de marchandises, régi par une loi spécifique de 1965,[17] inclut expressément la convention CMR, du fait d'une référence de cette loi de 1965, en raison du caractère international de l'opération de transport.

On retrouve ces fondements juridiques dans d'autres contentieux portés devant le juge anglais. Dans un jugement faisant la part belle aux faits dans l'esprit du droit de common law, on va donc retrouver également des éléments de codification nationale comme transnationale. Ici, de facto, faute d'inconduite (misconduct) caractérisée et en l'absence de fausse déclarations (misrepresentation) conséquentes sur la promesse de couverture de risques par une police d'assurance ou sur une promesse de remboursement, le juge concluait que la responsabilité du transporteur devait être limitée aux seuils maximums d'indemnisation dans les termes de la Convention CMR. Par une méthode différente, on en revient à une appréciation qui pourrait être estimée compatible avec les analyses du droit continental.

Le juge de la Convention CMR face à l'inflation normative des autres textes

Lorsqu'il est amené à trancher des litiges de droit des transports routiers internationaux de marchandises, le juge national est fréquemment confronté au phénomène de l'inflation normative. Il s'agit d'une situation particulièrement dénoncée en France.[18] En effet, C'est le nombre important de textes normatifs de toutes natures en droit français produits d'année en année qui est décrié, tant sur le plan quantitatif que sur le plan qualitatif. Le droit de l'Union européenne, ou une judiciarisation ainsi qu'une éventuelle demande

---

16 [2022] EWHC 1437 (Comm), Case No. CL-2020-000189.

17 Carriage of Goods by Road Act 1965, c. 37.

18 Pierre Januel, «2021, année record de l'inflation normative,» *Dalloz Actualité*, 19 avril 2022, <https://www.dalloz-actualite.fr/flash/2021-annee-record-de-linflation-normative>

de production de normes de la part du public ont pu être avancés comme causes de cette situation de foisonnement normatif, qui serait un frein à la qualité des normes, à leur visibilité et à la sécurité juridique.[19]

Par un arrêt en date du 4 septembre 2014, la Cour de justice de l'Union européenne semble apporter un élément de solution à l'inflation normative, pour le cas de superposition de normes transnationales dédiées à une même thématique, en ce qui concerne la Convention CMR.[20] Il s'agissait, sur le terrain de la compétence juridictionnelle, d'une éventuelle concurrence entre l'article 71[21] du règlement européen n° 44/2001[22] et l'article 31 de la

---

19 Cf. Philippe Martin, «L'inflation législative et la qualité de la réglementation», contribution publiée sur le site du Conseil d'État, <https://www.conseil-etat.fr/actualites/l-inflation-legislative-et-la-qualite-de-la-reglementation>, Christophe Eoche-Duval, «Plutôt que de perpétuer l'inflation normative, la France gagnerait à mieux appliquer les textes existants», *Le Monde*, 8 août 2022, <https://www.lemonde.fr/idees/article/2022/08/08/plutot-que-de-perpetuer-l-inflation-normative-la-france-gagnerait-a-mieux-appliquer-les-textes-existants_6137477_3232.html>

20 CJUE, 4 septembre 2014, affaire no. C-157/13.

21 Article 71 disposait comme suit: «1. Le présent règlement n'affecte pas les conventions auxquelles les États membres sont parties et qui, dans des matières particulières, règlent la compétence judiciaire, la reconnaissance ou l'exécution des décisions. 2. En vue d'assurer son interprétation uniforme, le paragraphe 1 est appliqué de la manière suivante: a) le présent règlement ne fait pas obstacle à ce qu'un tribunal d'un État membre, partie à une convention relative à une matière particulière, puisse fonder sa compétence sur une telle convention, même si le défendeur est domicilié sur le territoire d'un État membre non partie à une telle convention. Le tribunal saisi applique, en tout cas, l'article 26 du présent règlement (sur la vérification de la compétence et de la recevabilité); b) les décisions rendues dans un État membre par un tribunal ayant fondé sa compétence sur une convention relative à une matière particulière sont reconnues et exécutées dans les autres États membres conformément au présent règlement. Si une convention relative à une matière particulière et à laquelle sont parties l'État membre d'origine et l'État membre requis détermine les conditions de reconnaissance et d'exécution des décisions, il est fait application de ces conditions. Il peut, en tout cas, être fait application des dispositions du présent règlement qui concernent la procédure relative à la reconnaissance et à l'exécution des décisions».

22 Règlement (CE) no. 44/2001 du Conseil du 22 décembre 2000 concernant la compétence judiciaire, la reconnaissance et l'exécution des décisions en matière civile et commerciale.

Convention CMR.[23] L'article 71 concerné est aujourd'hui supplanté par le règlement européen n° 125/2012.[24]

A la suite d'une analyse circonstanciée, la Cour de justice de l'Union européenne concluait que l'article 71 du règlement n° 44/2001 doit être interprété comme signifiant que dans une situation où un litige entre dans le champ d'application tant du règlement que de la Convention CMR, telle que modifiée par le Protocole signé à Genève le 5 juillet 1978, un Etat membre puisse, conformément à l'article 71 alinéa 1er de ce règlement, appliquer les règles de compétence juridictionnelle de l'article 31 alinéa 1er de cette convention.

---

23 Pour sa part, l'article 31 de la convention CMR dispose, sur le même thème, comme suit: «1. Pour tous litiges auxquels donnent lieu les transports soumis à la présente Convention, le demandeur peut saisir, en dehors des juridictions des pays contractants désignées d'un commun accord par les parties, les juridictions du pays sur le territoire duquel a) le défendeur a sa résidence habituelle, son siège principal ou la succursale ou l'agence par l'intermédiaire de laquelle le contrat de transport a été conclu, ou b) le lieu de la prise en charge de la marchandise ou celui prévu pour la livraison est situé, et ne peut saisir que ces juridictions. 2. Lorsque dans un litige visé au par. 1 du présent article une action est en instance devant une juridiction compétente aux termes de ce paragraphe, ou lorsque dans un tel litige un jugement a été prononcé par une telle juridiction, il ne peut être intenté aucune nouvelle action pour la même cause entre les mêmes parties à moins que la décision de la juridiction devant laquelle la première action a été intentée ne soit pas susceptible d'être exécutée dans le pays où la nouvelle action est intentée. 3. Lorsque dans un litige visé au par. 1 du présent article un jugement rendu par une juridiction d'un pays contractant est devenu exécutoire dans ce pays, il devient également exécutoire dans chacun des autres pays contractants aussitôt après accomplissement des formalités prescrites à cet effet dans le pays intéressé. Ces formalités ne peuvent comporter aucune révision de l'affaire. 4. Les dispositions du par. 3 du présent article s'appliquent aux jugements contradictoires, aux jugements par défaut et aux transactions judiciaires mais ne s'appliquent ni aux jugements qui ne sont exécutoires que par provision, ni aux condamnations en dommages et intérêts qui seraient prononcés en sus des dépens contre un demandeur en raison du rejet total ou partiel de sa demande. 5. Il ne peut être exigé de caution de ressortissants de pays contractants, ayant leur domicile ou un établissement dans un de ces pays, pour assurer le paiement des dépens à l'occasion des actions en justice auxquelles donnent lieu les transports soumis à la présente Convention».

24 Règlement (UE) no. 1215/2012 du Parlement européen et du Conseil du 12 décembre 2012 concernant la compétence judiciaire, la reconnaissance et l'exécution des décisions en matière civile et commerciale.

Par une nouvelle norme de nature jurisprudentielle, le droit européen semblait mettre un terme à une incertitude concernant l'application de deux normes ayant en commun le même objet. Ce faisant, in concreto, il faisait état d'une marge d'appréciation des juridictions nationales confrontées à cette réalité d'inflation normative.Cette jurisprudence est d'actualité, l'article 71 du règlement 1215/2012 reprenant celui du règlement 44/2001. Le questionnement sur l'inflation normative n'est pas limité à l'ordre juridique français[25] ou au cadre de l'Union européenne, il est également l'objet d'études doctrinales de par le monde, par exemple au sein de la doctrine de droit suisse[26] ou encore de droit belge,[27] de droit espagnol,[28] de droit italien.[29] Il reviendra au final au juge national, confronté à un cas d'application de la Convention CMR, de composer en conséquence avec l'interférence des autres textes.

Interprétation du juge et truchement du droit interne

Devant les juges nationaux, la question du degré d'implication du droit interne dans l'application des dispositions de la Convention CMR se pose avec une certaine acuité, la méthode d'approche du litige par le juge national étant différente sur ce plan. Ainsi, par exemple, un juge belge noue son raisonnement sur la base de l'article 32 de la convention CMR en y associant son analyse de bon sens sans association particulière avec des normes de droit interne quand, pour rejeter un pourvoi, il retient qu'il «ne peut se déduire des articles 32.1, 32.1.b et 32.2 de la Convention CMR qu'une réclamation écrite qui a été introduite avant que la prescription prenne cours n'a pas d'effet suspensif,

---

[25] Voir, par exemple, Rachel Vaneuville, «Les enjeux politico-juridiques des discours sur l'inflation normative», *Parlement[s], Revue d'histoire politique* 11, no. 1 (2009): 80–91.

[26] Voir, par exemple, François Dessemontet, «La rédaction des lois, langage et système des lois suisses», *Les Cahiers de droit* 21, no. 3–4 (1980): 579–97.

[27] Voir, par exemple, Antoine Georis, «Quand la simplification devient compliquée: L'inflation normative en Belgique. État des lieux et perspective» (Faculté de droit et de criminologie, Université catholique de Louvain, 2022), Prom.: Philippe Coppens.

[28] Voir, par exemple, Isabel Lirola Delgado, «¿Inflación o deflación normativa en el derecho internacional?» *Revista de derecho internacional* (2022), <http://digital.casalini.it/5293295>

[29] Voir, par exemple, Angelo Maria Petroni, «Quale modello di semplificazione ?», *Rivista di diritto pubblico italiano, comparato, europeo* 19 (8 octobre 2008).

étant entendu que cette suspension n'a d'effet qu'à partir du moment où le délai de prescription prend cours».[30]

C'est dans le même esprit que le juge belge, sur la base de l'article 17 de la Convention CMR, décide que «La livraison d'une marchandise à une personne autre que celle qui peut prétendre à cette livraison constitue une perte totale».[31] Dans un arrêt de cassation, le juge belge revient à l'application de l'article 31 alinéa 1er de la Convention CMR sur la compétence juridictionnelle par priorité sur la clause contractuelle attributive de compétence.[32] Le juge suisse nourrit sa réflexion de conventions internationales telles que la convention de Vienne sur le droit des traités[33] et la convention de Lugano concernant la compétence judiciaire, la reconnaissance et l'exécution des décisions en matière civile et commerciale,[34] associées par exemple à ses lois internes de conflits de lois.[35]

Le juge luxembourgeois, sans référence au droit interne, décide notamment: «Il est constant en cause que les relations entre parties sont régies par la convention CMR, laquelle retient que le transport de marchandises réalisé en continuité, sans rupture de charge, par la combinaison d'un transport routier et d'un autre mode de transport, est en principe régi pour l'ensemble d'un tel transport par la CMR.» Ce faisant, il prône un principe d'application directe de la Convention CMR dès lors que ses conditions d'application sont réunies,[36] tout en nourrissant sa réflexion d'analyses de droit comparé propres au contexte du transport international routier de marchandises régi par la Convention CMR.

Sur la question de la suspension de la prescription en matière de transport routier international de marchandises régi par la convention CMR, le juge français associe les dispositions de cette convention à celles du Code civil, en jugeant que «La suspension de la prescription des actions relatives aux contrats de transports internationaux de marchandises par route est régie, en vertu

30 Chambre 1N, Cour de cassation, 9 juin 2016, affaire no. C.15.0352.N.
31 Chambre 1F, Cour de cassation, 11 avril 2016, affaire no. C.15.0183.F.
32 Chambre 1N, Cour de cassation, 21 février 2007, affaire no. C.06.0005.N.
33 BGE 138 III 708 S. 709.
34 BGE 138 III 708 S. 713.
35 BGE 132 III 626 S. 630.
36 Tribunal d'arrondissement de Luxembourg, chambre 6, 4 décembre 2008, décision no. 1259/08, numéros de rôle: 112818 et 116810.

de l'article 32 de la CMR, par la loi du tribunal saisi et donc en l'espèce par l'article 2234 du code civil».[37] Cette implication du droit interne est décisive pour l'action en responsabilité considérée, qui sera alors jugée non prescrite.

Le juge français, sur la base des articles L132-4 et L132-5 du code de commerce et de l'article 29-1 de la CMR, retient qu'il «résulte de la combinaison de ces textes que le commissionnaire de transport est responsable du fait du transporteur substitué dans la limite de l'indemnisation prévue par la CMR, sauf, en l'état du droit applicable avant la loi n° 2009-1503 du 8 décembre 2009, faute lourde de ce dernier», que «ne constitue une telle faute qu'une négligence grossière confinant au dol et dénotant l'inaptitude du transporteur à accomplir la mission qu'il a contractuellement acceptée», de sorte que la responsabilité du commissionnaire de transport doit être écartée.[38]

Faisant également référence au droit interne, le juge allemand renvoie, par exemple, aux dispositions des «Allgemeinen Vertragsbedingungen Kunst (AVK), qui sont des normes correspondant aux usages commerciaux allemands pour le transport, la livraison et le traitement des objets d'arts, en complément des articles 23 alinéa 3 et 25 alinéa 2 de la Convention CMR sur les seuils maximums d'indemnisation pour perte ou avarie des marchandises transportées.[39] Le juge autrichien fait également référence, outre la convention CMR, aux «Allgemeinen Österreichischen Spediteurbedigungen» AÖSp,[40] des normes autrichiennes se rapportant aux sages en matière de commission de transport, et à la loi Versicherungsvertragsgesetz VresVG sur le contrat d'assurance.[41]

Le juge espagnol,[42] pour étayer son propos dans le cas de la responsabilité du transporteur pour le fait dolosif de son sous-contractant, faire référence au fait que «même dans le cadre de la réglementation nationale, qui est utile pour contextualiser le régime du secteur, est énoncée ce qui n'est que la même règle (de l'article 47.3 de la loi 15/2009 du contrat de transport terrestre de

---

37 Cass. com., 8 février 2023, pourvoi no. 20-22.496.

38 Cass. com., 9 septembre 2020, pourvoi no. 17-11.522.

39 BGH, Urteil vom 17.12.2020 - I ZR 130/19.

40 OGH, 30 November 2016, Geschäftszahl 7Ob2/16v.

41 OGH, 30 November 2016, Geschäftszahl 7Ob2/16v; OGH, 29 März 2017, Geschäftszahl 7Ob91/16g.

42 Id Cendoj: 28079370282022100730 Órgano: Audiencia Provincial Sede: Madrid Sección: 28 Fecha: 24/06/2022 Nº de Recurso: 984/2020 Nº de Resolución: 497/2022.

marchandises, artículo 47.3 de la Ley 15/2009 del contrato de transporte terrestre de mercancías) selon laquelle le transporteur est responsable des actes et omissions de ceux dont il a recours aux services pour l'accomplissement de ses obligations, qu'ils soient dépendants ou même indépendants de lui». Il en déduit, dans ce cadre, l'application du délai de prescription de trois ans pour les faits de dol selon l'article 32 de la Convention CMR. Ainsi, le lien entre droit national et Convention CMR, au sein des jurisprudences nationales, est empreint de singularités qui relèvent de l'analyse de droit comparé, comme par exemple pour ce qui est de l'étude du «droit européen privé».

Influence du droit européen

Le droit de l'Union européenne exerce une relative influence quant au développement des jurisprudences nationales en matière d'application de la Convention CMR, comme par exemple pour ce qui est du traitement de la réalité de superposition de conventions internationales où est présent un texte de droit de l'Union européenne.[43]

A cet égard, le droit de l'Union européenne constitue un modèle, par exemple du fait de l'adhésion de l'Union européenne à de nombreuses conventions internationales de portées géographiques très étendues, en qualité d'organisation d'intégration économique régionale. Sur ce point, le retrait du Royaume-Uni de l'Union européenne permet d'observer une certaine cohésion entre termes d'harmonisation juridique internationale, portée par la jurisprudence. Ainsi, selon la jurisprudence anglaise,[44] dans un cas se rapportant au transport routier international de marchandises relevant de la Convention CMR, du fait du retrait du Royaume-Uni de l'Union européenne, les tribunaux de cette juridiction ne sont généralement pas liés par les décisions de la Cour de justice de l'Union européenne prises après le 31 décembre 2020, selon la section 6(1) de la Loi de 2018 sur le retrait de l'Union européenne, (le paragraphe 6(2) de cette loi stipulant expressément qu'un tribunal anglais «peut tenir compte» de telles décisions).

Cette jurisprudence rappelle que l'accord entre le Royaume-Uni et l'Union européenne fixant les modalités du retrait du Royaume-Uni de l'UE prévoit

---

43 Voir, par exemple, CJUE, 4 septembre 2014, affaire no. C-157/13.

44 [2022] EWHC 1114 (Comm), 4 April 2022, No. LM-2021-000064.

que les jugements de la CJUE rendus après le 31 décembre 2020 auront «force obligatoire dans leur intégralité au Royaume-Uni» s'ils sont rendus à l'égard des renvois faits par les cours et tribunaux du Royaume-Uni avant la fin de 2020 (conformément aux articles 86 et 89 de l'Accord de retrait).

Elle fait référence au paragraphe 4(1) de l'Accord de retrait, qui se lit comme suit: «Les dispositions du présent accord et les dispositions du droit de l'Union rendues applicables par le présent accord produisent à l'égard et au Royaume-Uni les mêmes effets juridiques que ceux qu'elles produisent au sein de l'Union et de ses États membres. En conséquence, les personnes physiques ou morales peuvent notamment s"appuyer directement sur les dispositions contenues dans le présent accord ou visées par celui-ci qui remplissent les conditions d'effet direct prévues par le droit de l'Union.»

Ici, le juge anglais souligne que l'Accord de retrait dispose en son paragraphe 4(2) que le Royaume-Uni assure le respect du paragraphe 4(1) «au moyen de sa législation nationale». La jurisprudence est donc appelée à concrétiser la cohésion recherchée dans le cadre de l'Accord de retrait. Le droit de l'Union européenne, quant à lui, lie en premier lieu les Etats membres de l'Union européenne et exerce une influence à l'échelle transnationale du fait des relations, telles que celles du transport routier international de marchandises, avec le cadre extracommunautaire.

Parmi les autres Etats de l'Espace Economique Européen, la Norvège est partie à la Convention CMR. La Suisse, qui prône une certaine exigence d' «eurocompatibilité» de son droit interne dédié aux activités internationales telles que le transport international routier de marchandises et où la Convention CMR a été signée, en est également partie. A l'évidence, les dispositions de la CMR connaissent un rayonnement à l'échelle paneuropéenne et même au-delà, la question de l'harmonisation juridique internationale qu'elle veut induire impliquant également des Etats récemment parties à cette convention, et où les juges nationaux sont également appelés à se positionner dans l'agencement de leur jurisprudence. Les disparités entre les jurisprudences de Etats parties vont de pair avec celles des jurisprudences locales de tous ordres.

Remarques conclusives

La réponse des jurisprudences nationales à la Convention CMR, en matière de transport routier international de marchandises, est une composante historique de l'évolution des normes commerciales. Cette évolution, dans un sens de "harmonisation juridique internationale, mérite d'être suivie d'autant plus que cette Convention CMR connaît un accroissement des Etats parties. Les juges nationaux sont ainsi appelés à développer davantage leurs méthodes interprétatives.

La Convention CMR dispose en son article 33 que «le contrat de transport peut contenir une clause attribuant compétence à un tribunal arbitral à condition que cette clause prévoie que le tribunal arbitral appliquera la présente Convention». On peut alors s'interroger sur l'avenir de l'option de l'arbitrage en transport international de marchandises, arbitrage présenté comme favorisé dans un esprit de promotion d'une liberté contractuelle s'étendant à une liberté de règlement alternatif des litiges. L'examen de l'abondance et de la cohérence des jurisprudences nationales en la matière suggère que ce mode alternatif de résolution des litiges ne semble pas apporter un surcroît de sécurité juridique par rapport aux normes établies par les juges nationaux en Eurasie.

Double Taxation Treaties before the Courts of Kazakhstan and Russia

Sagyngaliy Aidarbayev
Narxoz University

Ilya Lifshits
Russian Foreign Trade Academy

The introduction circumscribes the multiple challenges of interpreting the Double Taxation Treaties (DTTs). DTTs, as treaties submitted to the Vienna Convention on Law of the Treatise, are covered by articles 31-33 regarding interpretation. However, such DDTs are equally directly applicable and can be invoked by national authorities and judges. Moreover, there are also the OECD Model Tax Convention and its Commentaries, nonbinding instruments containing specific directives for the interpretation of DTTs dispositions. This multiple dimensionality creates the problems, the answer of which will be developed further in the paper In the second part of the article, the authors consider the role of DTTs within the legal systems of Kazakhstan and Russia. In the last and third parts of the article, the authors deal with the application and interpretation of DTTs by the national courts of Kazakhstan and Russia and summarize their findings with a conclusion.

Introduction

The interpretation of the provisions of Double Taxation Treaties (from now on referred to singularly as "DTT" and plurally as "DTTs") is undoubtedly a specific pressing problem that researchers have repeatedly noted.[1] On the one hand, such agreements are treaties, and Article 31-33 of the Vienna Convention on the Law of Treaties[2] fully apply to their interpretation: first, the provisions on interpretation following the conventional meaning of

---

1 See, for example, Reuven S. Avi-Yonah, «International Tax as International Law», *Tax Law Review* 57, no. 4 (2004): 483.

2 United Nations, *Treaty Series*, vol. 1155, 331.

the treaty's terms in their context and in light of the treaty's object and purpose; second, the provisions of Article 32 on the use of additional means of interpretation.[3]

Conversely, DTTs are particular treaties whose application is primarily based on terms and concepts originating from national legal systems and reflecting state practice.[4] Moreover, taxes represent the financial basis of state sovereignty, and the degree of "internationalization" of tax relations is minimal compared to other areas.[5] There are more than 3,000 double-taxation treaties.[6] However, such agreements are mostly bilateral treaties. Two taxation-related multilateral treaties have been signed within the framework of the OECD. However, these also represent a model for bilateral relations between states. The UN[7] and OECD[8] Model Conventions and their Commentaries undoubtedly have specific harmonizing effects. Nevertheless, the nonrepresentative composition of the OECD participants does not allow the provisions of the commentaries to be assigned the role of the only interpretative instrument.

All these circumstances, coupled with the absence of an international court with jurisdiction to try tax disputes, imply a significant degree of discretion in interpreting international tax treaties by national courts. In his review of the evolution of the concept of "international tax language," Johann Hattingh

---

3 Malcolm N. Shaw, *International Law*, 8th ed. (Cambridge: Cambridge University Press, 2017), 706–711; Jan Klabbers, *International Law*, 3rd ed. (Cambridge: Cambridge University Press, 2020), 57–59; Robert Kolb, *The Law of Treaties: An Introduction*, 2nd ed. (Cheltenham: Edward Elgar, 2023), 149–186; Christian Djeffal, *Static and Evolutive Treaty Interpretation* (Cambridge: Cambridge University Press, 2015).

4 *Klaus Vogel on Double Taxation Conventions*, 5th ed., vol. 1 (Alphen aan den Rijn: Wolters Kluwer, 2022), 229–37.

5 I. Lifshits, «Transgranichoe nalogooblozshenie: "Zolushka" mezshdunarodnogo prava, kotoraya mechtaet stat' korolevoi» [Transboundary taxation: "Cinderella" of international law which dreams to become a queen], *Zhurnal VSHÉ po Mezhdunarodnomu Pravu (HSE University Journal of International Law)* 1, no. 1 (2023): 37–49.

6 See Action 6 BEPS at the OECD website: <https://www.oecd.org/tax/beps/beps-actions/action6/> (last accessed on 14/12/2023)

7 *UN Model Tax Convention between Developed and Developing Countries 2021* (New York: United Nations, 2021) <https://financing.desa.un.org/sites/default/files/2023-05/UN%20Model_2021.pdf>

8 *Model Tax Convention on Income and Capital 2017* (Paris: OECD Publishing, 2017), <https://read.oecd-ilibrary.org/taxation/model-tax-convention-on-income-and-on-capital-2017-full-version_g2g972ee-en#page1>

notes that the conventional approach to interpreting the terms of a bilateral tax treaty based on a literal interpretation of the terms and purpose of such a treaty cannot be blindly applied in cases where it employs the concepts of a model tax convention.[9] Consequently, regarding international taxation, there are peculiarities in the interpretation of treaty terms, the conventional meaning of which is determined mainly by the OECD Model Tax Convention and its Commentaries. However, the suitability of an international tax language in this sense is complicated because the OECD is a closed, non-inclusive club with a composition that cannot be described as representative. The need to interpret DTTs is tremendous since such agreements are often applied in national legal systems. For example, Kazakhstan has DTTs with 55 DTT states,[10] while Russia has DTTs with 82 DTT states.[11] Such agreements can be applied directly in relations involving private individuals. Accordingly, national courts have to interpret DTTs, apply the provisions of the Vienna Convention, determine the meaning of its terms, and decide on the applicability of the Commentaries to the OECD Model Convention.

Role of DTTs as Treaties in the Legal Systems of Kazakhstan and Russia

Kazakhstan

A notable feature of the Kazakhstani legal system is that, according to the Constitution, the applicable law of the state, along with "the norms of the Constitution, relevant laws, other normative legal acts, international

---

9 Johann Hattingh, "An "International Tax Language for Tax Treaty Interpretation: Its Histories in Common and Civil Law Discourse," in *Building Global International Tax Law – Essays in Honour of Guglielmo Maisto*, ed. Pasquale Pistone (Amsterdam: IBFD, 2022), 17.

10 Conventions for the Avoidance of Double Taxation and the Prevention of Fiscal Evasion Concerning Taxes on Income and Capital (last amended on 29.11.2023): <https://kgd.gov.kz/ru/content/konvencii-ob-izbezhanii-dvoynogo-nalogooblozheniya-i-predotvrashchenii-ukloneniya-ot>

11 See information on the Ministry of Finance of the Russian Federation website: <https://minfin.gov.ru/ru/document?id_4=124786-spisok_mezhdunarodnykh_dogovorov_ob_izbezhanii_dvoinogo_nalogooblozheniya_mezhdu_rossiiskoi_federatsiei_i_drugimi_gosudarstvami_list_of_the_tax_agreements_for_the_avoidance_of_double_taxation_between_the_russian_federation_and_other_states>

contractual and other obligations of the Republic," also includes the normative (interpretative) resolutions[12] of the Constitutional Court and the Supreme Court (Paragraph 1 of Article 4).[13]

Resolution 3 of the Constitutional Council of the Republic of Kazakhstan (from now on referred to as the "RK") of March 6, 1997, clarified "the norm of Paragraph 1 of Article 4 of the Constitution of the Republic of Kazakhstan, which establishes that the applicable law includes normative decisions of the Supreme Court, should be understood to mean the Supreme Court of the Republic of Kazakhstan is authorized to issue normative resolutions only with regards to the application of legislative norms, including the norms of the Constitution, in judicial practice."[14] In other words, the Supreme Court of the Republic does not have the right to adopt new norms but can interpret existing legislative norms. Although the Supreme Court is deprived of direct law-making powers, its power to adopt legal interpretations that become a part of applicable law allows it to be a *de facto* legislator.

Such Supreme Court's normative resolutions are adopted after studying the practice of courts in applying Kazakhstan's legislation and treaties to ensure their uniform application. They contain explanations of the relevant norms and are mandatory for all state judicial authorities. The Supreme Court of Kazakhstan adopts normative resolutions on applying tax legislation by courts approximately every five years. Thus, on December 22, 2022, the Supreme Court of the Republic of Kazakhstan adopted Normative Resolution No. 9 – "On Certain Issues of Application of Tax Legislation by Courts,"[15] which

---

12 For a complete examination of the Supreme Court's normative resolutions, see the infra in this volume, Zhuldyz Sairambayeva, "Normative Resolutions of Interpretation by the Supreme Court of Kazakhstan."

13 Constitution of the Republic of Kazakhstan (adopted in a republican referendum on August 30, 1995) (with amendments and additions as of September 19, 2022), "https://online.zakon.kz/Document/?doc_id=1005029&pos=54;-52#pos=54;-52."

14 Resolution of the Constitutional Council of the Republic of Kazakhstan of March 6, 1997, No. 3 – "On the Official Interpretation of Paragraph 1 of Article 4, Paragraph 1 of Article 14, Subparagraph 3) of Paragraph 3 of Article 77, Paragraph 1 of Article 79 and Paragraph 1 of Article 83 of the Constitution of the Republic of Kazakhstan,"<https://adilet.zan.kz/rus/docs/S970000003>

15 Normative Resolution of the Supreme Court of the Republic of Kazakhstan No. 9 of December 22, 2022 – "On Certain Issues of Application of Tax Legislation by Courts," <https://adilet.zan.kz/rus/docs/P220000009S>

canceled the previous one. This current Normative Resolution of the Supreme Court of December 22, 2022, concerning treaties on tax issues emphasizes, first of all, the constitutional principle of priority of ratified treaties, the rules of which have priority over the rules of the Tax Code of the Republic of Kazakhstan (Paragraph 5 of Article 2 of the Tax Code).

Secondly, the Resolution in question emphasizes the Normative Resolution of the Constitutional Council of the Republic of Kazakhstan No. 6, of November 5, 2009,[16] which considers that normative decisions and other normative legal acts of international organizations, interstate associations, and their bodies, of which Kazakhstan is a member, have the same legal force as treaties and have priority in their application over the law of the Republic, including tax legislation.[17] The legal novelty introduced by the Normative Resolution of the Constitutional Council of the Republic of Kazakhstan in 2009 also applies to tax relations.

Thirdly, according to the Normative Resolution of the Supreme Court of December 22, 2022, if a treaty granted the power of taxation to the Government of the Republic of Kazakhstan, but this power was not implemented in national legislation, then national legislation had to be applied. The fourth important circumstance of the Supreme Court's normative resolution is that when the provisions of treaties are applied, the treaty effect extends to a specific group of subjects. Finally, the fifth provision establishes that the general rules of interpretation provided for by treaties and the legislation of the Republic apply to the interpretation of DTTs in situations where such rules of interpretation comply with the provisions of the Vienna Convention on the Law of Treaties (VCLT), to which the Republic acceded.[18]

---

16 Normative Resolution of the Constitutional Council of the Republic of Kazakhstan No. 6, of November 5, 2009 – "On the Official Interpretation of the Norms of Article 4 of the Constitution of the Republic of Kazakhstan concerning the Procedure for the Execution of Decisions of International Organizations and Their Bodies."

17 Normative Resolution of the Constitutional Council of the Republic of Kazakhstan No. 6 of November 5, 2009 – "On the Official Interpretation of the Norms of Article 4 of the Constitution of the Republic of Kazakhstan in Relation to the Procedure for the Execution of Decisions of International Organizations and Their Bodies," <https://adilet.zan.kz/rus/docs/S090000006>

18 Resolution of the Supreme Council of the Republic of Kazakhstan No. 2059-XII of March 31, 1993 – "On the Accession of the Republic of Kazakhstan to the Vienna Convention on the Law of Treaties of 1969," <https://online.zakon.kz/Document/?doc_id=1001807>

In conclusion, the actual, reviewed Normative Resolution of the Supreme Court of the Republic of Kazakhstan clarified five critical aspects in the application of DTTs by the judicial authorities of the Republic. The Normative Resolution of the Supreme Court of the Republic of Kazakhstan No. 1 of July 10, 2008 – "On the Application of the Norms of Treaties of the Republic of Kazakhstan" is also of great importance for judicial authorities in their application of treaties.[19] Thus, the content of this act provides for essential rules[20] and these provisions are fully applicable to DTTs.

Russia

Following the Constitution, the Russian Federation's legal system includes generally recognized principles and norms of international law and treaties.

---

19 Normative Resolution of the Supreme Court of the Republic of Kazakhstan No. 1 of July 10, 2008 – "On the Application of the Norms of Treaties of the Republic of Kazakhstan," <https://adilet.zan.kz/rus/docs/P08000001S>

20 In specific circumstances, courts within the jurisdiction of the Republic of Kazakhstan are obliged to be guided by the norms of international law (preamble of the Resolution). Treaties that do not require the publication of laws for application are directly applicable in the Republic of Kazakhstan. In other cases, along with the treaty, the corresponding law adopted to implement the provisions of the ratified treaty should be applied. If a conflict arises between constitutional provisions and ratified (or unratified) treaties to which the Republic of Kazakhstan is a party, priority in application belongs to constitutional norms (Paragraph 3). Officially published and effective treaties of the Republic of Kazakhstan are applicable. Official unpublished treaties relating to citizens' rights, freedoms, and duties are not applicable (Paragraph 5). Paragraph 10 of the Normative Resolution stipulates that when administering justice, courts must keep in mind that incorrect application by the court of the norms of treaties of the Republic of Kazakhstan may be grounds for the cancellation or modification of a judicial act. In addition, incorrect application of the norms of a treaty may occur because the courts need to apply the applicable norms of treaties, apply nonapplicable norms of treaties, or misinterpret the norms of treaties. Interpretation of the norms of treaties of the Republic of Kazakhstan, including the preamble, annexes, and any agreements or documents related to the treaty, must be carried out by a court of law in compliance with the rules provided for Article 31–Article 33 of VCLT according to the subject and purpose of the treaty. Finally, following Paragraph 16, if questions arise that require clarification of a technical and legal nature in the application and interpretation of the norms of a treaty of the Republic of Kazakhstan, one should use acts and decisions of international organizations, of which the Republic of Kazakhstan is a member, and contact the Ministry of Foreign Affairs of the Republic of Kazakhstan, the Ministry of Justice of the Republic of Kazakhstan, and the Prosecutor General's

The Law on Treaties of the Russian Federation explicitly states that treaties not requiring the adoption of internal legislative acts are directly applicable. Such agreements, which include DTTs, sometimes directly set different tax rates than those provided by Russian legislation. The norms of the Russian Federation's Tax Code reassess the provisions of the Constitution and specify the priority of treaty rules over the Code and its normative legal acts. These relevant provisions are reflected in judicial practice. For example, in the review of the court practice on the application of specific provisions of the Tax Code, the Supreme Court of Russia explicitly stated that the tax rate specified in the Convention for the Avoidance of Double Taxation with the Kingdom of Spain should be applied to dividends, and the tax authority had no grounds for applying a tax rate exceeding that established by the Convention to dividends.[21]

In another case, the Supreme Arbitration Court interpreted Article 7 of the Tax Code to apply DTTs when national legislation *conflicts* with international legal acts and establishes different legal regulations for specific taxation issues for residents of contracting states.[22]

Office of the Republic of Kazakhstan (for example, to clarify issues related to the term of a treaty, the list of participating states et cetera). These are the primary, most essential provisions of the Normative Resolution of the Supreme Court of the Republic of Kazakhstan No. 1 of July 10, 2008 – "On the Application of the Norms of Treaties of the Republic of Kazakhstan."

21 "Review of the Court Practice on the Application of Specific Provisions of Section V.1 and Article 269 of the Tax Code of the Russian Federation," (approved by the Presidium of the Supreme Court of the Russian Federation on February 16, 2017), Item 14, *Bulletin of the Supreme Court of the Russian Federation*, no. 9, September 2017.

22 Resolution of the Presidium of the Supreme Arbitration Court of the Russian Federation No. 8654/11 of November 15, 2011, on Case No. A27-7455/2010.

Application and Interpretation of DTTs by National Courts of Kazakhstan and Russia

Kazakhstan

As of November 23, 2023, the Republic of Kazakhstan has concluded treaties with fifty-five states to avoid double taxation and prevent tax evasion on income and capital taxes.[23]

The Government of Kazakhstan plans to conclude a DTT with Indonesia soon[24] and Israel.[25] Moreover, local legislation has implemented Action 3, "Controlled Foreign Companies" of the OECD project, which addresses Base Erosion and Profit Shifting.[26] In particular, based on paragraph 1 (1) of Article 294 of the new Tax Code, which was adopted in 2017, the tax authority annually publishes the list of the states that have DTTs with Kazakhstan and whose local corporate tax rate is greater than 75% of the relevant tax rate in Kazakhstan.[27]

Companies whose beneficiaries are from the states on the list are exempted from paying taxes related to controlled foreign companies. In this respect, on June 19, 2023, a new list containing 43 countries was approved.[28] The structure and main provisions of the DTTs concluded by Kazakhstan with

---

23 Conventions for the Avoidance of Double Taxation and the Prevention of Fiscal Evasion Concerning Taxes on Income and Capital (last amended on 29.11.2023): <https://kgd.gov.kz/ru/content/konvencii-ob-izbezhanii-dvoynogo-nalogooblozheniya-i-predotvrashchenii-ukloneniya-ot>

24 Draft resolution of the Government of the Republic of Kazakhstan «On Amendment of the Resolution of the Government of the Republic of Kazakhstan of 30.09.2019 No. 720 "On Signing of the Convention between the Government of the Republic of Kazakhstan and the Government of Republic of Indonesia for the Avoidance of Double Taxation and the Prevention of Fiscal Evasion Concerning Taxes on Income and Capital," <https://legalacts.egov.kz/npa/view?id=4404862>

25 Convention between the Government of the Republic of Kazakhstan and the Government of the Republic of Israel for the Avoidance of Double Taxation and the Prevention of Fiscal Evasion Concerning Taxes on Income and Capital (draft): <https://legalacts.egov.kz/npa/view?id=4020851>

26 OECD, Action 3 "Controlled Foreign Company" <https://www.oecd.org/tax/beps/beps-actions/action3/>

27 Code of the Republic of Kazakhstan No. 120-VI of December 25, 2017 – "On Taxes and Other Mandatory Payments to the Budget (Tax Code)" (with amendments and additions as of September 12, 2023), <https://online.zakon.kz/Document/?doc_id=36148637>

28 Order of the Deputy Prime Minister – Ministry of Finance of the Republic of Kazakhstan of 19.06.2023: https://base.spinform.ru/show_doc.fwx?rgn=151638.

foreign countries are based on the Model Convention on Taxes on Income and Capital elaborated by the OECD Committee on Fiscal Affairs.

The appropriate interpretation in the Commentary to the OECD Model Convention facilitates the correct application of the OECD Model Convention. Outlining the views of interested non-OECD countries, this Commentary contains a special section entitled "Non-OECD economies" positions on the OECD Model Tax Convention. Among 33 countries, the positions of Kazakhstan and Russia are reflected in each article of the document.[29] According to Paragraph I.3 of its Recommendation of October 23, 1997, the OECD Council recommended that member governments guide their tax administrations by the Commentaries to the Model Tax Convention as is regularly amended when applying and interpreting the provisions of their bilateral tax conventions based on the Model Tax Convention.

Given their status of non-legally binding advisory acts, the OECD Model Convention on Taxes on Income and Capital, and the Commentaries on its articles, we believe that the judicial authorities of the Republic of Kazakhstan do not have the legal obligation to apply these documents when adopting their decisions.

The Normative Resolution of the Supreme Court of the Republic of Kazakhstan No. 9 of December 22, 2022 – "On Certain Issues of Application of Tax Legislation by Courts" embraces this approach. In particular, following Paragraph 1 of this Resolution, tax legislation consists of the Tax Code and normative legal acts, the adoption of which is provided for by the Tax Code.[30] As laid down in Article 10 of the Tax Code of the Republic of Kazakhstan, normative legal acts regulating taxation issues are subject to mandatory official publication, for which they must first undergo state registration with the judicial authorities.

---

29 *Model Tax Convention on Income and Capital 2017* (Paris: OECD Publishing, 2017), <https://read.oecd-ilibrary.org/taxation/model-tax-convention-on-income-and-on-capital-2017-full-version_g2g972ee-en#page1505>.

30 Such normative legal acts include normative legal resolutions of the Government of the Republic of Kazakhstan, normative legal orders of the head of the authorized body in the system of tax authorities, normative legal orders of the Head of the Ministry of Foreign Affairs of the Republic of Kazakhstan, normative legal decisions of local representative bodies of regions, cities of republican significance and the capital on setting the rates of individual taxes and other mandatory payments to the budget.

The Supreme Court of the Republic of Kazakhstan explicitly addresses all judicial bodies of the Republic of Kazakhstan, stating that when hearing tax disputes, courts do not have the right to apply normative legal acts that do not comply with the listed conditions.

Neither the OECD Model Convention on Taxes on Income and Capital nor the Commentaries to its articles meet the requirements of these paragraphs of this Normative Resolution. As such, they cannot be applied by the courts of the Republic of Kazakhstan. However, given that the OECD Council has recommended that tax authorities be guided by Commentaries to the Articles of the Model Tax Convention when applying and interpreting the provisions of their bilateral tax conventions based on the Articles of the Model Tax Convention, it is our opinion that these authorities are entitled to use them.

It therefore follows that, according to Subparagraph 4 of Paragraph 2 of Article 19 of the Tax Code, tax authorities are obliged, within their competence, to provide explanations and commentaries on the occurrence, performance, and termination of a tax obligation. However, as noted in Subparagraph 8 of Paragraph 1 of the Normative Resolution, such clarifications, commentaries, and methodological recommendations, including those of the authorized body, are unrelated to normative legal acts. They are subject to assessment by the court, considering their compliance with tax legislation.

As such, the Supreme Court of Kazakhstan takes a very restrained position on applying acts of international organizations, of which Kazakhstan is not a member. That includes the OECD Model Convention and its Commentaries. Nevertheless, these documents can be applied by the judicial authorities of the Republic of Kazakhstan but only following explanations and commentaries, as well as methodological recommendations of the tax authorities, taking into account their compliance with the rules of the tax legislation of the Republic of Kazakhstan according to the court's assessment.

Concerning the compliance of the Republic of Kazakhstan's DTTs with the norms of the OECD Model Convention, Russian researcher A.A. Savitsky concluded that Kazakhstan's agreements with several countries contain some deviations from the OECD Model Convention.

In particular, the Agreement with India (Paragraph 2 of Article 24) contains a clause stating that the prohibition of discrimination against a permanent establishment does not apply to the right of the state where the permanent establishment is located to tax its profits at a rate exceeding the tax rate for resident enterprises of that state. Similarly, the Agreement between Kazakhstan and Turkey (Paragraph 2 of Article 23) restricts the application of the nondiscrimination regime to a permanent establishment only to the part of the profit that the state where the permanent establishment is located can tax after taxation of profits from entrepreneurial activities following Article 7.[31]

Between 2022 and 2023, several disputes related to the application of DTTs were heard by courts in Kazakhstan. The following disputes were of note: 1) the application of the mutual agreement procedure under DTTs for taxation of services; 2) the formation of a permanent establishment through the provision of services by a nonresident and the refund of corporate income tax (from now on referred to as "CIT") at the source of payment from the budget; 3) criteria for distinguishing royalties and services; and 4) dividend taxation procedure.

On April 28, 2023, the Judicial Board for Administrative Cases (from now on referred to as "JBAC") of the Supreme Court of the Republic of Kazakhstan published an "Analysis of Judicial Practice in Administrative Cases on Tax Issues," Part 2, about international taxation. The analysis covered administrative cases and judicial acts of the courts of Kazakhstan from June 2022 to May 2023. It concerned the application of tax law in the framework of lawsuits based on the Administrative Procedural Code of the Republic (from now on referred to as "APPC") on international taxation.[32] Below are two relevant examples.

Case #1: Exalo Drilling JSC

An example of the application of DTTs is a case related to applying the mutual agreement procedure in the taxation of services. Resolution No. 6001-22-00-6ap/1073, of January 19, 2023, analyses the following situation.[33]

---

31 A. A. Savitsky, *Tax Discrimination and Legal Regime of Nondiscrimination* (Ekaterinburg: n.p., 2019), 100–01.

32 Analysis of Judicial Practice in Administrative Cases on Tax Issues (Part 2: Issues of International Taxation) (April 28, 2023, Astana), *Bulletin of the Judicial Board for Administrative Cases of the Supreme Court of the Republic of Kazakhstan*, no. 1 (2023): 108–39.

33 ibid., 114-16.

Exalo Drilling JSC (nonresident) filed a lawsuit against the Department of State Revenue (from now on referred to as "DGD") with claims for invalidation of the decision of the state tax body on CIT and fines adopted as resulting from tax audits. By decision of the Specialized Interdistrict Administrative Court (from now on referred to as "SIAC") of October 19, 2021, and by the decision of the Judicial Board for Administrative Cases (from now on referred to as "JBAC") of April 11, 2022, the claim was dismissed.

The DGD charged the plaintiffs with 1) inflating deductions without supporting documents for KZT 69,323,048.00; 2) inflating deductions for general administrative and management expenses of the head office (from now on referred to as "OAUR") in the amount of KZT 1,134,712,456.00; and 3) unjustified application of a reduced CIT rate on net income of 10%, which led to additional tax in the amount of KZT 226,230,379.00.

In the cassation appeal, the plaintiff appealed to all these charges. The plaintiffs stated that the courts violated and incorrectly applied substantive or procedural rules. In particular, among all the other norms, the courts ignored Paragraph 3 of Article 4 of the Constitution, according to which treaties ratified by the Republic of Kazakhstan have priority over laws; additionally, the contested judicial acts were issued in violation of Paragraph 6 of Article 10 of the DTT between the Government of the Republic of Kazakhstan and the Government of the Republic of Poland, ratified on April 21, 1995.

The Judicial Board found that after the completion of the tax audit on November 1, 2020, on November 26, 2020, and following Article 25 of the DTT, the plaintiff appealed to the competent authority of Poland with an application for a mutual agreement procedure with the competent authority of the Republic of Kazakhstan (from now on referred to as the "Ministry of Finance of the Republic of Kazakhstan").

On December 20, 2020, a complaint was filed with the Ministry of Finance of the Republic of Kazakhstan. On February 3, 2021, the Ministry of Finance of Poland sent an email on the mutual agreement procedure with a copy of the plaintiff's statement to the State Revenue Committee of the Ministry of Finance of the Republic of Kazakhstan (from now on referred to as the "State Revenue Committee of the Ministry of Finance of the Republic of Kazakhstan"), which went unanswered due to the negligence of the State Revenue Committee staff.

On June 21, 2021, the Ministry of Finance of the Republic of Kazakhstan, without considering the Ministry of Finance of Poland's request, decided to leave the notification unchanged, and the plaintiff's complaint still needs to be addressed.

On August 23, 2021, the Ministry of Finance of Poland sent a second written appeal to the Ministry of Finance of the Republic of Kazakhstan, and an employee confirmed the receipt of this request. However, because the plaintiff had already filed an administrative claim with the SIAC by that time, this request also went unanswered. Under these circumstances, the Ministry of Finance of Poland initiated a procedure for a DTT-based mutual agreement.

According to JBAC, the filing of a claim by a Company to the court does not terminate the obligation of the Ministry of Finance of the Republic of Kazakhstan or its authorized representative, as represented by the State Revenue Committee of the Ministry of Finance of the Republic of Kazakhstan, to conduct a mutual agreement procedure. Based on these considerations, JBAC referred the administrative case as a new hearing to the court of first instance for a decision considering the result of the mutual agreement procedure.

Case #2: Potential Oil

One of the controversial issues in international taxation is dividend taxation. This issue was analyzed in the Resolution of the JBAC of the Supreme Court of the Republic of Kazakhstan on April 4, 2023, on Potential-Oil LLP's claim against the Department regarding recognizing notifications of tax audit results as illegal.[34]

It follows from the tax audit report that Bekstar, the founder, is registered in the British Virgin Islands. Between 2018 and 2020, the Partnership transferred 2018, 2019, and 2020 dividends to a Bekstar branch account in the Russian Federation. The Partnership withheld CIT at a reduced rate of 10% from the accrued dividends following the provisions of the DTT between the Republic of Kazakhstan and Russia. It was paid to the budget of the Republic of Kazakhstan.

---

34 ibid., 125-27.

The Department considered it *unjustified* to apply the provisions of the DTT between the Russian Federation and the Republic of Kazakhstan of July 3, 1997, to the income of the nonresident founder Bekstar in the form of dividends since the Bekstar branch is not a legal entity and cannot be considered a resident of Russia to apply the DTT.

Bekstar is registered in a state with preferential taxation. Therefore, per Article 646 of the Tax Code of the Republic of Kazakhstan, the company is subject to taxation at its source of payment at a rate of 20%. Rejecting the claim, the court of first instance noted that the presence of a document confirming residency is an insufficient basis for applying the provisions of the DTT since, following the provisions of the DTT, the relevant person is not recognized as a resident since only a branch was registered in the Russian Federation and not Bekstar itself.

However, the court of appeals did not agree with the conclusions of the court of first instance on the following grounds. According to Paragraph 2 of Article 646 of the Tax Code of the Republic of Kazakhstan, the income of a person registered in a state with preferential taxation included in the list approved by the authorized body and defined by Article 644 of the Code is subject to taxation at the source of payment at a rate of 20%.

Paragraph 5 of Article 2 of the Tax Code states that if a treaty ratified by the Republic of Kazakhstan establishes provisions other than those contained in this Code, the said treaty shall apply.

Article 10 of the Convention states that dividends paid by a company resident of a contracting state to a resident of another contracting state may be taxed in that other state. However, such dividends may also be taxed in the contracting state, where the company paying the dividends is a resident following the laws of that state. However, if the recipient is the beneficial owner of the dividends, then the levied tax will not exceed 10% of the total amount of the dividends.

The treaty will apply as provided in Paragraph 4 of Article 666 of the Tax Code of the Republic of Kazakhstan, provided that the nonresident submits a document confirming their residence to a tax agent. From the documented response of the Federal Tax Service of the Russian Federation (from now on referred to as the "Federal Tax Service of the Russian Federation") of September 17, 2021, it follows that the foreign company Bekstar has been a tax resident of the Russian Federation from October 2, 2017, to the present.

The Department concluded that the Bekstar branch cannot be a resident of the Russian Federation based on the response of the Federal Tax Service Directorate for the City of Moscow. This response shows that the Bekstar branch (and not the company itself) has been an income-tax resident of the Russian Federation since October 2, 2017.

However, the court thought this response contradicts the above information from the Federal Tax Service since Bekstar, not its branch, is registered for tax purposes in the Russian Federation. According to the Civil Code of the Republic of Kazakhstan, branches and representative offices are not legal entities (Paragraph 3 of Article 43); they are endowed with property by the legal entity that created them and act based on the provisions approved by it. Consequently, branches do not have the right to dispose of the property of a legal entity; as such, even though dividends are transferred to the branch‘s account, the right to dispose of them belongs to the legal entity itself, that is, Bekstar, which is the owner and recipient of these dividends.

From the response of the Federal Tax Service of the Russian Federation of March 18, 2022, it follows that dividends paid from sources in the Republic of Kazakhstan to Bekstar, which is a tax resident of the Russian Federation, may be taxed within the territory of the Republic of Kazakhstan at a rate not exceeding 10%.

It follows from the meaning of Paragraph 7 of Article 645 of the Tax Code of the Republic of Kazakhstan that, regardless of the form and place in which dividends were paid, the income is considered to have been received by a nonresident of the Republic of Kazakhstan. The court of appeal came to the correct conclusion that Bekstar's residence in the Russian Federation was confirmed by official documents issued by the authorized body of the Russian Federation; the company is not exempt from taxation in the Russian Federation; and therefore, the Partnership lawfully applied the provisions of the DTT and withheld the CIT in the amount 10% of nonresident income.

Under such circumstances, the JBAC of the Supreme Court of the Republic of Kazakhstan found no grounds for satisfying the cassation appeal or the cassation petition and upheld the court of appeal‘s decision. As such, the courts concluded that the branch is not a separate legal entity and that the legal entity itself receives the dividends received by the branch. Accordingly, the Supreme Court confirmed that the income of the BVI branch can be applied to the DTT with Russia since the company is registered for tax purposes in

Russia, and the tax residence of the branch does not exist independently of the residency of the entire company.[35]

The review of judicial practice on applying DTTs in Kazakhstan shows that the judicial authorities of the Republic of Kazakhstan need to apply the Commentaries to the OECD Model Convention on Taxes on Income and Capital. The failure to apply it is apparently due to the small number of court cases related to the use of DTTs compared with other categories of tax disputes.

Russia

In contrast, the courts of the *Russian Federation* have developed relatively straightforward approaches to the interpretation of DTTs and the use of the Commentaries to the OECD Model Convention. Even though Russia, like Kazakhstan, is not an OECD member, Russian courts assess Commentaries to the OECD Model Convention as a document expressing a "generally accepted approach."

For example, when defining the concept of "capital" to apply a reduced dividend rate, the court, in one of the cases, referred to the Commentaries with exactly this qualification and noted that the tax authority should have taken into account the amount of the loan provided to the company as a contribution to the capital of a Russian organization (Subparagraph "D" of Paragraph 15 of the Commentaries to Article 9 of the Standard Model of the OECD Convention on Income and Capital Taxes).[36]

In another case, the Presidium of the Supreme Arbitration Court referred to the Commentaries as the Model Convention, stating that the latter is "a framework document establishing general principles and approaches to

[35] Analysis of Judicial Practice in Administrative Cases on Tax Issues (Part 2: Issues of International Taxation) (April 28, 2023, Astana), *Bulletin of the Judicial Board for Administrative Cases of the Supreme Court of the Republic of Kazakhstan*, no. 1 (2023): 256.

[36] "Review of the Practice of Consideration by Courts of Cases Related to the Application of Certain Provisions of Section V.1 and Article 269 of the Tax Code of the Russian Federation" (approved by the Presidium of the Supreme Court of the Russian Federation on February 16, 2017), Item 14, *Bulletin of the Supreme Court of the Russian Federation*, no. 9, September 2017.

the elimination of double taxation."[37] I.V. Khavanova identified four main methods of using terminological techniques in the interpretation of international model tax agreements: the Introduction of conventional terminology, references to national legislation, the admission of interpretation within the framework of mutual agreement procedures, and official commentaries on the articles of the model convention[38]

It is important to emphasize that Russian courts interpret the provisions of the DTT with the general objective of countering tax abuses. In cases where, after analyzing a particular transaction, the courts conclude that the real purpose of the parties to the transaction was to reduce taxes payable to the budget, they deny the taxpayer the right to apply the preferential tax rates provided for by the DTT.

For example, the following situation was considered in several cases: a Russian taxpayer paid dividends to shareholders and withheld tax at the payment source at a reduced rate provided for by the DTT (5 or 10%). As part of the audit, the tax authority discovered that a company registered in a jurisdiction with which Russia had an existing DTT (for example, Cyprus) immediately redirected the received dividends in total to a jurisdiction with which no such treaty existed (for example, the British Virgin Islands). On this basis, the tax authority denied the Russian taxpayer's right to apply a preferential tax rate on dividends withheld at the source and increased the tax to a regular rate of 15%. As part of the case challenging the tax authority's decision, the court faced the need to interpret the DTT norm on the beneficial owner of income in the form of dividends.

As a result of interpretations based on the literal meaning of the terms, the purpose of DTTs, and the OECD Commentaries on the Model Convention, the courts concluded that the beneficial owner of the income in the considered case is not the company that was formally a shareholder (registered on Cyprus) but another company that ultimately received the amount of dividends (registered on BVI).[39] When qualifying the status of a shareholder,

---

37 Resolution of the Presidium of the Supreme Arbitration Court No. 7854 of November 15, 2011, on Case No. A27-7455/2010 ("Northern Kuzbass").

38 I. A. Khavanova, *Russia's Double Taxation Prevention Treaties* (Moscow: ID Iurisprudenzia, 2016), 91.

39 Resolution of February 7, 2017, of the Ninth Arbitration Court of Appeal on Case No. A40-113217/16 (Severstal); Ruling of the Supreme Court of the Russian Federation No.

the courts applied the term "conduit company" used in Paragraph 2 of the Commentaries. The courts applied a similar interpretation of DTTs, providing for the need to identify the beneficial owner of the income in other cases, including those relating to the taxation of interest on deposits or loans.[40]

Conclusion

International tax concepts are increasingly used in Russia and Kazakhstan. Treaties, particularly DTTs, are part of each country's legal system and are directly applicable. Moreover, in the Russian Federation, the courts are aware of the possibility of applying the OECD Model Convention and its Commentaries as international taxation or generally accepted principles. The Commentaries, while only an interpretative instrument of the OECD-recommended Model, are used by Russian courts as part of an international tax language.

For now, the OECD Convention may be applied by courts in Kazakhstan only indirectly – via tax authorities" recommendations and interpretations based on the OECD commentary. Such recommendations should, however, not contradict tax legislation. Nevertheless, the next step in developing Kazakhstan court practices in interpreting international tax terms and provisions will be directly applying the OECD Commentary as an authoritative source. Implementing international tax reform under the auspices of the OECD and expanding the UN's participation in international tax cooperation will strengthen the internationalization of the tax domain. That will likely result in the conclusion of new multilateral treaties and the broader use of documents from international organizations (primarily the OECD) in interpreting treaties. That will hopefully lead the national authorities of the Republic of Kazakhstan and the Russian Federation to speak increasingly the language of international taxation and use it to interpret treaties and domestic legislation.

304-KG17-17349 of December 25, 2017, on Case No. A27-20527/2015 (Krasnobrodsky-Yuzhny); Ruling of the Supreme Court of the Russian Federation No. 304-KG18-19526 of December 3, 2018, on Case No. A27-27287/2016 (Polosukhinskaya Mine). See the file index of Russian arbitration cases: <https://kad.arbitr.ru/>

40 See an overview of such cases in the Letter of the Federal Tax Service of Russia of May 6, 2019, No. CA-4-7/8448@, <https://www.consultant.ru/document/cons_doc_LAW_325224/>

Notes on Contributors

Didier GUEVEL est Professor émerité de droit privé et sciences criminelles a l'Université de Sorbonne Paris Nord. Il est aussi doyen honoraire de la faculté de droit, sciences politiques et sociales.Ses recherches se focalisent sur le droit des affaires, et le droit patrimonial de la famille. Parmi ses nombreuses publications il faut mentioner *Droit du commerce et des affaires* (Paris: LGDJ, 2017).

Luc-Michel NIVÔSE est Conseiller honoraire à la Cour de cassation, exerçant des fonctions juridictionnelles à la cour d'appel de Paris. Il enseigne à l'Institut catholique de Paris (depuis 2022) et il est aussi ancien professeur associé à l'Université Sorbonne-Paris-Nord (2011-2022).

Remus TITIRIGA is a Senior Researcher at the Department of Law, of the University of the West, in Timisoara, Romania. He has a PhD in EU Law from the Université Nancy 2, France. He specializes in Trade Law, Data Protection, and Internet Law. His publications include "Autonomy of Military Robots: Assessing the Technical and Legal ("jus in Bello") Thresholds," *The John Marshall Journal of Information Technology and Privacy Law*, Vol. 32, No. 2 (2016): 57-87.

Maxime CHARITE est Maître de conférences à l'Université Le Havre Normandie. Il est docteur en droit public de l'Université du Mans. Il est auteur, entre autres, de *Excès de pouvoir législatif et excès de pouvoir administratif: Étude comparée de l'office des juges constitutionnel et administratif français* (Paris: Mare & Martin, 2023).

Louis-Philippe GRATTON holds a PhD in Law (Université Toulouse 1 Capitole, France) and is a Data Protection and Privacy Consultant. He is also an Associate Member, LexFEIM, Université Le Havre Normandie. His publication include "Artificial Intelligence and Algorithms Regulations in China" in *Eurasian Legal Systems in a World in Transition*, edited by Pierre Chabal, Zhuldyz Saraimbayeva, Hye-Hwal Seong, and Remus Titiriga (Bruxelles: Peter Lang, 2024).

Sandie CALME holds a doctorate in Law from Paris 1 Panthéon Sorbonne University and an LLM from Frankfurt am Main, Germany. She has published in the fields of international, European, comparative, and transport law. She is the author of, among other publications, "L'essentiel du droit des transports" (Paris: Gualino Lextenso Éditions, 2012).

Sagyngaliy AIDARBAYEV is a Professor at the School of Law and Public Administration at Narxoz University. He is a Doctor in International Public Law. His research areas include international trade and economic law. His publications include "International Legal Regulation of Government Procurement for Sustainable Development in the Framework of the WTO," *Rivista di Studi sulla Sostenibilità* 2021 (2): 95-109.

Ilya LIFSHITS is an International Law Professor at the Russian Foreign Trade Academy. He holds a Doctorate in International and European Law. His research area covers international financial and tax law, sustainable finance, and international trade law. He is the author of the monograph *International Financial Law and European Union Law: Interaction and Mutual Influence*.

Zhuldyz SAIRAMBAEVA is a Professor of International Law at Al-Farabi Kazakh National University. Her field of expertise is international economic law.

Yesbol OMIRZHANOV is Associate Professor of International Law at Al-Farabi Kazakh National University. He works on problems of theory and history of the state and law. He is the author of the monograph, *Azat Movement and the History of Political and Legal Thought of Kazakhstan*.

Cultures juridiques et politiques

Editors: Stéphanie Rohlfing-Dijoux, Otmar Seul

ISSN: 2235-1078

Toute forme de culture ayant une dimension politique et juridique, la Collection publie des travaux, tels que des thèses, synthèses de recherches, ouvrages collectifs et actes de colloques se proposant de faire connaître les systèmes politiques et juridiques contemporains et leur implications sociales et sociétales. La Collection se focalise sur les interférences entre le politique, le juridique et le socio-culturel dans le contexte de la globalisation et de la mondialisation, en prêtant une attention particulière aux processus d'intégration politique et d'harmonisation juridique en cours dans l'Union européenne.

The series publishes works on culture with a political and legal dimension that are intended to reveal the contemporary political and legal systems and their social and societal implications. The series focuses on the interconnections between the political, the legal and the sociocultural in the context of globalization, paying particular attention to the processes of political integration and legal harmonization underway in the European Union. Proposals for revised doctoral theses, edited collections and conference proceedings are all welcome.

Cultures juridiques et politiques

Vol. 1 Stephanie Rohlfing-Dijoux (éd) La Transmission de Terminologie et de Concepts Juridiques dans l'espace Européen. Allemagne / France / Russie 2012, ISBN 978-3-0343-1094-9

Vol. 2 Otmar Seul & Tomas Davulis (éds./Hrsg.) La Solidarité dans l'union Européenne / Solidarität in der Europäischen Union. Actes de la 5ème Université d'été francogermano-lituanienne et européenne en sciences juridiques Vilnius, 3-10 juillet 2008 / Tagungsband der 5. DeutschFranzösisch-Litauischen und Europäischen Sommeruniversität in den Rechtswissenschaften,Vilnius 3.–10. Juli 2008 2012, ISBN 978-3-0343-1122-9

Vol. 3 Ralf Alleweldt, Raphaël Callsen, Jeanne Dupendant (eds.) Human rights abuses in the contemporary world. Tri-National Workshop,Tbilisi, September 2011 2012, ISBN 978-3-0343-1147-2

Vol. 4 Stefanie Bouquet La réglementation européenne relative à la discrimination fondée sur l'âge: conséquences sur le droit du travail français. Préface du Professeur Joachim Gruber, Université Paris Ouest - Nanterre La Défense 2012, ISBN 978-3-0343-1174-8

Vol. 5 Izabela Krasnicka & Magdalena Perkowska (éds.) How to Become a Lawyer? 2013, ISBN 978-3-0343-1290-5

Vol. 6 Kerstin Peglow et Géraldine Demme (dir.) La protection des intérêts privés sur le marché intérieur. La situation des consommateurs et entrepreneurs. 2015, ISBN 978-3-0343-1615-6

Vol. 7 Sam Lyes Crimes internationaux et immunité de l'acte de fonction des anciens dirigeants étatiques. 2015, ISBN 978-3-0343-1690-3

Vol. 8 Fabien Bottini, Harold Gaba et Pierre Chabal (dir.) Le régionalisme et ses limites. Regards croisés franco-kazakhs. 2016, ISBN 978-2-87574-335-0

Vol. 9 Otmar Seul, Kaïs Slama, Kerstin Peglow (Hrsg.) Kulturvermittlung und Interkulturalität, ein deutschfranzösisch-tunesischer Dialog. Politische, rechtliche und sozio-linguistische Aspekte 2017, ISBN 978-2-8076-0133-8

Vol. 10 Stephanie Rohlfing-Dijoux (ed./dir.) Developing Intraregional Exchanges through the Abolition of Commercial and Tariff Barriers. Myth or Reality? L'abolition des barrières commerciales et tarifaires dans la région de l'océan Indien. Mythe ou réalité? 2017, ISBN 978-2-8076-0126-0

Vol. 11 Sagyngaliy Aidarbayev, Pierre Chabal, Zhuldyz Sairambaeva (dir.) Mutations de société et réponses du droit. Perspectives franco-asiatiques comparées. 2017, ISBN 978-2-8076-0187-1

Vol. 12 Tomas Davulis (ed.) Labour Law Reforms in Eastern and Western Europe. 2017, ISBN 978-2-8076-0416-2

Vol. 13 Tai-Uk Chung, Zhuldyz Sairambaeva, Pierre Chabal (eds.) On the Asian and European Origins of Legal and Political Systems. Views from Korea, Kazakhstan and France 2018, ISBN 978-2-8076-0732-3

Vol. 14 Manuel Goehrs Coopération transfrontalière et intégration européenne. Contribution à l'étude du principe fédéraliste 2018, ISBN 978-2-8076-0409-4

Vol. 15 Amandine Cayol, Zhuldyz Sairambaeva, Pierre Chabal (eds.) T he challenge of change for the legal and political systems of Eurasia. The impact of the New Silk Road 2020, ISBN 978-2-8076-1382-9

Vol. 16 Christine Canazza, Stéphanie Rohlfing-Dijoux, Otmar Seul (eds.) L'Union européenne face au vieillissement de la population active. Analyse et perspectives autour de la discrimination sur la base de l'âge et des conditions de travail. 2020, ISBN 978-2-8076-1454-3

Vol. 17 Patric Kra Ehe und Familienschutz in Zeiten des demografischen Wandels. Ein Rechtsvergleich zwischen dem deutschen und ivorischen Einkommensteuerrecht. 2021, ISBN 978-2-8076-1469-7

Vol. 18 Amandine Cayol, Hye-Hwal Seong, Remus Titiriga, Pierre Chabal (Eds.) Eurasian challenges to international economic law. New developments after Brexit and in the context of the COVID-19. 2022, ISBN 978-2-87574-467-8

Vol. 19 Stéphanie Rohlfing-Dijoux & Rajendra Parsad Gunputh (Eds.) T he Intercultural Approach to Covid-19 Management In Germany, France and the Indian Ocean countries. 2023, ISBN 978-2-87574-790-7

Vol. 20 Remus Titiriga, Hye-Hwal Seong, Zhuldyz Sairambaeva & Pierre Chabal (Eds.) Eurasian legal systems in a world of transitions. Economic prosperity or disparity, and the return of politics in international law. 2024, ISBN 978-3-0343-4822-5

Vol. 21 Remus Titiriga (ed.), Courts applying the law Tribunaux appliquant la loi. Perspectives from Europe and Asia Perspectives d'Europe et d'Asie. 2025, ISBN 978-3-0343-5555-1

FSC
www.fsc.org
MIX
Papier | Fördert
gute Waldnutzung
FSC® C083411

Kolibri 360 GmbH
Ferdinand-Jühlke-Straße 7
99095 Erfurt, Deutschland
produktsicherheit@kolibri360.de

Druck:
CPI Druckdienstleistungen GmbH
im Auftrag der
Kolibri 360 GmbH
Ferdinand-Jühlke-Str. 7
99095 Erfurt